A Dream of Everest

A Dream of Everest

Edmund C. Neuhaus

iUniverse, Inc.
New York Lincoln Shanghai

A Dream of Everest

iUniverse books may be ordered through booksellers or by contacting:

iUniverse
2021 Pine Lake Road, Suite 100
Lincoln, NE 68512
www.iuniverse.com
1-800-Authors (1-800-288-4677)

Because of the dynamic nature of the Internet, any Web addresses or links contained in this book may have changed since publication and may no longer be valid.

The views expressed in this work are solely those of the author and do not necessarily reflect the views of the publisher, and the publisher hereby disclaims any responsibility for them.

ISBN: 978-0-595-43972-0 (pbk)
ISBN: 978-0-595-88292-2 (ebk)

Printed in the United States of America

To Olga, my wife
A gutsy gal who helps make everything possible

Contents

Introduction ix

CHAPTER 1   The Dream Begins 1

CHAPTER 2   Culture Shock 21

CHAPTER 3   The Clouds Have Rocks in Them 33

CHAPTER 4   The Trek Begins 44

CHAPTER 5   Window to Everest 69

CHAPTER 6   Acclimatization Gets Tougher 106

CHAPTER 7   Few Walks in the World More Wonderful 126

CHAPTER 8   Altitude Takes Its Toll 146

CHAPTER 9   Contemplating the Himalayas 159

CHAPTER 10   Energies Restored 173

CHAPTER 11   Kathmandu Belly 184

CHAPTER 12   A Dream Fulfilled 192

Afterword 195

Selected Bibliography 197

Introduction

The telephone call left me stunned and excited. It was from my son Eddie, who proposed that we go to Nepal the following year in March and trek to Mount Everest, the highest peak in the world. He grew up with Pop dreaming of going to Everest, and he got the idea when several of his college friends told him of their extensive travels in Nepal. My immediate reaction was mixed: I desperately wanted to go but was fearful of such a gigantic undertaking. How could the two of us handle the physically arduous itinerary on our own and cope with strange food, bad drinking water, unsanitary conditions, high altitudes, and a possible medical problem in an impoverished country? My wife, Olga, reassuring and encouraging, reminded me of our son's abilities as a certified ski patroller, paramedic, and accomplished backpacker. I could not help feeling safe and secure traveling with and relying on Eddie. Moreover, I was in excellent health and in good physical shape from my years of skiing and sailing.

I was very disappointed when, several weeks later, Eddie called to say that he had to cancel. A much sought-after fellowship had been offered to him, and it would begin during the time of our trip. He was working toward his doctorate in clinical psychology and could not refuse the offer.

I was crushed and in a funk. But Olga, in her upbeat manner, would have none of it, and she announced that she would go with me. Somehow we would make new plans to do the trek. I didn't know whether to laugh or cry over the disappointment and her seeming irrationality. Nevertheless, we discussed how we might be able to do the trek together, and we thought of going with a tour group. Eddie encouraged us and recommended Overseas Adventure Travel (OAT) in Cambridge, Massachusetts. As if it was destined to be, OAT had a nineteen-day trek to Everest planned in early March; the cost of everything, including airfare, was about nine thousand dollars for two people. The trekking group consisted of six couples hiking the traditional route to the Everest foothills. After arriving in New Delhi after a fifteen-hour flight from New York, there would be a ten-hour overnight layover until the next morning's brief flight to Kathmandu. After acclimatization in Kathmandu at six thousand feet, the group would fly an hour to Lukla at 9,482 feet to begin the trek that would end at 18,192 feet on Kala Pattar, which is considered to be the best viewing site of Everest. Treks and mountain-climbing expeditions are usually scheduled in the spring, before the summer monsoons bring torrential rains that make trails impassable and dangerous.

Self-doubt began to plague me. Both Olga and I, a few years shy of sixty, had no camping experience. We had never slept in a tent (except for my basic infantry training in World War II) and had never lived at high altitudes, except for skiing in the Swiss Alps. Our route would cover a distance of about eighty miles and go from nine thousand feet to eighteen thousand feet. The possibility of coming down with altitude sickness would be on our minds constantly. Hiking six to eight hours a day on twisting, rocky trails with precipitous drops to the valleys below, we would have to adapt to a climate ranging from freezing temperatures at night to comfortable temperatures in the sixties (Fahrenheit) during the daytime.

Olga and I reassured ourselves that we would be in good professional and experienced hands. Besides, we had several months to prepare for the trek and get in shape physically and emotionally. A general medical exam was required to prove that we were in good health, and various immunization vaccinations were needed to protect against infectious diseases. OAT would arrange air travel, brief hotel accommodations, and permits to travel through Nepal's isolated villages. Scores of Sherpas with yaks would carry and unpack our gear, strike our tents daily, and cook three meals a day for us. Each trekker only needed a backpack while hiking. For twelve trekkers, this seemed like a luxurious way to hike. All we had to do was walk and walk amid the spectacular mountains towering from eighteen to twenty-two thousand feet close above us, with Mt. Everest looming in the distance.

Despite the reassurances, pervasive doubts and anxieties nagged at us. Could we cope with the physical demands and mental challenges of the trek? Would we remain healthy? Would we be able to keep up with the more experienced trekkers and achieve the goal of Kala Pattar? We would do our best and keep in mind our son's motto: "Go for it."

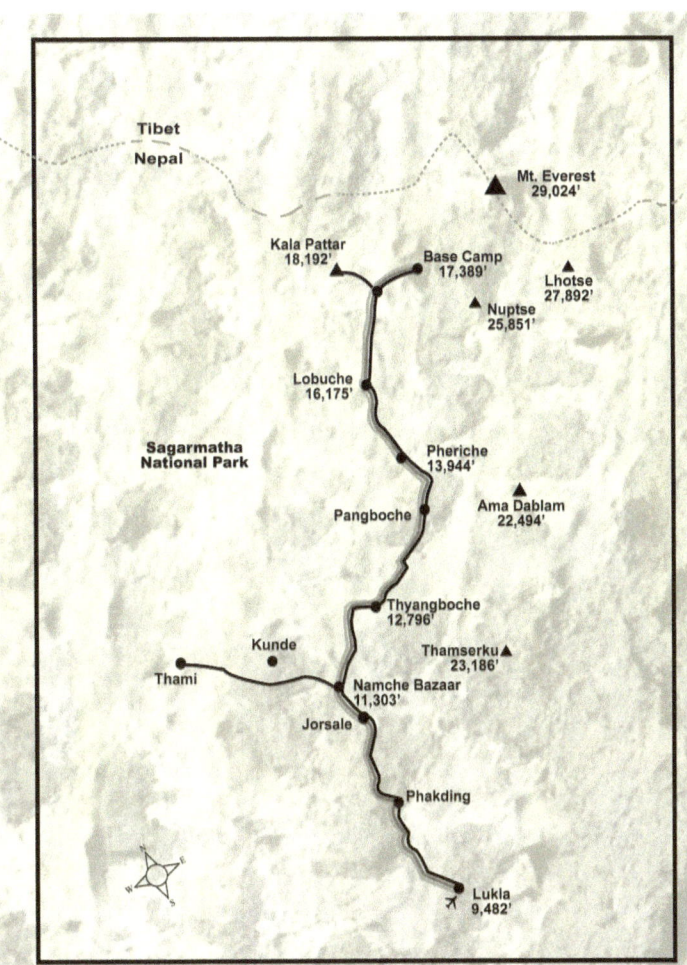

Tibet

Nepal

Mt. Everest
29,024'

Kala Pattar
18,192'

Base Camp
17,389'

Lhotse
27,892'

Nuptse
25,851'

Lobuche
16,175'

Sagarmatha
National Park

Pheriche
13,944'

Pangboche

Ama Dablam
22,494'

Thyangboche
12,796'

Kunde

Thamserku▲
23,186'

Thami

Namche Bazaar
11,303'

Jorsale

Phakding

Lukla
9,482'

West to east

1

The Dream Begins

Kathmandu! Finally, after a fifteen-hour flight that landed at midnight in New Delhi and an uncomfortable night in the airport's waiting room, we took off at 9:00 AM for the two-hour flight to Kathmandu, the capital of Nepal. From the north side of the small jet, the great Himalayan summits appeared like tiny white peaks on the distant horizon. My mind was a jumble of excitement and thoughts about the great climbers, mountains, and Nepalese villages I'd read about for nearly a lifetime: Mallory, Tillman, Shipton, the pioneering climbers who laid the groundwork for the ultimate conquest of Everest; the exotic-sounding places of Namche Bazaar, Khunde, and Tengboche; and the magnificent mountain ranges flanking them. Above all, the thought of finally seeing Mt. Everest and the Himalayas, the highest peak and mountain range on the face of the Earth, kept me in a state of tension and excitement.

The reality of our immediate surroundings and physical exhaustion, however, constantly intruded on our excitement. An atmosphere of neglect and shabbiness pervaded the airplane. And a breakfast of tough tandoori chicken served on a tray that still showed the food stains and crud of a previous meal added to our anxiety about sanitary conditions to come. These thoughts came naturally after the interminable night at the New Delhi airport. Arriving there at nearly midnight, we had spent the night in an airless and windowless concrete-walled room. The huge fans turning lazily under the twenty-foot ceiling had provided only an appearance of relief from the stifling atmosphere. Sleep had been difficult for most of us. The dank and humid conditions and the strangeness of this new world had allowed only the most fitful periods of sleep or relaxation.

Although we were thirsty, everyone viewed the dirty communal drinking fountain in the corner of the waiting room with repulsion and even horror—especially when some native would drink from the fountain with a cup that floated in a bowl of purplish red water that we assumed was colored by an antiseptic. We were anxious enough about the safety of drinking the luke-warm bottled soda and beer we bought from a grubby airport stand without having this display of public drinking under our noses. Our squeamishness was soon put to another test—a public toilet. Our first encounter, however, with the Asian public "water closets" did not live up to the horror we antici-pated. The men's-room floors, walls, and urinals were covered in square tiles of blues and greens, cool and soothing colors that failed to overcome the pow-erful stench of urine that overwhelmed the senses. A quick peek at the toilets showed the Western-style seat and not the Asian-style hole in the floor—a slight reprieve until the real thing that was soon to become a part of our daily existence in the field. With these thoughts about the challenges to come and anxieties about adjusting to the customs of an impoverished Asian culture, we landed in Kathmandu, the capital of Nepal, where our group of trekkers would meet its guides, become oriented, and prepare for our journey—the trek to the foothills of Mt. Everest.

Kathmandu lies in a valley at an altitude of 4,500 feet and is surrounded by gently rolling hills. Its airport, once called Gaucher ("cow pasture"), had pale orange stucco walls and white roofing, with vines of pink flowers and plants that imparted a warm welcome to its visitors. No sterile, sleek, or impersonal airport atmosphere here—more like a small country airport decked out for a special celebration, except for the waiting for baggage and the crowding and pushing to get through customs. But these harried moments quickly gave way to elation when we were greeted by our American guide, Jim, and his staff, who had a wreath of flowers for each trekker. The long, tiresome journey was soon to be over. The thought of a comfortable hotel and rest would soon be a reality—but not before the wildest taxi ride imaginable, one that would leave us mentally exhausted.

In groups of four, we were tightly packed with our gear into small Toyota taxis that would drive us through the heart of Kathmandu until we reached our hotel forty-five minutes later. The taxi snaked through narrow streets no wider than two car widths and crowded with people, rickshaws, bicycles, cows, dogs, and chickens. For most of the ride, we sat terrified as the taxi seemed to aim with varying bursts of speed at oncoming cars that would be missed by inches in passing. Screams and groans erupted from us as we thought ourselves in the hands of a maniacal driver who was bent on self-destruction. The constant horn blowing added to the noise of the passengers' exclamations and the endless accelerations and gear shifts. Taxis represented at least 90 percent of the cars in Kathmandu, and as they approached one another or any obstacle in their path, the drivers would hit their high-pitched, tinny-sounding horns with brief staccato bursts. As if by magic, people, animals, and vehicles suddenly moved to avoid the swerving cars that narrowly missed them. When we began to realize that our driver was highly skilled and that this dangerous driving pattern was normal for Kathmandu, our hysterical shrieks gave way to uncontrollable laughter. Nevertheless, none of us was ever so glad to be done with a taxi ride. Not even one of the many new immigrants who recklessly drive New York City taxis had given us such a fright. The bad reputation of German, French, Italian, and New York drivers can't compare to the daring, reckless, and indifferent driving style of the Kathmandu taxi driver. At one point in this ride, we careened past a line of natives clothed from head to toe in white, who were carrying a coffin covered in white and decked with flowers—a funeral procession that symbolized our fears of the moment.

At long last, nearly forty hours after our Thursday afternoon departure from JFK, we arrived intact at our hotel. Situated on a bluff on the western outskirts of the city and overlooking Kathmandu, the Hotel Varja seemed an oasis of tranquility amid the teeming natives and the traffic we had just negotiated. Like an old Hollywood movie set, the hotel sat inside a dull pink-walled compound whose gates were guarded by a brightly colored kiosk. Uniformed guards patrolled the entrance and smartly saluted entering guests. Any minute now, I expected to see Gary Cooper and the Bengal Lancers walk by in review. In the space of a few hours since landing in Kathmandu, our senses were bombarded by strange and unanticipated impressions. I was struck by the realization that this country was quite distinct from Western culture, and that our customs and beliefs would provide no safe guide in understanding and adjusting to this alien culture. More important, I knew that imposing our ways and needs on these people could prove disastrous to enjoying and experiencing Nepal. Invoking our values would only result in the all-too-human tendency to pigeonhole and categorize, a reaction that sets up stereotypes that diminish the vividness and richness of any experience. Here in these unfamiliar surroundings, I better understood why we invoke stereotypes: to ward off the newness with its sense of threat, because it is different from our world. It is sad to see how readily we become defensive and kill spontaneity when confronted by new and different worlds. No great insight here, but it was a thought I wanted to keep in mind, lest I fall into the blasé attitude of the "sophisticated" traveler who never leaves his own psychic and cultural backyard.

Fatigued but too excited to rest, we welcomed the news that after getting our room assignment and safely depositing our luggage, there would be a meeting with our trek leader and his staff. Under a hazy, hot sun in the humid weather of an early Kathmandu afternoon, we gathered on the hotel's rooftop terrace, enclosed by brick and stone walls overlooking the surrounding countryside and city. This was the group's introduction to Jim Traverso, a twenty-eight-year-old Bostonian who was to prove a remarkable leader, capable of coping with any problem or need with incredible patience and efficiency. Unflappable and businesslike, Jim outlined the trek's goals and gave guidelines on adjusting to Nepal.

Although we all tried to listen intently, I felt distracted by the jet lag dulling my senses, and by my own curiosity to absorb the newness enveloping us. While Jim was earnestly talking about the two days of rest and orientation at Kathmandu, my eyes and ears were busy trying to take in everything around us, from the most trivial things, like the tray of refreshments we were served, to our physical surroundings and the people who would become such an integral part of our lives over the next twenty days. As I greedily drank the glass of cool soda water enlivened with freshly squeezed lime, I thought about how much more pleasing and refreshing was this local thirst-slaking drink than our infinite variety of sodas. I recalled that we called this a Lime Rickey, a drink probably as old as the first appearance of seltzer, and noted that this simple and inexpensive drink was so much more satisfying than the Perrier with lime of a sophisticated culture. I had to travel halfway around the world to an impoverished country to appreciate how satisfying the simplest things can be.

Even the faded and weathered dark rose-colored bricks and smoothly worn stone, which were set in slightly crooked lines and patterns, were pleasing in their primitive simplicity. The hotel's architecture of low archways, curving stone stairs, small courtyards, and fortresslike constructions, with towers set in each of its four corners, made me feel like a guest in a cozy medieval castle. Perched on a small hilltop, the castle seemed aloof and protected from the chaotic and bustling city surrounding it. Here, three stories high on this rooftop terrace, the midday haze made the distant city below, the enveloping faded green mountainside, and the straw-roofed native huts appear like an impressionist painting.

I was impatient for Jim to finish the orientation so that we could be free to wander Kathmandu's streets. The people conveyed an easygoing, good-humored, and hard-working quality. Eager to please and be helpful, they were deferential, not in a submissive way, but in a proud manner. Generally short of stature and well built, with skin color ranging from light cream to brown to pitch black, with high cheekbones, dark peering eyes, full lips, and sensual looks, the Nepalese are a striking and handsome-looking people. These ruminations were at the back of my mind as I listened to Jim tell us of the challenges before us, and how we should prepare for them psychologically. It became readily apparent that Jim loved Nepal and its people. He emphasized the importance of understanding and accepting Nepalese values if we wanted to get the most out of our trek. Proudly, Jim spoke of his choice of the hotel: a truly native non-Westernized hotel that would quickly give us a genuine sense of the Nepalese. The more Jim talked, the more one realized that Jim had "gone native" in the best and most complimentary sense: after several years of residing in Kathmandu, Jim had become accepted and fully integrated into Nepalese culture. A forceful champion of the Nepalese, Jim described this primitive and impoverished culture. He cautioned us to be aware of slow service, bad plumbing, Asian-type toilets with their rectangular cutout in the floor, the hazards of eating uncooked foods and of drinking water that wasn't boiled or bottled, and the begging children.

Before we ventured into the city, Jim had to inspect our trekking gear. He wanted to be sure that we had all the proper clothing and accessories that were recommended by the trekking organization. It was no cursory inspection, but a careful check of every item of clothing and accessory in our cargo bags. I felt like the army recruit in basic training of years ago, fearful of a reprimand, as Jim examined the gear, asking questions and making comments about their usefulness. Had we brought the proper balance of light and heavy-weight pants, jackets, and shirts for the constant shifts in weather? Where was our rain outerwear? Had we broken in our new lightweight biking boots?

"The polypropylene long johns will prove invaluable. Don't forget sun screen lotion and hats for the intense sun. Your ski parkas will keep you warm in the chill of the evening." He continued in this vein until everything had been seen and checked. Even the snacks were commented upon. As I expected, our quantity of nuts, raisins, cheese, crackers, and chocolate was somewhat excessive and created extra weight. But Jim allowed it, noting that everyone's anxieties about food had caused us to bring an overabundance of snacks. It would not go to waste, in any event, since the Sherpas would gladly consume the leftovers. Our anxieties also had made us pack an abundance of toilet paper and take along every conceivable drug that would combat colds, fevers, diarrhea, and altitude sickness. Slightly chagrined at these excesses, we were, nevertheless, proud to have passed this inspection. We could relax, since there was no need to scurry around Kathmandu to buy gear we hadn't brought along. This equipment inspection and informal questioning exemplified Jim's professionalism and competence in everything he undertook. His was a great responsibility: to lead a group of twelve trekkers of varying ages, capabilities, and backgrounds to a land of high altitudes and rugged terrain that provided neither adequate medical resources nor the everyday conveniences of Western life.

Still too excited to rest after the luggage inspection, we decided to take a walk in this strange new land. Eagerly but anxiously, a few of us left the hotel compound and walked down the dusty dirt road that led to the neighboring streets. We first came to a stone bridge pockmarked with crumbling stone, holes, and a three-foot-high metal guard railing that had sections torn out. This hundred-yard-long bridge of cracking concrete and mounds of rubble looked as if it had been destroyed by a bomb. It crossed a river that was now a dried riverbed with a shallow stream no wider than thirty feet. The river scene below included desiccated cows drinking and defecating, dead animals lying on their sides with bloated bodies, and natives washing laundry and filling water containers while also taking care of their toilet and washing needs. Stunned into silence, we stared incredulously at this panorama of primitiveness. From the riverbed rose a putrid stench that caused us to gag and added to our stupefaction.

Leaving the bridge, we found it impossible to avoid the physical and psychological distress that enveloped us at every turn. Just like the taxi driver who had driven daringly through the crowded streets, we had to move quickly to avoid the taxis, bikes, and animals in our path. Ramshackle wooden and concrete houses flanked the narrow streets. Usually no higher than two stories, most of these attached houses looked rickety and in disrepair. Sections of walls were unfinished or caved in, spaces for windows remained open or were covered with cardboard, and gaps in roofs were the norm. Most striking was the primitive construction of these neighborhood buildings that tilted to one side. Wooden siding, brick walls, and roofing rarely showed the symmetry of seams and angles that should join together. Doors hung awry, and house entrances were curblike steps of varying heights. Colors in all shades of brown and gray reinforced the drab quality these houses projected. How similar these Nepalese streets were to the vandalized buildings of the South Bronx of New York City. "Streets" is a euphemism for the narrow, winding dirt roads that are littered with mounds of dirt, animal dung, and clumps of garbage. These streets are also frequently torn up for the laying of underground pipe. Nowhere in the world can one escape the ongoing construction; from the streets of Manhattan to those of Kathmandu, the pedestrian seems eternally plagued by road repairs.

The first native adults and children we encountered that afternoon haunted and disturbed us with their vacant and emaciated looks. For the most part, they seemed oblivious to tourists. With one exception: begging children looked at us with a mixture of curiosity and supplication. Begging was usually left to children who would suddenly appear from nowhere, stand in your path, and boldly shove a hand in front of you. We remembered the admonition Jim had given us at the orientation: Ignore children who beg, for to give them money can upset the fragile economic balance that exists in this impoverished land, where the native wage is not much higher than a dollar a day. On the other hand, begging by crippled adults is acceptable. The Nepalese have rationalized that since its society does not provide for the disabled, begging is allowed, because it functions as a form of social welfare.

Paradoxically, poverty and an air of industriousness assailed our senses. These natives seemed constantly busy and in motion. Men, women, and children were all engaged in productive tasks. Someone was always scurrying by with a huge basket on his or her back. Many natives walked stooped over, as their heavy loads were carried in the traditional way, with a headband support. Even the smallest children carried baskets much larger than themselves, threatening to topple them over. Others were busy selling from small shop stalls, which were usually on the ground floors of their houses. These stalls were like miniature stores, no larger than a small room, and stocked with their specialty of groceries, lotions, vegetables, fruit, or meat. Most of the shop items looked old and unappealing with their faded labels and shriveled cartons. The butcher stalls repulsed us, as slabs and sides of beef and butchered fowl were displayed on the dirt floor, oozing blood and smelling putrid. Vegetables and fruits were the only appealing items, displayed neatly in patterns of bright contrasting colors and groupings that made pleasing geometric designs. On closer view, however, this appetizing scene gave way to disgust as one saw the stale produce mixed with the fresh and observed the flies and dust that settled on everything.

Effective sanitation or cleanliness appeared to be sorely lacking. The natives washed their clothes with water drawn from small springs and water holes polluted by garbage and animal waste. Poorly and simply clothed, men wore pants and sport shirts, while women were dressed in blouses or shirts and long dresses to below the knee. Most clothes looked secondhand and cast-off, usually in drab shades of tan and gray. However, some children and adults stood out dramatically in this dreary landscape because of their colorful dress, such as a bright red sweater, deep blue pants, flowered dress, or multicolored blouse. These vivid colors were a pleasing contrast indeed and a momentary lift to our saddened spirits. To me, this handful of colors symbolized the human spirit and individuality in refusing to succumb to the dreary and destitute atmosphere.

The air of Kathmandu was pervaded with swirling dirt that settled upon everything and everybody. People looked grimy with dirt, especially those barelegged in shorts and the partially naked infants and young children. It was impossible to avoid the dust that was blown about by the afternoon breezes and kicked up by scrambling rickshaw drivers and darting taxis. This dusty atmosphere gave off a dead and unclean odor permeated with a mixture of ordure, rubble, and pollution. At times, the smell of decay and dust was so bad that it made me gag.

After a few hours of wandering about, we returned to the hotel in a state of shock, traumatized by the poverty, filth, stench, and dilapidation that assailed our senses. I became aware of a strange reaction during the walk: after several initial exclamations of disbelief, no one spoke much. We walked back to the hotel in silence, each preoccupied with his sundered emotions. One of our group remarked that compared to the poorest third world countries in Africa, the marginal and impoverished living conditions of this Kathmandu locale were the worst he'd ever seen. It was with relief that we saw the hotel rising in the distance on a hilltop, like a haven of safety and comfort, walled off from the destitute neighborhood that we had just experienced. I was plagued by a disturbing thought: *If this is the capital of Nepal, what is in store for us in the uncivilized mountain country through which we'll be trekking and living the next twenty days?*

The Hotel Vajra turned out to be a dubious haven of comfort. In the few hours before meeting Jim, Maura, and Ved for our dinner meeting at 7:30, each of us was to become disappointed with this native hotel. Although the Vajra was steeped in native charm and local color, with its small brick courtyards, marble floors, stone walls, futon beds, and flower gardens, this charm slowly gave way to disillusionment. Our Western washing, toilet, and space requirements were quite at odds with these fascinating lodgings. Eager to rest and freshen up after the long, fatiguing trip and depressing afternoon walks, we all experienced varying degrees of inconvenience with our accommodations.

Bathrooms were the major problem. Most had water leaks coming from the toilet, the shower stall, or some mysterious hidden pipes. As a result, the crooked and cracked tile floor was always wet and usually flooded with an inch of water. Toilets did not always flush. Bath towels looked unclean; their white color had faded to gray, and the fabric had worn to a paper-thin texture. Yet water faucets worked, and hot water was available.

The short, narrow beds with futon mattresses were comfortable and adequate. However, the musty bed odor and soiled dark red mattress coverlets were not conducive to relaxing. In compensation, we had a spacious room with large, airy French-type windows. It was furnished sparsely but pleasingly with a chair, a table, and an Oriental rug partially covering the polished dark wooden floor. We learned that our room was the choicest and that the other rooms were like closets that would have comfortably accommodated the trekking gear without the addition of people—an exaggerated description, but one that fitted well the disgusted reactions of the weary travelers. Nevertheless, we all slept well that first night in Kathmandu until the dogs started barking.

Around midnight and through the early morning hours, packs of dogs howled incessantly. During the day, dogs were underfoot everywhere, reacting indifferently to people. At night, though, they seemed possessed, if their endless snarling and barking was any indication of their spirits. No one could give us any explanation of their nocturnal howling, nor did other people seem concerned about this nightly phenomenon. Our best speculation was that both domesticated and wild dogs, which roamed the countryside, came out to forage and fight for food after the natives turned in.

Before retiring, we dined in the Vajra's restaurant with Jim, Maura, and Ved, who gave us a more detailed orientation about Nepal, the trek, and our plans for the next few days. This after-dinner orientation was to become a ritual with Jim. Even on the trek, when we would find ourselves dead with fatigue, Jim would patiently and concisely outline the next day's trekking goals, points of interest, and potential problems. This first orientation focused on the immediate itinerary, and he gave guidelines about food, drink, equipment, and the plane flight to the trek's starting point. The group would have two days in Kathmandu to rest and become acquainted with a new culture before the forty-five-minute flight into Lukla at 9,200 feet, where the trek would begin.

During the few days in Kathmandu, most of us walked the streets of the exotic city, shopped in the endless variety of fascinating stores, and just watched the teeming crowds of people and animals go by. At 4,500 feet with temperatures ranging from the sixties to the nineties, Kathmandu also offered a chance to acclimatize gradually to a high altitude and warmer weather than the raw winds and cold temperatures of March in New York. If we wanted physical conditioning, Jim suggested a bicycle tour around Kathmandu's perimeter or hiking in the hills of a nearby state park. Having gotten this far in good physical and mental shape, I rejected these activities as being too strenuous. I feared the possibility of a physical mishap and becoming fatigued before the trek. I just wanted to rest, relax, and walk through this exciting city. Walking would be enough exercise for us at this point. When several of the group spent the hot and muggy next day bicycling and hiking in the nearby hills, Olga and I became insecure about our physical condition, compared to the others. We were quite worn out by the long journey and wanted to do nothing but rest before the trek, which was to be one of the most physically and emotionally stressful challenges of our lives.

Food and drink would present constant challenges. Jim warned against eating fresh food such as fruit, salads, and uncooked vegetables. Water and local drinks were also to be avoided. If we consumed these at an unacceptable local hotel or restaurant, we chanced a case of diarrhea or dysentery. Jim explained that in the better restaurants and hotels, all water was boiled for twenty minutes and vegetables were cooked enough to kill off the harmful bacteria. Since milk and cream are not boiled, Jim also prohibited us from eating ice cream anywhere. Much of the high infant mortality rate and the shortened life expectancy of the Nepalese can be attributed to the primitive and poor sanitary conditions that contaminate all food and water in Nepal. It was odd to view the everyday things of life, which we take for granted in our Western world, with apprehension and doubt.

For the next two days in Kathmandu, we had to remain patient and keep mentally prepared for the trek while we acted like tourists getting acquainted with the local customs. As Jim described the trek that evening, I sensed an undercurrent of impatience and tension among the group, who were eager to get on with it. The excitement grew as Jim began outlining what we could expect during the next twenty days in the field.

The trek would begin in Lukla, a small village at 9,200 feet, reached by an early morning mountain airplane flight. Each day, the group would hike to a new campsite. Averaging six hours of walking daily, we could walk at our own speed. Since the trails were clearly marked and the Sherpas would keep a vigilant but unobtrusive watch over us, there was little chance to become separated from the group. A typical day's hike consisted of endless descents and ascents, trudging down into valleys, crossing ravines and gorges, and going up and up to one rise after another. Walking at altitudes that ranged from ten to twelve thousand feet, we would rest every third day in order to avoid altitude sickness and ensure proper acclimatization. The trek's goal was Kala Pattar ("black rock") at 18,250 feet, which offered the closest and best full view of Mt. Everest. This viewing site would be approached from the final campsite, Lobuche, at sixteen thousand feet, and demanded a rigorous climb of nearly eight hours. The group would leave Lobuche at 4:00 AM in order to reach Kala Pattar by noon and have an hour of viewing before the afternoon clouds obscured Everest and the surrounding peaks.

Repeatedly, Jim stressed that the most serious potential problem was altitude sickness. Despite decades of mountain research with the most advanced physiological technology, no one could predict how high altitudes would affect a person. The best knowledge we had lay in methods of prevention: gradual or slow acclimatization, proper physical condition, and adequate nourishment. Jim advised that we drink at least two quarts of liquids a day and always eat something, although we might have little appetite at these high elevations. Even experienced mountain climbers will suffer altitude sickness for a few days until they become acclimated and shake off the disabling symptoms. Lassitude, fatigue, nausea, headaches, loss of appetite, pulmonary edema, coughing, and rapid breathing are the signs of altitude illness. To help prevent and minimize mountain sickness, the trekker should avoid overexertion and take things slowly. If altitude sickness does occur, an immediate retreat to a lower altitude and rest is crucial. Despite these cautions, Jim noted that we might still feel mild distress because of the high altitude and briefly experience dizziness, weakness, appetite loss, or general malaise. When I expressed little concern over this problem and remarked that I was used to skiing at heights of ten to eleven thousand feet with no difficulty, Jim emphasized that living twenty-four hours a day, compared to several hours of skiing at that altitude, is a completely different experience.

To guide us and take care of our needs, our trekking group would have a complement of twenty Sherpas, including a sirdar (or leader), several guides who would stay with us on the trail, porters, and kitchen crew. To carry equipment, food supplies, and our duffel bags, the group had the services of twelve *dzopkyo*, a smaller version of a yak, the beast of burden used throughout the mountain country of Nepal. Each morning, the group would be awakened at 6:00 AM by a Sherpani, or kitchen girl. Carrying a kettle of tea, she would pour the day's first cup of tea that would combat the morning chill and help us get moving. Breakfast would be an hour later at seven o'clock, allowing time for washing, dressing, and packing gear.

Although the daily amenities of life would be met, their implementation would be limited to the basics, at best. For washing, boiled hot water would be dispensed from a five-gallon can with a homemade faucet. Just enough should be taken to quickly wash our hands and faces, since water would not be plentiful. If need be, however, we could have a basin of hot water to shave. Toilets were small huts built of stone and wood, varying in size from that of a closet to a small room. This Asian outhouse would have a rectangle cut out in the middle of the floor, which was usually strewn with hay. By comparison, a typical outhouse with its wooden bench was a luxury. No such comfort here. Learning how to squat properly over this target would take some getting used to and practice.

A special note on clothing reflected a cultural norm that surprised us: women trekkers were requested to wear skirts when hiking. Although slacks would be acceptable, the Nepalese disapproved of women wearing tight-fitting or revealing clothes. Jim explained that trekkers were more welcome and accepted if they conformed to the local custom. A more practical reason concerned the matter of answering the demands of nature, which would be easier for women wearing skirts than slacks.

Dressing for the day was also to be a new experience for me. The amount and kind of clothing we wore and took along in our day packs would depend upon the weather, the altitude, and one's physical condition. As Jim explained, we had to avoid becoming overheated yet not become cold. What we wore during the early morning hours to ward off the mountain chill would be different from our midday attire when the mountain sun was intensely warm. Therefore, clothing should be a system of layers. As weather conditions changed, an additional layer of clothing could be removed or added. For example, after walking for hours in warm sunlight, a descent into the shadows and turbulent wind of a river gorge would bring a temperature drop that would make you yearn for a sweater and jacket. From there, hiking to the heat and dust of a rising, rocky trail would leave you perspiring and shedding clothes. Layering clothes helps you adjust to sudden temperature changes and, most importantly, prevents you from catching cold. This once-in-a-lifetime trek made us anxious about remaining physically healthy, since the slightest illness would have more serious consequences here on a Himalayan hiking trail than back home in suburbia.

The importance of having proper clothing was emphasized before the trek when a list of required clothing was mailed to each of us. Anyone found lacking any of the clothing requirements was firmly instructed to purchase the missing item in Kathmandu before we moved out. Jim explained his philosophy: it is better be over-prepared for severe weather conditions than to be under-equipped and suffer ill effects that could ruin your trek. We needed clothing to cope with summer temperatures, the quickening cold of the evening (eating dinner in unheated and windy Sherpa homes), and the possibility of rain or a snowfall. Also, our clothing should wash and dry quickly and absorb the perspiration that would flow freely from us during the day. We were to have no synthetics, only 100 percent wool and cotton, with the exception of long underwear and jackets that could be made of the revolutionary, man-made materials of polypropylene and bunting. These fabrics can actually absorb and throw off perspiration (moisture wicking), preventing one's body from becoming clammy and chilled. The basic trekking clothes included a down parka, an outer shell garment, long underwear, a wool jacket, hiking trousers and shorts, a few cotton shirts, some changes of underwear, gloves, and hats. Hiking boots, an extra pair of shoes such as sneakers or moccasins for relaxing at the end of the day's trek, and wool socks and liners composed the footgear. The single most important piece of gear, hiking boots, needed to be broken in, well fitting, and ankle high to stand up to a day of hiking on all kinds of terrain, steep grades, and descents. Needless to say, any serious foot problem would be a major tragedy.

At the end of each day's hike, the Sherpas would pitch everyone's tents, which would be ready and waiting for our weary bodies as we arrived at a campsite. Sleeping bags, preferably of down material, were rated for temperatures down to five degrees below zero Fahrenheit. Evening temperatures could be expected to be around freezing, but they might drop to below zero at the sixteen-thousand-foot campsite. Immediately after breakfast, the camp would be struck and quickly disappear as the Sherpas and animals carried everything away to the next campsite. Despite each Sherpa being burdened with loads averaging sixty pounds of food and kitchen equipment, they would arrive at the new camp destination hours before the group. Being greeted by their smiling faces and the ever-ready mugs of tea and biscuits would become a daily ritual that would lift the spirits of the most fatigued trekkers—usually Olga and me. The untiring good humor, helpfulness, and solicitude of the Sherpas were incredible and a joy to behold.

In addition to this gear, each trekker would take along several essential accessories: toilet articles, a quick-drying towel, two plastic water bottles, a flashlight and tent light with spare batteries, and a pocket knife. Special emphasis was placed on having dark sunglasses, a hat, sun screen, and lip salve to protect against the intense sun at high altitudes, which could cause serious sunburn. Certainly, everyone had cameras and loads of film, but I hadn't counted on seeing Jack, a fellow trekker, burden himself with a tripod throughout this arduous trek. The tripod was packed in a homemade, light-weight, shiny, silver metal container that hung from the bottom of Jack's day-pack. We could always spot Jack on the trail, no matter how far away, by the gleam of this futuristic-looking silver container in the distance. It was an odd but somehow comforting sight to see this insignificant bit of Western technology bouncing up and down on an isolated Himalayan hiking trail.

To protect against any of the many illnesses and health problems which could occur, we were required to bring a medical kit with every possible pre-cautionary medication: aspirin, Tylenol, codeine, an antihistamine, and an antibiotic, to treat cold symptoms, fever, minor pain, headache, and infection. For diarrhea, dysentery, and stomach upset, we took Pepto-Bismol, tincture of opium, and tetracycline. Although there are many other prophylactic and therapeutic products for such stomach disorders, diarrhea is an acute and time-limited problem that should be allowed to run its course without excessive medication.

Coping with altitude sickness became a controversial issue, especially between the two physicians in the group, since it worried everyone. The majority believed that our gradual acclimatization schedule, plus a large liquid intake and adequate eating to insure proper nutrition, would be sufficient preventive measures. The minority held that the drug Diamox would be beneficial in warding off and treating symptoms of high altitude. Those of us who frowned on such medication, however, were secretly relieved to know that Nas, an experienced trekker and surgeon, had a large supply of Diamox, which he generously offered to anyone.

Since the trek would take us to the World Health Organization's "rural and remote areas," we had to follow immunization recommendations. One of the curses of civilization is that we must be shot full of inoculations in

order to prevent illnesses. For Nepal, we had to be immunized against diph-
theria, tetanus, polio, typhoid, and hepatitis. Besides, we had to begin a
weekly regimen of taking antimalaria pills that would continue six weeks after
our return home.

Our last item of supplies consisted of a variety of snacks that would supple-
ment our meals. At high altitudes, you tend to lose your appetite, and snack
foods should be on hand. Olga and I took peanuts, granola bars, cheddar
cheese, raisins, peanut butter, crackers, and our very favorite Swiss Lindt
chocolate bars. As each of us had a small pharmacy of drugs, we all had mini
mobile candy and grocery stores in our packs.

All our clothing, footwear, medical supplies, accessories, and food needed
to fit into a cargo or duffel-type bag that could be no larger than three feet
long and a foot and a half in height. It needed to be rugged enough to be mis-
handled repeatedly by porters and animals. Each morning after breaking
camp, the bags would be slung on either side of a *dzopkyo* until the next
camp destination. Arriving at a new campsite, we would see the duffels neatly
placed in front of our respective tents. Seeing them was like coming home as
they represented all our possessions. Not only did we live out of them, but
they also became comfortable pillows for sleeping and propping ourselves up
to read in the tent at night. To see them being flung around, hanging from
the sides of our beasts of burden, misshapen and bulging and becoming dirt-
ier every day, called to mind the advice of a trekking guide: "One's cargo bag
should be strong enough to withstand being thrown from a second story and
stomped on over and over again." This exaggerated advice was more than
confirmed by the beat-up and filthy condition of our bags at the trek's end.

While listening raptly to Jim describing these details and concerns of the
trek, I became increasingly aware of the group as a unit. It wasn't until we
arrived in Kathmandu that we assembled fully as a group. By evening, I began
to get a sense of group identity and some initial impressions of the people we
were to live with during the next three weeks of arduous living conditions and
physical challenges. What struck me most was the serious, determined, and
efficient manner everyone projected. All revealed a deep sense of commit-
ment to achieving the trek's goals of arriving at the foothills of the greatest
mountain on Earth. Talking about our goal, which would demand much self-
discipline, generated a mood of controlled excitement and quiet apprehension. Although we were as different as any twelve individuals could be, we
seemed to be a pretty self-assured and independent group of people. That old

cliché, "rugged individualist," came to mind as I observed my trekking colleagues.

The youngest trekker was fourteen-year-old Kirt, who was accompanied by his father, Nas. At first, I wondered about the appropriateness of a teenager being included in a group of adults under these atypical daily living conditions. My concern quickly vanished as I got to know this bright, warm, witty, and spontaneous young man. A pleasure to be with, Kirt intuitively blended just the right amount of youthful brashness and deference to the adults. He knew his own mind and spoke it, yet he was able to mix harmoniously with individuals who could have been his parents. It was no easy task, but it was one that this exceptional boy of slight build, jet-black hair, and sparkling eyes took easily in stride.

A young married couple in their early thirties, Donna and Jim from Connecticut, provided the down-to-earth, easygoing, and joking manner that is so necessary to a group's morale. Donna, a hospital psychiatric social worker, was skinny and frail in contrast to Jim, a construction engineer, who looked like an overweight football lineman. They both seemed in less than excellent physical shape for what was ahead, an impression that quickly proved wrong as they left me in the dust with their vigorous trekking pace. I still smile when I remember Donna in her long flowered cotton skirt, knee socks, and baseball cap, and Jim with his bright red polypropylene long johns underneath his khaki shorts. As their colorful appearance made me smile, so did their wisecracking give me the lift I needed when the going became difficult for me.

The only other "youngsters" were a couple from Minnesota in their late thirties. Betty, a supervising hospital nurse, and John, a psychiatric social worker, were the epitome of the friendly but quiet and reserved midwesterner. Both had many years of backpacking and trekking experience, and John had years of mountaineering experience. I was to be ever grateful to John, who in his low-key and unassuming but firm manner explained how to maintain a slow but steady pace, and showed me the mountaineer's rest step. This basic technique proved invaluable when the trek had me puffing and feeling unable to put one step after another.

Our young middle age trekkers began with Nas, Kirt's father, in his late forties, an orthopedic surgeon residing in New Jersey. A wonderful human being, Nas made me feel privileged to know him. Ever ready to be of help and give of himself, Nas was the complete professional: supremely confident, knowledgeable, and ready to take charge. In a nonchalant but dominant manner, Nas was always in the center of things, offering advice and encouragement. Physically, Nas was made of steel. Even when suffering from a bad cold, Nas never seemed tired or out of sorts. At times, I felt mildly resentful and envious of his endless stamina and even temperament.

A long-time medical colleague and climbing friend of Nas was John, an Englishman residing and practicing orthopedic surgery in London. In his forties, John was an accomplished rock climber whose physical energy and stamina were boundless. Quiet, unassuming, and introverted, John set a torrid and driven pace throughout the trek. As the official physician of the trek, his gentle and caring manner soothed many trekkers' physical ailments and concerns. A friendly and teasing professional rivalry existed between Nas and John. When Nas was advising the group to take medication to combat possible altitude sickness and recommending other active therapeutic measures, John adopted the conservative wait-and-see approach, recommending no medication until necessary. Hearing their interchange, I thought how unfortunate it was that we had to bring our civilized controversies along to burden us in a land where decisions allowed for few options.

Another trekker in superb physical condition, and with the gung-ho attitude of Nas and John, was Abby, a widow in her early fifties hailing from Connecticut. I felt that she viewed everyone who was not up to her physical standards with condescension, especially Olga and me. Around Abby, I felt like an athlete on a team who failed to live up to the coach's expectations. A tough-minded and stern woman, Abby was a superb physical specimen. Even on rest days, Abby, Nas, and John took off for extra half-day side treks, the thought of which just added to my physical and mental exhaustion. Watching them stride briskly, at a pace I could not even dream of maintaining, made me feel envious and inadequate. Usually, they would arrive at a new campsite about two hours before Olga and me. Not only were they faster on the trail, but they also seemed tireless and nowhere close to the fatigue I felt at day's end.

Jack and Caryl and Olga and I completed the group. All in our late fifties, we found that we were practically next-door neighbors, living just ten minutes apart in adjacent Long Island suburban towns—a strange coincidence indeed. A professor of engineering on sabbatical, Jack took everything in a calm, methodical, and analytical fashion. Nothing ruffled Jack, who exuded competence and confidence. More easygoing was his wife, Caryl, whose slow and regular pace reflected her laid-back attitude. As I compared myself to this lightly built man and chubby, chain-smoking woman, I felt an edge of physical superiority. This feeling quickly vanished when I learned that Caryl and

Jack had been trekking and camping out West for at least a decade. They were instrumental in teaching us a crucially important trekking lesson: to walk at a regular, consistent pace, no matter how slowly, so that one avoids stopping to rest. Too-frequent resting interferes with one's metabolism and makes it difficult for the body to get started up again. I still see Caryl walking at a snail's pace, hardly stopping, and passing nearly everyone who began at a rapid pace that could not be sustained all day.

From the moment we planned the trek, Olga and I never stopped wondering whether we were physically fit enough to cope with living in a tent for twenty days and trekking to a height of eighteen thousand feet. Anxious because we had no overnight outdoor camping experience, we became obsessed with our physical condition. We rationalized that our fairly active outdoor life (skiing, walking, and sailing), healthy physical constitutions, and intense desire would see us through. Several telephone calls to Overseas Adventure Travel, the trekking organization in Boston, discussing our apprehension, were met with emphatic reassurances. We were told that even inexperienced trekkers in their late sixties had made the trek. Despite these reassurances, a pervasive anxiety about our lack of camping and mountaineering experience preyed on our minds.

Always the optimist and positive thinker (and a good foil to my overly objective and skeptical outlook), Olga pooh-poohed my doubts and anxieties. When we first met our fellow hikers, Olga was quick to observe that we looked in much better physical condition than they, and she said that I should stop worrying about our ability to keep up with them. I could not, however, let go of my worries, which were somewhat reinforced during the two rest days in Kathmandu. While Olga and I rested from the forty-hour journey and walked leisurely around Kathmandu, shopping and sightseeing, most of the group took a strenuous bicycle tour of the city, and some went on a vigorous hike in hills overlooking the city. None of this fazed Olga; once settled on a course of action, she remained undaunted and determined to succeed. More important, her cheerful and positive attitude helped her ignore and overcome the toughest obstacles. Olga is a gutsy gal who doesn't give up easily.

We began preparing for the trek, both physically and mentally, the summer before. From our vacation home in Chittenden, Vermont, situated at an elevation of two thousand feet and surrounded by the lush Green Mountains, we took daily hikes into the forest and mountain trails. It was a short drive to the ski slopes of Pico Peak and Killington, where I learned to ski at the age of forty, and there we climbed ski trails, which were overgrown with long grass, berry bushes, and wild flowers. Arriving at Killington's summit of 4,400 feet, I wondered how it would be walking in Nepal at over ten thousand feet, flanked by mountain peaks rising to over twenty-five thousand feet. Gazing at the endless view of the rolling and verdant Green Mountains and valleys, like seductive, hazy, blue green ocean waves in the sky, one thing seemed certain to me: nothing could be more beautiful. The Himalayas would be huge and awesome with a beauty of their own. There was no need to compare nature with nature. The beauties of nature aren't consumer products trying to outdo each other. The eternal allure of nature is that beauty is found everywhere, from the smallest wildflower to the tallest redwood tree, the trickling forest stream to the endless ocean, the low, earth-hugging hills to soaring alpine mountain peaks. Nature, like an emotion, should not be analyzed and catalogued, lest we lose its essence.

In addition to scrambling around the forests and mountains of Vermont, we walked endlessly on weekends back home on Long Island. Residing on the south shore of Long Island in North Bellmore, thirty miles from NYC, we had a short drive to Jones Beach, where we hiked the long stretch of beaches. For hours, with daypacks, we trudged up and down the sand dunes until our legs ached. In the fall and winter, devoid of summer crowds, the beach and ocean take on a quiet and desolate beauty. Unfortunately, at the end of several hours of trudging in the sand, we were too exhausted and sweaty to appreciate it any longer. (Now, the thought of walking on the beach leaves me less than enthusiastic.) I never realized how tiring and difficult it would be to walk for hours in sinking sand, and as I came to hate every minute of it, I consoled myself with the thought that it was getting my legs and lungs in shape. During fall weekends, we also drove to Bear Mountain on the Hudson River near West Point, and there we hiked the many rocky and steep trails to the summit. Enveloped by the striking colors of autumn foliage, this was a great day's outing and provided excellent conditioning, since the rocky terrain and grade approximated the Nepalese trails. In retrospect, this physical conditioning was crucial in helping us keep up with the physical demands of the trek, but it most certainly should have been much more extensive in view of the extreme fatigue we experienced during most of the trek in Nepal.

Both Olga and I felt that our mental outlook was equally important to the physical preparations. Our enthusiasm for the trek knew no bounds. A day didn't pass without our talking about the coming trek, and for me, seeing Mt. Everest was a boyhood dream. Not only were we enthusiastic, but we also felt confident of being successful. Although Olga chided me for my apprehension, our attitudes and thoughts about the trek were positive. My most serious concern was making the trek's goal of Kala Pattar, the black rock summit of eighteen thousand feet from which one has the closest and least obstructed view of Mt. Everest. That day's hike would consist of breaking camp at 4:00 AM in pitch darkness, followed by an eight-hour climb to Kala Pattar. After an hour of viewing and resting, we would have a four-hour descent to our campsite. This would be the most arduous and longest day of the trek, with at least twelve hours of climbing on terrain more steep and rocky than any of the previous trails. It turned out that my anxieties about this day were not farfetched and unrealistic.

2

Culture Shock

Our first full day in Kathmandu was given over to sightseeing, shopping, and resting. Rising early, we had a familiar breakfast of orange juice, fried eggs, and toasted thick white bread. The hotel dining room was a charming, sparkling-clean room, decorated in white, blue, and gold Buddhist designs and murals. The cool, soothing, and tranquil atmosphere was somewhat marred by a pervasive unpleasant acrid odor that seemed to be a mixture of curry, kerosene oil, and rancid butter. After breakfast, most of the group opted to rent bicycles and tour the city. Not only were Olga and I too tired to go biking, but the thought of navigating on bicycle through the teeming traffic of Kathmandu was mildly frightening. It would be like snaking through a Manhattan midtown traffic jam, with rickshaws, animals, and trolley cars thrown in. We settled for a leisurely stroll through bustling streets of shops that led to the famous Monkey Temple, a Buddhist shrine on top of the hill overlooking Kathmandu, a half hour's walk from the hotel through dusty, hard-packed dirt streets. Its golden dome, rising above the western edge of the city, was a beautiful and haunting sight, especially at twilight, when the gold became suffused with a rosy, shimmering glow.

Now in early March, signs of the oppressive summer heat to come were already in the air. In the mornings, a haze covered the city that made the golden heat of the sun feel clammy and uncomfortable. I remembered that Nepal is at the same latitude as Miami, Florida, and is characterized by a subtropical climate. It was hard to believe when thinking about the distant, forbidding, snow-covered Himalayas, but it was easy to accept when dressing for the already humid heat of Kathmandu in March. Olga, dressed in a cotton shirt and skirt, and I in khakis with a light sport shirt, made our way through the narrow, winding, and dusty streets leading to the Buddhist temple of Swayambhunath.

Already perspiring lightly from the humidity and still tired from jet lag, I was unhappy to see that the three hundred flagstone steps leading to the temple were fairly steep and at least twenty stories high. Climbing up the steps, we were welcomed by monkeys sliding up and down iron handrails flanking the ten-foot-wide worn and chipped tan stone steps. Darting about playfully, these monkeys reminded us that the temple is also called the Monkey Temple because of their presence. Small groups of young children were scattered about the steps' entrance, waiting to beg as tourists approached. A determined and stubborn boy of about ten years with unkempt black, overgrown hair, a faded, soiled blue denim shirt, and blue jeans attached himself to us as a self-appointed guide. It was hard to ignore his determination and the charm of his sparkling eyes and toothless grin. Strangely, the children we observed seemed much younger because of their physically stunted appearance, even though their sad-looking and pleading eyes made them look older.

Arriving breathless at the top of the steps, we entered the temple grounds, which consisted of a cluster of shops, houses, and smaller temples built in a variety of different architectural styles. Swayambhunath's huge stupa, a dome-shaped white concrete structure with a golden-spired tower soaring into the dark blue sky, dominated this temple-village. This stupa was built two thousand years ago and is thought to be the oldest in Nepal. Overlooking the city, it was a breathtaking sight, which was made more exciting and mysterious by the large, elongated blue eyes of the Buddha painted on the squat base of the tower. We were to see innumerable stupas of all sizes throughout Nepal, with the eyes of Buddha following us everywhere. Symbolically, the Buddha's eyes represent our conscience always watching us. This religious motif was reinforced by a large wall of gold and black prayer wheels set in a wrought-iron trellised structure. Looking at the forbidding and scowling eyes of Buddha made me want to spin the prayer wheels in obeisance—conscience doth made cowards of us all. (Even here on the other side of the world, religion invokes fear to instill ethical behavior.)

Physically and emotionally, our senses were overwhelmed by this hodge-podge of buildings, the myriad of intense colors, and the odors of incense, charcoal fires, and feeding animals. The inhabitants of this temple-village looked even more impoverished when viewed against this richly dramatic backdrop. It was as if a group of itinerant actors had walked onto the wrong stage set. Yet these temple villagers went about their business in the passive, calm, and detached manner that characterized most Nepalese. Not our intrepid child guide, however, who excitedly dashed around, pointing things out to us. He led us to a small shrine that made up the northeast corner of the grounds. Before entering, visitors had to remove their shoes as a sign of respect and deference to the god within. Entering this dimly lit interior, we were greeted by chanting, atonal music, incense, flickering candles, and shoving people. Upon leaving the shrine and ambling about with a tourist's curiosity and naivete, we could not help but wonder about the experiences to come. What would be in store for us in the next few weeks, if so much awe and excitement had already been generated in less than two days in Kathmandu?

As we left Swayambhunath and descended its steep steps, we were greeted by many more monkeys that romped about on our arrival. Their mischievous glances called to mind a guidebook's advice to be wary of them lest they snatch any packages we might be carrying. Appealing and comical as monkeys are, they seemed to project a sinister and distrustful quality to me. When we said good-bye to our doughty guide at the Swayambhunath street entrance, where twenty-foot high colorful stone goddesses looked over us, I was taken aback by the boy's reaction to the ten rupees (about seventy-five cents) I had given him. With a flash of a smile, he turned on his heels and ran away as quickly as he had come. How naive I was to be disappointed in his quick flight. I thought we had forged some emotional bond after spending the morning together. It was another instance of culture shock, I rationalized, telling myself that his reaction was appropriate: he rendered a service, was reimbursed, and departed to look for other customers. However common and prevalent begging is in a poverty-stricken culture, it will always upset me to see young children reduced to such a degrading condition. Even as a soldier in occupied Europe after World War II, where begging children were commonplace, I was angered that the world allowed this to happen to children. In my own childhood, I had often wondered why adults treated children so punitively and disrespectfully. This concern led to my lifelong interest in understanding human behavior and to my becoming a psychologist. Although I know the intellectual and theoretical answers, after a lifetime of clinical practice, I still become enraged at man's inhumanity to children. I consoled myself with the thought that these begging and scavenging children exemplified the incredible strength and will of humans to adapt and survive.

Thirsty, hungry, and hot from this exhilarating morning at the Swayambhunath temple, we were sorely tempted to buy bottled soda and oranges from one of the many tiny shops that dotted the narrow streets. Although the fruit, vegetables, and soda bottles looked colorful, fresh, and inviting, we remembered Jim's warning to avoid fresh produce, and we resisted the temptation. It wasn't too hard to resist when we viewed the shops in their dilapidated and grimy setting and saw the tattered appearance of most shopkeepers. We saved our appetite for lunch at the hotel dining room, where we had odd-tasting grilled cheese sandwiches and refreshing limeade.

Feeling refreshed, we planned an afternoon of shopping and souvenir hunting. Despite the exotic and exciting ambiance of Kathmandu, we were preoccupied with the thought of the trek and the flight tomorrow that would begin the adventure that had brought us halfway around the world. Shopping and sightseeing were just marking time. This was dramatically reinforced as we passed shops with mountaineering equipment and clothing displayed from floor to ceiling. Near the center of town stood a row of about twenty trekking and mountaineering travel agencies. Their names (Everest Travel Service, Himalayan Exploration, Mountain Travel, Trans-Himalayan Tours, Sherpa Trekking, Yak Travel, Yeti Travel) and advertising posters only heightened our excitement and impatience to be on our way. Our own Overseas Adventure Travel agency (OAT) of Cambridge, Massachusetts, was squeezed in a small office with the barest of furnishings. It stood in marked contrast to the hype and commercialism of most trekking agencies, and we wondered whether we had chosen wisely. But in the little time we had interacted with Jim and the OAT staff, we were impressed with their professionalism and careful attention to every detail. We were further reassured by one of those coincidences that happen to everyone.

On a street corner, we met a young, emaciated Englishman who had just returned from Kala Pattar, our trekking destination. Hanging on to his every word, we found that he had trekked by himself, picking up a Sherpa guide here and there, eating and sleeping along the trail. He bemoaned his lack of planning and schedule, which didn't allow for a gradual acclimation to the high altitudes. Not only did he suffer from altitude sickness, but also from bouts of diarrhea and an upset stomach caused by his careless drinking and eating habits. When we described our itinerary, he complimented us on our choice of OAT. It seemed that most of the foreigners in Kathmandu were either, like us, marking time before a trek, or those who had returned from a trek. All conveyed either an impatient eager-to-get-on-with-it manner, or an air of quiet triumph and self-satisfaction.

Except for the innumerable cluttered shops with their ambiance of dirt, detritus, and odors, shopping in Kathmandu was no different from anywhere else in the world. In Nepal, wood-carved and silver-inlaid prayer wheels, oriental rugs, furs, jade, and original paintings on parchment were priority items on most tourists' shopping lists. Many college students from the West financed their stay in Nepal by purchasing several oriental rugs at an average price of fifty dollars and selling them back home for several hundreds of dollars each. The favorable exchange rate—about sixteen rupees for a dollar—tempted everyone to buy readily in Nepal. This translated into about ten dollars for a colorful handmade sweater, two dollars for a woolen ski hat, and ten dollars for an excellent dinner for two in a local native restaurant. A moderately priced hotel room for two ranged from twenty to thirty dollars per night, while one in a luxury hotel averaged sixty dollars. The lure of a bargain serves as an excuse to buy many of the souvenirs that initially are so appealing and later become just so much junk. Despite the dire poverty in Nepal, every conceivable type of consumer good was available. Although pharmaceutical items and film for cameras were difficult to find, they were obtainable if you looked hard enough. The only item we could not find was firecrackers, for which our teenage trekker, Kirt, searched in vain.

Although British mountaineering groups have been arriving in Nepal since the 1930s, the country was closed to foreign visitors during World War II and reopened again in 1951. Foreigners have since flocked to Nepal in increasing numbers, and over a hundred and twenty-five thousand tourists now arrive annually. Other than the prevalent T-shirts, Coca-Cola, pizzas, and similar consumer goods and foods, Nepal has been minimally touched by Western ways and ideas. A few major Western influences, however, stand out: the emphasis on improved personal hygiene, sanitation, and education. Wherever we walked in Kathmandu, we came across a scattering of private schools, easily recognizable by their students' neat and well-groomed attire and appearance. Children in local public schools looked like a motley group, unwashed, uncombed, and dirty, whereas pupils in private schools looked spankingly clean and neat. It's a truism in Nepal that improved education brings better personal hygiene and chances for a longer life. Because of the pollution and unsanitary conditions, about half of Nepalese children die by their fifth birthday, and living to a ripe old age is not to be expected.

That afternoon of sightseeing and shopping found us buying the usual amount of obligatory presents for friends and family: sweaters, scarves, T-shirts, trinkets, and a bagful of woolen Sherpa-made ski hats, with their typical geometric design (a Greek key variation). As dutiful parents, we found a plush three-by-five-foot oriental rug at thirty-five dollars for our married daughter, and for our son a *cholo*, a woolen jacket similar to a Nehru coat. A local native garment, the *cholo* had to be custom made, since none on the rack would fit our strapping six-foot son. Eager to please, the tailor would deliver it to the hotel the next day. The cost for this custom-tailored *cholo* would be 145 rupees, or about nine dollars. We paid and asked that it be held until we returned from the trek, since tomorrow morning we would be flying to Lukla for the beginning of the trek. Like most consumer goods anywhere in the world, little of what we bought was actually made in Nepal, but instead came from neighboring Tibet, China, and India.

Nepal is primarily an agricultural nation, attested to by an infinite variety of street stalls purveying produce. Displayed in baskets and crates piled in tiers were colorful melons, oranges, lemons, limes, carrots, radishes, onions, cabbages, and potatoes that delighted the eye. Most of these stalls fronted the ramshackle and deteriorating apartment dwellings of the shopkeepers. The bright and varicolored produce against the background of decay made an incongruous scene. Above the teeming crowds in these narrow streets were occasional colored banners hanging twenty feet high, secured to poles, and stretching across the street's width. This was a local form of advertising, written in native or English words. For example, a typical advertising banner, neatly printed in bright green on a shabby white cloth background, is reproduced below:

Many of the banners were done up in pastel hues of pink, lavender, or green, adding to the colorful market displays on the street below.

Everywhere we walked, the filth, poverty, and shabbiness seemed to be dressed up in compensating colors and striking contrasts. The colorful produce contrasted sharply with the dirty streets and deteriorating houses. The naked and unwashed children sported ribbons in their hair or an item of new clothing that stood out against their dirty bodies. A newly painted rickety window frame, splintered door, or crumbling wall was like a beacon shining in the dilapidation.

The dress of the people also boggled the senses. There was no typical dress, no uniformity, no usual attire. The only common denominator of Nepalese dress in Kathmandu was its total lack of conformity, its individuality and unpredictability. The women, dark skinned with straight jet-black hair and beautiful sensual features, wore multicolored flowered or patterned dresses or blouses and skirts, or baggy pants covered by knee-length smocks, or native saris that covered the body in swirls of different-colored cloth from neck to ankle. No Nepalese woman, however, ever wore shorts, which were seen as being immodest and offensive to native religious standards. In contrast to women, the men displayed a greater range of dress. T-shirts of all colors, light-colored cotton slacks or faded blue jeans, ski sweaters and jackets, shorts and colorful sport shirts, Nehru jackets, and Western-style business suits made up a typical cross section of men's clothing. Most strange was the sight of a middle-aged man walking proudly dressed in a Western sport jacket over tight leg-fitting native cotton slacks and sporting the native *topi* headgear. The *topi* is the traditional Nepalese hat, distinguished by a high, flat crown, conelike in shape (akin to a fez), and brimless. Customarily made in dark or white cotton cloth, *topi* also come in patterned hues and shapes that conform closer to the head. Like the woman's sari, it projects an aura of exoticness and distinction. Men's hats also included the popular baseball caps with contrasting colors. Like everywhere else in the world today, T-shirts and hats sported a particular logo or advertising legend. How startled we were when we saw the writing on the T-shirt of Kanchha, the nineteen-year-old Sherpa who was to become like a second son to us, and our lifesaver on the trek; his faded orange T-shirt was from our own Yosemite National Park and bore the words GO CLIMB A ROCK. The unbelievable coincidence was not that Kanchha's shirt came from America, but that it was identical to the one our son had worn last summer. We saw this as a good-luck omen, and so it turned out when things became scary and threatening on the trek.

At that time of year in Kathmandu, early March, the weather was like an early New York summer, with much humidity and temperatures in the seventies to eighties. Although most natives dressed in light garments, many wore woolen sweaters, jackets, and outer garments as if it were cold. Probably this warmer attire was to ward off the dankness of the narrow, sunless streets that still held the cold of winter. Everyone, however, wore the same kind of footwear, either sandals or sneakers, and some children and adults padded about shoeless. It was hard to believe, while walking in the hot, crowded streets of Kathmandu, that the highest and coldest mountains on Earth are in Nepal.

Until now, whenever I thought of Nepal, the image of snow-covered, cold, forbidding Himalayan peaks came to mind, never an idea of the warm, balmy climate in which we now found ourselves. Harder to grasp was that just south of Kathmandu existed a tropical jungle preserve, Tiger Tops, where all kinds of jungle animals could be observed. Even the huge, welcoming white sign with its bright red letters at Kathmandu Airport gave no inkling of a tropical climate as it proclaimed: WELCOME TO NEPAL—THE LAND OF MAGNIFICENT MONUMENTS AND MOUNTAINS.

The day of shopping and sightseeing left us fatigued as well as excited and unnerved by the strange new impressions that constantly bombarded our senses. In my feverish desire to absorb all this newness, it seemed apparent that the strain and tension of taking pictures of everything prevented me from fully experiencing this different world. It is difficult to be a photographer and a genuine observer-participant at the same time. Looking at a culture through a camera lens gives one the narrow and constricted view of the lens and the photographer's subjectivity, however beautiful and atmospheric the pictures. At best, photos can only approximate the reality. This realization often made me put my camera aside so that I could more fully experience the people, places, and customs of exotic Kathmandu.

The more we let an experience come to us, the less we interpose ourselves—whether it be with a camera, a prejudice, an anticipation, or an expectation—the more we can enjoy and understand that new sensation. It is similar to what I remembered the maharishi emphasizing when instructing people how to meditate: "Take it as it comes." Or in the words of the Beatles, "Let it be." As a psychotherapist, I found that whenever I explained this concept of being—just allowing ourselves to experience an event without imposing our own rigid and subjective ways—the reaction was one of puzzlement. Regrettably, cultural conditioning and our own prejudices restrict us in experiencing life fully.

A vivid example occurred while I was taking pictures. Some Nepalese did not want their photos taken, and they became angered when a camera was pointed their way. I reproached myself for this indiscretion, forgetting that this appealing subject was a person with feelings and thoughts that the camera's lens disregarded. Those Nepalese who refused to have their pictures taken believed that a photo was destructive, as it captured their soul and took part of themselves away; thus their fearful looks and angry gesticulations at picture-taking tourists. From that first occurrence, I made a practice of asking permission, usually by gestures, of every Nepali whom I wanted to photograph.

We returned to the hotel late in the afternoon, laden with flimsy paper and plastic shopping bags filled with all sorts of gifts. Too tired to walk back, we debated about taking a rickshaw. The idea of someone struggling to pull us up and down hills through the treacherous traffic and narrow alleys was not appealing and seemed inhuman. But we rationalized away our own cultural prejudice and hired one. Unfortunately, the experience was unpleasant and confirmed our initial repugnance. The rickshaw driver was a scrawny, under-nourished middle-aged man who strained and puffed with all his might as he trotted through the bumpy dirt streets. Every time he came to a hilly section, he stopped to catch his breath and regain strength. The rickshaw was a fragile two-wheeled contraption that looked as if it had been improvised and built over two oversized bicycle wheels. Pulled by two long wooden guide bars attached to the hub of each wheel, the rickshaw did not ride easily over the road. The jostling was akin to being in a human mixmaster. Relieved that we were in sight of the hotel perched on a hilltop, we were surprised when the rickshaw driver stopped and announced that this was as far as he would go. Gesticulating that he couldn't make it up the hill, this bedraggled and exhausted man seemed on the verge of collapse. Perhaps we were naive, but we could not see his reactions as an attempt to defraud a tourist. Guilty that we were a part of this scene, we could not look the poor man in the eyes, and we quickly paid him. With much relief, we scrambled out of the rickshaw, even though it meant a tiresome, dusty, ten-minute climb uphill to the hotel compound.

What an enervating day it had been. Back in the hotel, we washed and rested for the evening ahead. The entire group was to be treated to a dinner at one of Kathmandu's popular restaurants, Rum Doodle. Washing and resting were not so easily accomplished. The leaking toilet was still not fixed, and the bathroom floor was slightly under water. Apprehensive about the water, we debated taking a shower. I needed to rid myself of the dust and perspiration that clung to me, and so I braved the shower, being careful not to swallow any water. Olga toweled herself down, as she would not trust the slippery, wet, crumbling tile floor of the shower stall. Using the bathroom was neither the pleasant nor refreshing experience it should have been. Resting was also diffi-cult in a smelly and soiled-covered futon-type bed. But we soothed ourselves with the thought that by tomorrow afternoon, we would be on the trail.

As we gathered that evening to leave for the restaurant, we learned that most of the group had bicycled around Ring Road, the outer highway that cir-cles Kathmandu, for several hours. And in the afternoon, John and Nas took off with Ved, the Nepalese representative of our trekking agency, to climb the steep hills behind the hotel. Jim couldn't believe their stamina and the torrid pace they had set. Hearing about everyone's physical activities, I wondered anxiously how we would compare to them on the trek. This nagging anxiety was somewhat diminished at dinner when I noticed them dozing off. At least they weren't superhuman, and they could feel as tired as we did.

A moderately priced restaurant, Rum Doodle consisted of a large, dark-paneled, dimly lit room with wooden tables, benches, and chairs. Situated in the heart of the Thamel shopping district, it is a meeting place for trekkers and offers a cross section of Western and Asian dishes. Many of us chose the popular steak, since meat would not be on our trekking diet. Although the meals were pretty acceptable, I found the food tinged with an odd flavor that seemed to be a mixture of charcoal and mild curry flavoring. Also, the texture of everything from bread to meat was much coarser and tougher than Western food. Kirt had a hamburger at Rum Doodle that was a disappointment because of its large chunks of beef. Noodles, rice, and french-fried potatoes were invariable side dishes. One of the most typical meals or dishes everywhere in Nepal is *dal bhat tarkari*, which is made of rice, lentils, and curried vegetables. All these ingredients get mixed together and can produce a tasty, well-cooked dish. But on the trek, it often was a mushy or pasty mixture with varying degrees of spiciness. Chicken made in every conceivable way and curries of all kinds were on every menu.

Although all kinds of liquor were available, we drank the local yeasty beer that helped quench the thirst that never seemed to leave us. The criteria for being considered a better restaurant, like Rum Doodle, require food to be fresh and well prepared from a hygienic viewpoint, and water to be safe for drinking. It is not enough that water is boiled; it must boil for at least ten minutes in order to kill off the bacteria. Most restaurants in Nepal do not follow this practice, and improper food preparation can cause diarrhea and hepatitis.

Our dinners at Rum Doodle were tempting to look at but varied in taste. None of us expected Western food standards, yet the different tastes, textures, and seasonings took time to get accustomed to. Jim emphasized that our stomachs might feel queasy for days until we got used to the food. The steak, for example, was stringy and a little tough, and strongly flavored; the spaghetti was overcooked, gluey, and accompanied by an acrid-tasting tomato sauce. Potatoes and bread were the most palatable food we had eaten so far. In this city of three hundred thousand people, there was an endless variety of food.

It is unbelievable, but in Kathmandu, which most people have never heard of, and which has little of the comforts and technologies of modern life, you can find most of the foods of the world. In addition to native food, a visitor can easily sample Tibetan, German, Japanese, French, Mexican, and Italian cuisine. Recently, pizza parlors have appeared in the crowded streets, and newly established pastry shops have introduced pies and cakes to a land that has no tradition of bakeries. I was astounded by the amazing variety of ethnic and international restaurants and food shops that existed in the narrow byways of Kathmandu. Even a Good Humor ice cream bicycle-type wagon (with a huge ice cream cone painted on a ground of pale yellow) could be found ting-a-linging through the streets. The product was comfortingly familiar, but the name seemed as exotic as the land: Himali ice cream. I nearly gave in to the temptation to buy one, but I recalled that ice cream could easily cause a stomach upset, since milk cannot be properly boiled. There was even a Mom's Health Food store featuring soy burgers, enchiladas, honey, whole wheat bread, and all the staples and foods you'd find in a New York or California health store.

When dinner ended at Rum Doodle, Jim outlined the plans for tomorrow's departure and the beginning of the trek. Although we were all tired from our day's sightseeing and on the verge of sleep from the food and drink, everyone listened intently to tomorrow's itinerary: an early breakfast, a truck ride to the airport, a 9:00 AM flight to Lukla, beginning the trek after lunch, and reaching the first campsite at around 5:00 PM, followed by dinner in the field. Impatient to return to the hotel to pack and get ready for the morning's departure, I wanted this evening to be over. My impatience made me forget my resolve to avoid any more rickshaw rides, but since this was the only available mode of transportation back to the hotel, we reluctantly climbed in the carriage. This time, however, the driver was an athletic-looking young man who exuded strength and muscle power. Our observation proved true with a vengeance as he trotted through the streets, pulling the rickshaw at a healthy clip. Hanging on for dear life and cursing ourselves for taking another hairy ride, we felt the rickshaw bounce and careen at a merciless pace. There was no need to worry, though, we told ourselves, as accidents were quite rare.

Safely in the hotel again, we made our preparation for the morning. All gear and clothes would go with us except for what the trekking guidelines euphemistically called "city clothes." We would leave behind enough clothes to be worn when we returned to Kathmandu after the trek—for men, slacks and sport shirts, and skirts and blouses for women. Packed in a duffle, the city clothing would be stored at the hotel. For tomorrow's first trekking day, I chose climbing shorts and a cotton shirt. Olga picked a cotton skirt that came to her ankles, especially suited for trekking, and a light woolen sweater. Both of us wore polypropylene undershirts and bunting jackets, the amazing new man-made materials that were warm yet porous, preventing the buildup of perspiration, and lightweight hiking boots.

In our daypacks, we stored sweaters, gloves, scarves, hats, snacks, and a 35 mm Spotmatic Pentax for me, and a Sure-Shot camera for Olga. The most important items in our daypacks were the two one-liter Nalgene (plastic) bottles required for our daily supply of drinking water. Everyone laughed when I confessed that I had filled our bottles with New York drinking water before leaving JFK airport. As it turned out, the laugh turned to envy when I was able to forestall, by a day, drinking the stale-tasting and kerosene-flavored water boiled for us every morning by the Sherpa kitchen staff. As our trekking experience would repeatedly demonstrate, we would not only learn to appreciate more the innumerable everyday things we took for granted, but also begin seeing them in a new light. For example, everyday drinking water for us is plentiful, clean, and fresh tasting (at least for us New Yorkers) and free from any health dangers. Not so for the poor and underdeveloped countries, whose people avoid drinking water and use it primarily as an ingredient for making coffee or tea.

3

The Clouds Have Rocks in Them

Monday, March 4, 1984, the day of the trek, finally arrived. The early morning was warm, humid, and hazy, like typical Kathmandu mornings this time of year. The group rode to the airport in various passenger cars loaded with gear piled in the trunks and strapped on their roofs. When we arrived at 8:00 AM, the airport was a bustle of activity and resembled a huge storage room with baggage piled everywhere, mostly equipment belonging to trekkers and climbers. It was an impossible crowded scene including people of all nationalities, dress, and baggage. How we ever got through the weighing and cursory baggage inspection so quickly and smoothly was a testament to the efficiency and know-how of our trek leaders, Jim and Ved, who knew how to deal with the native airport bureaucratic personnel.

From the time we arose that morning, everyone was preoccupied with the same nagging apprehension: would the weather enable a takeoff and allow a landing at Lukla? Lukla is a tiny mountain Sherpa village located on a small 9,200-foot-high plateau enveloped by mountains and drifting clouds. Only two daily flights to Lukla were scheduled by Royal Nepal Airlines Corporation, and these departed between 7:30 and 9:30 AM. After that time, the weather makes landings and takeoffs too hazardous. Because of the unpredictable weather, it was not uncommon for the earlier Lukla flight to turn back because of poor visibility and the later flight to succeed in landing as the weather cleared. No pilot ever knew whether he'd be successful in reaching Lukla because of the constantly changing cloud cover. Although the plane might leave in clear weather, the short forty-five-minute flight could suddenly encounter clouds and wind drafts that made a landing dangerous. The classic remark by a pilot, reported by Stan Armington in his *Trekking in the Himalayas*, explains the situation perfectly and succinctly: "We don't fly through the clouds because in Nepal the clouds have rocks in them."

The remote villages to which these planes fly have tiny airstrips that are quite tricky and difficult to approach without the additional problem of weather. For example, Lukla's dirt airstrip is a rock-strewn twelve-hundred-foot-long by fifty-foot-wide landing area that rises from its western to eastern end at an angle of ten degrees, and the western perimeter drops off into a valley thousands of feet below. The plane has exactly enough fuel for a return trip to Kathmandu and fifteen minutes of circling time to decide whether it is safe to land. The pilot has no instruments, only his eyesight and experience to rely on. Therefore, a decision to land has to be made quickly in view of the lack of technological aids and limited fuel. The passengers' eager anticipation and excitement must be totally ignored in the decision process. It is better to have delayed and angry trekkers than none at all.

Despite this dire description of the possible consequences of this plane flight, Royal Nepal Airlines had an incredible safety record in flying to these isolated and distant tiny mountain villages. Only one fatal accident had ever occurred: while taxiing for a takeoff, the plane suddenly and inexplicably exploded, killing all its occupants. It was an ironic catastrophe, since the victims included Louise Hillary and her preteen daughter, the family of Sir Edmund Hillary, the first mountaineer to conquer Mt. Everest. (Hillary and his family had decided to live in Nepal to devote their lives to developing health and educational facilities in order to improve the lives of the Sherpas, whom they had come to love and admire.) This unusual record of airline safety was the result of the extremely cautious and conservative attitude of the pilots. In a conversation with one of the pilots, I was told that they would refuse to take any chances and would abort the flight whenever there was the slightest doubt about the weather. A small airplane, limited to only visual approach techniques, has little room for error flying in narrow valleys, flanked by mountains that soar above twenty thousand feet. Therefore, delays of several hours or days could be expected when a trek involved flying into an isolated mountain village.

All of these thoughts went through our minds as we boarded the twin-engine Otter STOL (short takeoff and landing) aircraft that carried no more than nineteen passengers. Brightly painted with red and blue stripes on its tail against a white fuselage and wings, this plane looked like a toy model in an age of huge jets. We scrambled into the plane excitedly, trying to get the best seats to view the distant Himalayas. The crowded atmosphere inside accentuated the smallness of the plane. Every seat was taken, and Ved and Jim sat on duffel bags jammed behind the last row of seats. There seemed to be only enough room to get in and out of the plane. Still, the plane's interior surprised me with its neat and attractive white and blue plastic cabin interior and simulated wood molding. We were surprised to be greeted by a chubby and pretty stewardess dressed in a dark red flowered sari. (Chubby dark midriffs that were bared whenever the hostess bent over to serve a passenger seemed to be the rule when flying with sari-clothed air hostesses.)

Flying at about ten thousand feet, we saw the terraced valleys below looking parched from a lack of rain, since the monsoon and rainy season had ended the previous September. The unending hills and valleys over which we flew appeared uninviting because of their ugly shades of brown and wrinkled appearance. Except for an occasional patch of new grass, there was little evidence that spring would soon be here. The entire landscape below looked stark, lonely, and forbidding. I was relieved and glad that we were flying into Lukla rather than having to hike this depressing countryside. Walking to Lukla from Kathmandu, which many trekkers do, would have taken about twelve days instead of a forty-five-minute plane ride.

After ten minutes of flying, the great Himalayan peaks came into view in the distant north. A magnificent range of endless snow-covered mountains rose in the distance like a majestic background, contrasting with the foreground of arid valleys and ugly brown and black hills. As we flew closer, clouds began drifting lazily over the distant valleys, and puffs of clouds were rising from the valleys below. Even though these great mountains looked like miniature peaks in the distance, they still presented an awe-inspiring vista. When Mt. Everest and its surrounding peaks rose on the clear blue horizon, I became spellbound. Flying from the west at our particular angle, we could see more of its triangular summit than we would see during the trek, when most of Everest, except for the summit, would be covered by the Nuptse mountain range. Everest was quickly recognizable by the plume of cloud that usually streams from its gigantic summit; otherwise, from a distance, the largest mountain in the world neither looks different nor stands out from the enormous peaks surrounding it. My eye remained fixed on this panorama until the plane's angle of flight shut it out. I couldn't believe that we would soon be walking into those distant valleys among those tremendous mountains. My mind and emotions were a jumble of excitement and apprehension about the adventure that would begin as soon as the plane landed.

As the plane was making its approach to Lukla, a greater concentration of clouds began to appear. Suddenly, the plane was going back in the opposite direction from Lukla. Our puzzled looks were soon answered by Jim, who explained that the pilot had decided not to chance a landing, because of the increasing cloud cover. Stunned by this disappointing news, we were thrown into a gloomy silence. It was hard to understand why the pilot refused to land. To us, the clouds seemed fleecy and not at all thick enough to impair one's vision.

We were a sad, let-down, and angry group as the plane headed back to Kathmandu. Jim was wise and sensitive enough to let us stew, and he avoided giving further explanations. He simply stated that tomorrow would be another day and that we'd try again; we couldn't fight the weather in this mountainous country, or we'd be on the losing end. Unfortunately, the flight back had clear, sunny weather, which made the aborted landing harder to understand and exacerbated our sullen mood. By the time we landed in Kathmandu, the group's moroseness had given way to overt grumbling and irascibility. The warm, clear weather that greeted us as we left the plane only added insult to injury.

There was no use in brooding over it anymore. I realized now why the trek had three extra days figured into the schedule: for the expected and unexpected contingencies that might occur. I could also understand how scores of trekkers could be backed up at Lukla by flight delays, and how the disappointed hikers could be affected by periods of near-rioting and hysteria, which often occurred during crowded trekking seasons. What soon dawned on all of us was the happy realization that whatever problems or emergencies arose would be efficiently and promptly handled and resolved by Jim and Ved with a minimum of fuss. Had we been on our own, this problem and others to come would have been magnified and overwhelming. The quiet competence and professionalism of Jim and Ved would, time and time again in the days to come, be crucial to the trek's success and the group's harmonious spirit. Right now, however, no one felt any harmony as we grumbled our way out of the airport and into the taxis to take us back to the hotel. Jim tried to encourage us to visit the famous Bodhnath Temple, just a short walk from the airport, since their annual New Year's festivities with sacred dancing and other forms of exotic rituals were under way. With the exception of a few, most opted to return to the hotel to nurse their grievances and sulk.

After getting resettled at the hotel and having a quick lunch, Olga and I decided to walk to town and see the famous Durbar Square area of Kathmandu. For us, the best way to get the feel of a city is to see it on foot. Walking through the different streets and areas of a new city gives one a firsthand flavor of its pulse, people, and customs, one that can't be obtained on a tour bus or with a guided group. Walking sets the stage for the thrill of the unexpected and the chance to come face to face with all kinds of people: shopkeepers, schoolchildren, policemen, and local residents. We tried to avoid fellow tourists, who seemed always too ready to talk about back home and regale us with their value judgments of what they've just seen. It's a rare tourist who can allow himself to experience a new country on its own terms and who will attempt to understand and accept its customs. An air of superiority and a patronizing attitude seem always to characterize the Western tourist's reactions, which are usually manifested in the comparison-competition game: our ways and things are much bigger and better than your ignorant, inferior, and backward ways—as if life was mostly an accumulation of material objects and technological conveniences.

Going from the hotel to Durbar Square involved a circuitous route that took us through rundown residential areas and the overcrowded shopping district of Thamel, past the Royal Palace hidden behind a stone wall and tropical foliage, to the wide, impressive main boulevard, Durbar Marg, flanked by modern hotels and government buildings set among parklike grounds, to New Road, the street that takes one into the old section of Kathmandu. Passing the modern hotels like the Annapurna, I became depressed by the Western-style sleek, commercial, impersonal buildings that clashed with the seductive charm and warmth of this old, exotic city.

Fortunately, the encroaching impersonal quality and coldness of modern commercialism was quickly forgotten as we turned into New Road. The density and diversity of human beings and shops were incredible to behold. Everything made by man and machines was here: household goods, fabrics, jewelry, books, magazines, and any gadget you could imagine. The alleyways and streets teemed with tourists and native shoppers gazing at goods that were crammed into every nook and cranny and spilled out into the streets. To me, a New Yorker, it was a mixture of Times Square, Delancy Street, Chinatown, and upper Broadway, and then some—what a sight! What a maelstrom of people and consumer goods! The infinite variety of colors and background of noise also battered our senses, which were constantly being assaulted by new sensations. Except for the creaking rickshaws and animal sounds, the noise was similar to any busy city, as shouting voices, squealing car horns, and blaring radios assailed our ears.

Whenever we stopped to look or entered a shop, we were soon asked the universal question: want to buy? No matter where we go on this globe, we can't escape the depressing reality that materialism and consumerism, buying and selling, seem to be the most pressing and conspicuous human activity. Although trading goods has been with us since time immemorial, I wondered whether it was characterized by the coldness and impersonal quality of today's commercialism. The crowds in today's shopping malls appear detached as they shop in air-conditioned and chrome-plated surroundings. At least here in Kathmandu, buying and selling was rooted in a genuine human interaction that was far removed from the robotlike and inhuman quality that pervades much of our consumer behavior.

There was nothing impersonal about the bustling crowds and extraordinary shops of New Road and its nearby twisting alleyways. Everything seemed more than life-sized, like a photograph blown up and magnified many times, especially as we finally came upon Durbar Square, the epitome of medieval Kathmandu. *Durbar* means "palace" in Nepali, and this sprawling square was the site of the old Royal Palace. Akin to an outdoor museum, the square was a group of pagodas; Indian, Tibetan, and Chinese-style temples and monuments; and statues of varying sizes and coloration. More than fifty temples and monuments were scattered, with little architectural unity, over this brick-paved square. The temples rose two to three stories high; their gilded roofs and contrasting intense reds, blues, golds, and white struck the eye with a kaleidoscope of colors. Some were built on tiered plinths, or stepped platforms, which were draped with beggars, lounging tourists, natives, and shopkeepers who displayed their goods and produce on the temple steps. Droves of pigeons and birds swooped boldly among the crowds and made aviaries of the temple's nooks and crannies. Most striking were the stone monuments, sculptures, and masks that adorned every temple. Many of the statues of lions, horses, and deities appeared grotesque, fierce, and repulsive. Like gargoyle figures, they sprouted distorted limbs and features that were made to look more ugly and frightening by being painted in clashing bright primary colors. Erotic woodcarving of gods, goddesses, and animals (usually monkeys) depicted in various sexual positions also adorned several temples. Durbar Square was a fascinating hodgepodge of man's artistic creativity, religious piety, myths, and commercialism.

Leaving Durbar Square feeling quite exhilarated, we passed the infamous Freak Street area, a former hangout of hippies and a maze of low-priced hotels, rooming houses, food shops, and restaurants. In the 1960s, Kathmandu experienced an invasion of hippies from all nations. Today, although the hippies and their culture have gone, Kathmandu still draws an unbelievable mix of foreign visitors. What chiefly drew the hippie swarms were the easy availability of drugs and the permissiveness of the Nepalese. The simple, down-to-earth, primitive lifestyle of Nepal also contributed to its allure for the hippie generation, who sought freedom from bureaucratic intervention and opportunities to indulge themselves however they pleased. Certainly life in Nepal twenty years ago was stripped to its essentials, an easy temptation for self-indulgence. Perhaps, too, these seemingly sophisticated hippies viewed Nepal as an opportunity to be exploited because of the country's backwardness and innocence. As Nepal introduced legal restrictions against drugs, the flower children of the sixties gradually left, and today there are neither signs of a drug culture nor the self-indulgence and irresponsibility of those times. Most typical of Nepalese society was its simplicity and primitiveness, and a lifestyle that reflected hard work, respect for others, and a constant struggle to cope with poverty. I'm not sure that the hippies could have coped, in the long run, with the challenges that this impoverished culture presented.

While walking back to the hotel, we could not resist buying another small handsome rug with a dark blue and gold border design, which was an outrageous bargain at thirty dollars. Of all the innumerable goods available in Kathmandu, rugs, whether made in Tibet, China, India, or Nepal, are one of the best bargains available. A common practice is to buy several to cart back home, where they fetch prices three or four times higher. But such bargains are becoming rare as goods from the Far East are flooding commercial markets throughout the world. Since prices of foreign products are now fairly comparable wherever one buys, today's tourists fool themselves when they think they have gotten a super bargain. Despite these thoughts, we returned to the hotel feeling a sense of accomplishment in obtaining such a beautiful piece of work. Our exciting afternoon in Durbar Square and old Kathmandu helped us forget the disappointment of the morning, and it put us in better spirits for tomorrow's attempt to fly into Lukla.

Tuesday morning was like a replay of the previous day: the same warm, hazy early morning, the long taxi ride to the airport, the weighing in, the crowding, and worrying whether we would take off. Anxiety and impatience pervaded the group but gave way to a surge of relief as we were told the flight was on. I walked to the plane in a daze, hoping and praying we would make it this time. As we took off and approached our destination, the tension of the group mounted. Circling Lukla, we saw the valley below and the steep mountainsides, clear and cloudless. What a shock it was to see how little room there was for a plane to maneuver among the walls of mountains and narrow valleys.

Suddenly, the plane was dropping below the huge mountainsides, aiming for a small, insignificant strip of land that was Lukla's runway. The toy plane touched down and hit the runway with a jolt, rattling and bouncing until it taxied to a stop. We had made it! The realization that we had landed gave way to a wild, hysterical reaction: clapping, shouting, yelling, and whistling. Excited as children at a party, we disembarked, laughing, exclaiming, and jostling one another playfully. Not only was our arrival a special occasion for us, but it seemed to be one for the natives of Lukla as well. Scores of them had lined the upper edges of the airstrip, observing the landing and our behavior with interest and amusement. Although they had seen thousands of landings and trekkers and climbers over the years, another plane with its new load of visitors was probably still an exciting event in their isolated existence.

Seeing the airstrip made it readily apparent why the landing was a rocky one. About twelve hundred feet long and fifty feet wide, bordered by sections of four-foot fence posts painted white on top, the airfield was made of hand-packed dirt strewn with stones and small rocks. Far from flat and smooth, it canted at a slight angle and had a rise of over a hundred feet from one end to the other. Only twenty years old, the Lukla airport was the brainchild of Sir Edmund Hillary, who supervised its construction, which is described in his autobiography, *Nothing Venture, Nothing Win.* Committed to helping the Sherpa people develop better educational and medical facilities, Hillary sought an alternative to the time-consuming sixteen-day hike from Kathmandu into Sherpa country. Hillary was approached by a group of Lukla farmers who believed they had a parcel of land suitable for an airfield, an astonishing proposition from mountain people who had no experience of flying. After Hillary's investigations of the Lukla area, he purchased a six-acre plot for 6,350 rupees, or $634, in 1964. He then employed over a hundred Sherpa men and women to hack out the brush and dig and cart away boulders and rocks. As landfill was put in place, cows with ploughs loosened and graded the soil. Unhappy with the soft surface, Hillary hit on the idea of having fifty Sherpas "link arms and stamp their way backwards and forwards across the field." After two days of this improvised Sherpa dance, "the earth received a most resounding thumping." Built in four weeks, the Lukla airfield accelerated tourism into Sherpa country and the Everest region. This was a mixed blessing for Hillary, who wrote that he was pleased by the inroads of increased schooling and medical care but tormented by the fact that easier access for tourists had led to the blights of civilization: denuded forests, litter and rubbish strewn about campsites, begging children, and the erosion of Sherpa values and community spirit.

Gawking like awed tourists as we deplaned, we immediately reached for our cameras to take pictures of each other and our new surroundings. Lukla seemed more like an airstrip with houses than a village of any significant size. I was soon to learn that its scores of scattered houses, barns, and farm huts made it one of the larger mountain villages when compared to the typical Sherpa village. Nearby farmland was beginning to show patches of green grass, budding trees, and pale pine trees dotting the valleys and lower mountain walls. Huge dark-hued mountain walls, rocky pinnacles, and snow-covered summits encircled Lukla. Still not in high mountain country, we were nevertheless impressed by the immensity of these craggy peaks and ranges.

Our immediate destination was the Lukla Hotel, a low stone and wooden-beamed ranch-type structure, a short walk from the plane and overlooking the airstrip. Here we would have lunch before starting out on our first trail. The day was clear, with bright sunlight warming the gentle mountain valley breezes. The weather couldn't have been more beautiful. As we walked to the hotel, I began puffing and huffing mildly, probably due to the effects of suddenly arriving at an altitude of 9,200 feet and scrambling hurriedly around to take pictures. I also became aware of a stillness that seemed to magnify the grandeur of the mountainous landscape. The quiet became apparent after the plane took off to return to Kathmandu and the native onlookers dispersed, leaving us by ourselves on this rocky plateau. Finally, we were all alone with the endless valleys, gorges, and mountains. The only semblance of civilization was the sight of two native policemen dressed in dark tan matching trousers and shirts, topped by rakish brown berets, and swinging swagger sticks as they patrolled the area. Their presence was necessary to watch over the plane loads of trekkers and equipment that filled Lukla. The only sound we heard was the flapping of prayer flags arranged in several layers atop fifteen-foot-high poles. Reminding me of a sailboat's halyards and sails flapping in a stiff breeze, these flags were dirty and shredded. Their appearance deflated my idealized and stereotyped notion that prayer flags would be an impressive sight, not dirty, tattered rags streaming in the wind.

A short walk brought us to the Lukla Hotel, which was a low-slung stone structure with a tin roof; it was built in a cockeyed octagonal shape about twenty-five feet in diameter. Its main entrance led into a lobby-cum-dining hall. A white cloth sign with crooked block lettering reading WELCOME TO SHERPA COOPERATIVE HOTEL LUKLA hung from the top of the stone chim-

ney. It was funny to see this greeting amid such primitive and isolated surroundings. Set back fifty feet from the airstrip, the hotel sat in a low
depression of earth with a backyard of pine trees and steep-rising mountains.
The dirt-packed front yard sported three circular wooden tables with rickety
chairs and several sawed-off logs as added seating. Sections of broken white
picket fencing and stunted, sickly looking bushes made the grounds of the
hotel look like a downtrodden picnic area.

We dumped our daypacks on the tables and sat down to admire the stunning view and wait for lunch. As we sat sunning ourselves, Jim asked that we
gather as a group so that Ved could take each of our cameras to snap a group
shot. Although we groaned as each trekker's camera demanded another pose,
this picture-taking was a ritual that symbolized Jim and Ved's caring and
thoughtfulness. I wondered how we would look after the trek and how we
would fare hiking the trails that led into the great Himalayas that loomed in
the distance.

It was past 11:00 AM when we sat down to lunch in the hotel's dining
room. On entering the twenty-by-thirty-foot wood-paneled room, we were
greeted by a bar with a variety of whiskeys and other liquors standing in rows
on a wall shelf. Mountaineering pictures, a calendar, a mailbox, personal
snapshots, mementos, and a tip box flanked the counter and adorned the
walls. Nothing uncivilized here! In the middle of the room were five knee-
high, five-foot-long mahogany tables and wooden stools and chairs with cush-
ions of pale grey and yellow oriental design. Several rows of short multicolored drapes hung from the ceiling, from whose center hung an ornamental
lamp fixture. Against the walls were several shabby grey couches, in front of
which were low cocktail tables of striking red, blue, and white oriental motifs.
A handful of mountaineering posters were tacked on the walls between the
large picture windows. The room's central focus was a stone fireplace, whose
ten-foot-wide mantel was made to look like an altar. Ceremonial lamps were
planted on each end of the mantel, like sentinels. On the wall behind the
fireplace, a large Buddha figure was painted in tan against a black background and white religious symbols. Despite the odd mixture of many styles
and cultural influences, the dining room/bar/lobby projected an inviting and
warm quality. This room exited onto a long, narrow, unlit wood-paneled hallway to a dormitory area consisting of small beds and cots. Off this hallway was
the ultimate sign of luxury: six private rooms, each with two beds, a dresser,
and a small bathroom with a toilet and sink. We smiled at these bare and sim-

ple accommodations, not knowing how precious and desperately sought after they would be on our return fifteen days later.

While waiting for lunch, Jim presented each of us with a map of the Khumbu region, where the trek would take us. Folding out like an automobile highway map, this large, simple, mimeographed map showed all of the trekking routes and topographic details of the Khumbu. Jim outlined the entire trek from village to village. All the Sherpa villages, mountains, and rivers I had read and fantasized about were right there on the map, real and concrete, just a trek away. It was a strange and exciting sensation to mark the trails and villages that were to become our daily destinations. The trek would start after lunch, to the first campsite only four hours away—a warm-up for the daylong treks to come. While we lunched, our contingent of Sherpas and yaks would go on ahead to set up the camp.

4

The Trek Begins

Looking at our maps, we marked the trails as Jim explained each day's destination and hiking characteristics. This afternoon's objective would be a campsite due north on the western bank of a tributary of the Dudh Kosi river fed by melting snows of Everest. The following day would be the first full trekking day and, according to Jim, one of the toughest, as the trail ascended one ridge after another to Namche Bazaar, the capital of the Khumbu region in which Everest is located. At Namche Bazaar, we would have a rest day and experience the spectacular view of Everest and its neighboring peaks. A day of rest is a day of options, usually giving a trekker a chance to unwind, recover, and recharge one's energies. It's also a time to have laundry done, get a much sought-after homemade shower, and take a side trip if one has any energy left.

From Namche Bazaar, instead of going directly north to the Everest region, the group would detour west to Thami. Why spend precious energy, I wondered, going out of our way? A day of acclimation and training and an interesting hike among narrow rock cliffs and boulders were the reasons. After Thami, the fourth afternoon would find us in Kunde, back on the trail that heads toward Everest. Then we would make a long trek to Tengboche, situated on a plateau, with a famous Buddhist monastery and a stunning view that looks down a valley to Everest. Our second rest day would be at Tengboche, where we would gather strength and prepare for the next few days.

The final phase of the trek would take us near the famous base camp of Mt. Everest. Leaving Tengboche, the group would descend into the Imja Khola valley enveloped by the summits of Everest, Lhotse, Nuptse, and Ama Dablam looming twenty-five to twenty-nine thousand feet above us. The next three days would bring us to campsites at the isolated villages of Pengboche, Dingboche, and Lobuche, closer and closer to Everest. There would be no villages beyond Lobuche, and shelter and humans would be difficult to find. Lobuche, at nearly seventeen thousand feet, would serve as our base camp to climb our final goal, Kala Pattar, at 18,450 feet, which provides the closest and best view of Mount Everest. This climb would be the most challenging and strenuous part of the trek. At 5:00 AM, the ascent to Kala Pattar would begin in order to arrive at around noon, which would allow for thirty to sixty minutes of viewing before the clouds obscured the view. This schedule would allow sufficient time to return to Lobuche, where we would arrive at around 5:00 PM, nearly twelve hours later—a good day's trek in the mountains.

Jim concluded this briefing by reassuring us that we would all probably make it to Kala Pattar, but he emphasized that it would be much rougher and physically demanding than a usual day's trek. I wondered, with much apprehension, whether Olga and I, who were much older and less experienced than the others, could take such a grueling day. Could we make it to Kala Pattar—a twelve-hour day that would begin in darkness with temperatures that might be below zero and on terrain much steeper and rockier than usual? It was a worry and a question that would haunt us throughout the trek.

There are essentially two approaches to trekking: a backpacking do-it-yourself approach, or an organized trek arranged and supervised by a professional trekking agency. The backpacking version consists of trekking without a guide or porters and requires making your own sleeping and food arrangements. Going on your own is feasible and challenging but will test your fortitude and patience, especially when dealing with the red tape of visas and trekking permits. Bureaucracy will even follow you into mountain villages, when the permit is checked by local police outposts. Also, when traveling alone, you may run afoul of Nepal's many regulations, of which one could easily be unaware. For example, if you happen to engage a Sherpa, you will have to arrange the details of pay and an itinerary, and you also must insure him against accidental death. Upon entering the vast Everest National Park, you will have to follow fuel regulations. The hiker must carry his own fuel, usually kerosene, since firewood is prohibited because of soil erosion and the scarcity of wood. Conflicts and confusion are inevitable under such circumstances, and if you're inflexible and unwilling to negotiate and compromise, your trek will be fraught with tension and annoyance.

Trekking with a professional agency, on the other hand, relieves one of many burdens: myriad details of food, sleeping arrangements, obtaining permits, establishing an itinerary with specific campsites, hiring and dealing with Sherpas and porters, and coping with any emergencies. An organized trek provides you with three meals a day, tents that are set up at each campsite upon your arrival, campsites relatively safe from intruders, and the experience and competence to deal with most problems or personal needs that may arise. An interesting example, which no one likes to contemplate, is knowing that you will be flown out by helicopter (contacted by radio or a runner) in the case of a life-threatening medical problem. Incidentally, the cost for such a joyride is five hundred dollars, and every trekker has to sign a waiver agreeing to an emergency evacuation if necessary.

Many trekking agencies exist and are easily found in the advertisements of national magazines. The agency we chose was Overseas Adventure Travel (OAT) of Cambridge, Massachusetts, which has its own crew of Sherpas and porters. Their USA representative and our trek leader, Jim Traverso, resided in Kathmandu but visited the States a few months a year to develop and prepare treks. A coleader and senior staff member of OAT was Ved, a Nepalese man who resided in Kathmandu. The combination of Jim and Ved proved unbeatable, as their combined know-how and contacts easily overcame every problem and contingency, from getting overweight baggage accepted at the airport to greasing the right palm to ensure a return flight at Lukla. What a relief it was to know that all our energies could be directed to the physical and emotional demands of hiking and not be expended on the practicalities of the trek. Exclusive of air travel to Nepal (flying Air India to Delhi and a connecting Royal Nepal Airline to Kathmandu), a trek of twenty-five days, including three days' accommodations in Kathmandu, cost $1,480 per person, or about seventy dollars per trekking day; with air fare, the cost was doubled.

Increasingly, the Nepalese have become dependent upon trekkers, climbers, and tourism for their income. Today, many Sherpas receive their chief source of income from climbing and trekking expeditions. A Sherpa who acts as the chief guide, the sirdar, earns about fifty rupees, or slightly more than three dollars a day, plus food and accommodations. Porters and kitchen workers earn two dollars for lugging your equipment and preparing your meals. Since the trekking season usually runs about eight months from October to May, and many compete to be employed by a trek, the Sherpas are limited in what they can earn from trekking tourists. The haze, heat, and monsoon weather from June through September significantly curtails trekking during the summer. Hardy souls, however, exist who undertake monsoon treks, where mud, rain, and floods are the rule, keeping you constantly soaked. Other than just being eccentric, the only reason to trek during the summer monsoon months in Nepal is to see the spectacularly lush plant and animal life. As a trekking map warned about this time of year, "In Nepal, all paths and bridges are liable to disappear or change at no notice due to monsoons, acts of God, etc."

A concern of every visitor to this primitive and poor country is the question of safety: how safe is it to hike alone or in a small group through the isolated regions of the Himalayas? The answer is a resounding "Don't worry!" Crime such as robbery and assault is relatively rare in Nepal. However, since the number of trekkers and climbers has increased, one needs to be cautious about leaving equipment and clothing lying about a campsite. In nearly three weeks in the field, none of our group lost anything. In fact, the porters were scrupulously careful, when breaking camp every morning, to see that nobody left anything behind as they took down the tents and put cargo bags on the yaks.

While eating lunch, we saw a trekker come in to order lunch. He looked pretty run down and fatigued. It was odd seeing a solitary westerner in the middle of nowhere, but we would see many single trekkers on the trail during the next few weeks. His aloof and preoccupied air did not invite more than a nod of acknowledgment and left our curiosity unsatisfied. He was served a plate of large golden brown french fries. In the coming days on the trail, we would learn that potatoes are Nepal's main food staple, and few meals, including breakfast, would be without them.

Our lunch finally came: plates piled high with rice mixed with slivers of vegetables and tiny pieces of meat. Perhaps it was because we hadn't eaten since early morning, but that simple savory plate of rice turned out to be one of the tastiest dishes I have ever eaten. Unfortunately, no seconds were offered, and no one asked for more. It seemed as if we intuitively sensed that food was scarce in these mountain villages, and we gratefully settled for whatever was served. There was nothing scarce about tea, though; we could drink all we wanted. I'm not a tea drinker, but this dark, full-bodied, freshly brewed tea laced with honey or sugar was a most satisfying drink. Our daily cup of tea would become a welcome and eagerly anticipated companion throughout the trek. Its soothing and filling taste approached a therapeutic quality for me, as it would reinvigorate me and combat my exhaustion in the days to come.

It was now after 1:00 PM, lunch was over, and we were eager to be on the trail. Our destination was the village of Phakding, about four hours distant, where our first campsite would be. It was a good feeling to put on our day-packs and finally be off. Setting out from Lukla, we began a long descent into one valley after another. The surrounding countryside near Lukla consisted of terraced farms precariously set among the rock and dirt mountainsides.

Heading north, the main trail was a simple dirt road, the width of a sidewalk and strewn with small rocks and stones. Although the trail was hard-packed dirt, we constantly kicked up dust and soot.

This time of year was the peak of the dry season; the monsoon weather and last rainfall had ended six months before, in late September. Everything was dry, brittle, and dusty. The pine and fir trees looked pale and sickly; the ever-present juniper and rhododendron bushes were stunted and oddly shaped. It was a desolate and primitive landscape, not attractive or appealing, but the excitement about being here masked the drabness around us. There was little of nature's beauty here. The trails, hills, and mountains were depressing shades of gray, black, and brown. What little green foliage and grass there was appeared faded and dull. This dirty and impoverished landscape confirmed my belief that nature can also be ugly. To equate nature with only beauty and attractiveness is a myth. Such a view robs nature of its eternal power. Nature can attract and repel. It can be forbidding and repulsive—traits which in themselves can fascinate.

The trail to Phakding gradually descended about one thousand feet into a canyon of the surging and turbulent Dudh Kosi river. Fed by the melting ice and snows of the Everest region, this river snakes its way down valleys that we would constantly cross. The river's name means "milk river," for the foamy white rapids made by its boiling and roaring action. Like the mountains enveloping us, the Dudh Kosi would initially be a companion rarely out of sight or earshot. In this lower region and time of year, however, the river was like a backwater and often shallow, so that it appeared as a sandy and boulder-strewn riverbed. Recently, sections of the river had been tackled by white-river enthusiasts who canoed through its most treacherous and challenging routes.

The sunny, clear weather in which we started out had turned into overcast skies. Increasingly, the mountains around us became enveloped in low-hanging dark, heavy clouds. The skies looked threatening and ready to burst with rain, and the hills and valleys took on an even more depressing and ominous semblance. We were to learn, however, that this would be a daily characteristic of the weather: the mornings bright and clear until early or late afternoon, when the cloud cover moved in and obscured the craggy mountains.

After an hour on the trail, the group's pace and trekking pattern emerged, characteristics that would remain much the same throughout the next fifteen trekking days. Although we would start out together, by the end of the first hour, the twelve of us would be strung out on the trail, with nearly a mile between the first and last trekker. Nas, his son, Kirt, John, and Abby headed the pack, usually setting a rapid, smooth pace typical of the experienced and superbly conditioned trekker. They would soon be out of sight of us ordinary mortals. I quickly realized that trying to keep up with them or anyone else was foolhardy and self-defeating. Finding one's own trekking pace and sticking to it was crucial in remaining efficient and healthy. Jim advised us to maintain a steady pace without too many rest stops and starts, which create additional strains on the body. Steadiness of pace, not speed, is most important. The steady, plodding hiker is the one who will always outlast and outperform the one who rushes ahead with no thought of maintaining a regular rhythm. This became immediately apparent to me when, feeling most exuberant and chipper at the outset, I pushed myself into high gear and tried to keep up with John. For half an hour while walking together, we talked about his professional life as a surgeon in London under socialized medicine. As I listened to his experiences and learned how badly the mentally ill fared under this system, I became uncomfortably aware that I could not keep up with John's brisk pace. I was becoming winded and tired, and I wanted badly to stop talking and slow down. I was quite relieved when John, probably sensing my predicament, excused himself and took off at his usual blistering pace in front of the group. It was now around 5:00 PM—already a long, arduous day since rising at 6:00 AM in Kathmandu and arriving in Lukla at midmorning.

To help and accompany us were several guides whose presence would go a long way in making the trek successful. Jim and Ved would remain an elusive presence, either staying behind or rushing ahead to supervise and check on staff and logistics. Every trek has a sirdar who serves as the chief Sherpa guide. Our sirdar was Nahwang, a handsome, twenty-two-year-old, self-assured, relaxed Sherpa who exuded competence and a quiet friendliness. Another sirdar, Nahtang, joined the trek, as he was en route to his parents' home in Thamel, a village on our itinerary. Nahtang, also in his early twenties, was quite tense, anxious, and preoccupied, despite his friendliness and obvious desire to please. We were surprised to learn that he was suffering from a bleeding ulcer, a medical problem that was just beginning to emerge in this primitive land.

A few other Sherpa guides hiked along with the group to assist in whatever way needed. Because of our lack of trekking experience, Olga and I were assigned Kanchha, a nineteen-year-old Sherpa guide who watched over us and remained by our side throughout the trek. Of modest build and strikingly handsome with straight jet-black hair, laughing deep blue eyes, and a sparkling smile, Kanchha became our inseparable companion. More than any-one, Kanchha helped us forge ahead when we were totally exhausted and felt as if we couldn't take another step. As the trek progressed and got more diffi-cult, Kanchha never left Olga's side. He was seldom more than a stride away and always ready to help her navigate the steep and treacherous sections of the trail. With affection and deep concern, he began to call Olga "Mama," while I became "Papa." What a wonderful and beautiful young man was this Kanchha, who could hardly read or write, spoke and understood only a mini-mum of English, but who would see to our safety and well-being daily with all the competence one could wish for.

As we trekked we found Kanchha and the other guides sources of fascinat-ing information about Nepalese customs and cultural lore. A few of the cus-toms in which we were immediately instructed concerned the Nepalese greeting and the small religious temples that were found scattered throughout the trail. Nepalese greet one another by placing their hands before them in a praying position, bowing their heads, and saying *"Namaste"* (nah-ma-stay), which translates literally into "I salute the God in you." It is a greeting based on religious beliefs and respect for another human being. Whenever we passed natives on the trail, they would sing out, *"Namaste."* At times it just sounded like "stay," as the first two syllables would be swallowed. The sing-song word and the respectful tone in which it was uttered always made me feel peaceful.

On the trail, we constantly passed different-sized temples called chortens or stupas. Built to pacify the gods or evil spirits, a chorten is made of stone and has a square base topped by a bell-shaped dome that tapers to a spire no higher than fifteen feet. Prayer flags and the eyes of Buddha are found on most chortens. Some are also decorated with colorful paintings, metal sculp-tures, and gilded towers. The chortens reminded me of the religious shrines along the roadsides of many rural and mountain villages in Europe. We were admonished to always pass on the left side and never to touch or take their prayer flags or prayer stones. The tattered prayer flags and nondescript stones might look insignificant to Western eyes, but to the Nepalese, they represent powerful supplications to the gods and demons.

After passing many chortens, hearing many *namastes*, and being awed by the strange scenery, we were nearing our first campsite. The trail had been easy, as it descended gently most of the way. By late afternoon I was becoming tired because of the unaccustomed sustained hiking at this nine-thousand-foot altitude and the excitement of the long day. I was relieved to see in the distance a bridge and a group of blue tents by the river's edge. The scene looked like a picture-book campsite set on a stage before us. Here was our first bridge crossing, and I thought with some apprehension about the wobbly and swaying bridge crossings I had seen in pictures and read about. About a hundred feet long and wide enough to touch the rails with outstretched arms, the bridge was fairly sturdy despite a gentle sway. It was built of wooden planks and railings, and reinforced underneath each end with logs. The river twenty feet below, a tributary of the Dudh Kosi, was littered with rocks and debris. The area gave an impression of desolation that was heightened by the dark, hovering clouds and the scrublike vegetation. This countryside was still showing the devastating effects of a 1977 avalanche from Ama Dablam, a peak near Everest, which caused a wave of water thirty feet high to roar down to the Dudh Kosi valley. The flash flood washed away parts of the trail, several bridges, and a part of the village of Jorsale, killing three of its villagers. Clearly, these mountain villagers were at the mercy of nature.

To my dismay, our campsite was not the idyllic-looking group of blue tents sitting just across the bridge; it was still beyond the bend, fifteen minutes away. It was odd seeing this reassuring sight of tents and nearby shacks in the middle of nowhere. Like a local deli, the two shacks were selling snacks, local beer, tea, and even Coca-Cola. The thought of food and drink assuaged my fatigue and annoyance that we still had a way to go. Suddenly, as we rounded a bend, there was our camp. Set in a clearing surrounded by rocks and boulders, scrub brush, and a steeply rising cliff as a backdrop, our tents were set in two neat rows. It was a depressing and grubby-looking place that made our multicolored tents of faded orange, green, tan, brown, and maroon stand out dramatically and incongruously.

More than half of the group was already scrambling about, taking pictures and getting settled, when I arrived. I just wanted something to drink and to lie down and rest. What a relief it was to see our duffel bags intact and neatly lined up in front of the tents, and the inviting look of the thin foam mattresses inside each tent. Every arrival into camp was immediately greeted by a Sherpa offering a mug of tea and a biscuit.

As I sat on a rock, drinking my tea, I took in the rest of our surroundings. Immediately behind the tents was an elongated kitchen tent, where fires were blazing and Sherpas were busy preparing for dinner. Next to the tent was a long wooden overhang, like an oversized carport, with braided bamboo siding that housed gear and the yaks who were feeding nearby. A rock-lined dirt path wound thirty feet in front of the campground to a communal toilet, a dilapidated five-foot-square wooden structure set a few feet above the ground so that waste dropped onto the straw spread below. How would I navigate this path and the shaky steps of rock that led to the entrance in the middle of the night when nature called? I was too tired to worry about that now.

Off to the side was a small house made of stone and wood where, in an hour, we would have dinner. Everywhere I looked, I was struck by the incredible number of pebbles, rocks, and boulders of all sizes and shades of color. Huge boulders, oddly shaped and as large as ten to twenty feet in diameter, seemed to have been set randomly around the campsite. Even the scrub brush, evergreen trees, and shrubs fought a losing battle to the combination of slate and granite formations on the steeply rising hills behind the camp. I had often thought that all the stones in the world were located in the hills and forests of Vermont, especially around my country home, where the least amount of digging would unearth stone after stone. My thinking was irrevocably revised: this Nepal countryside had to be second to none in rock deposits. There were so many diverse kinds of rock that one might think it was a natural crop that bred and proliferated indiscriminately.

While I ruminated about this primitive geography, Olga arrived looking more chipper than I felt. It was now 6:00 PM, and the weather was turning colder. The chill and damp of early evening at these high altitudes necessitated a quick change of clothes. Long pants, sweaters, down vests, and ski parkas or outer jackets became de rigueur for evening wear if you wanted to combat the cold and be warm and comfortable. Sartorially, we were an oddly dressed group, with our clashing colors and variety of garments. I changed into woolen pants and a bunting jacket; Olga donned long johns and a skirt, a sweater, and a lightweight wool-lined parka. We also got out of our boots and put on moccasins or sneakers after the day's trek, in order to prevent any foot problems. A foot discomfort or injury, however minor, would be a major disaster. Walking is the only means of transportation besides being carried by a yak, whose loads never include human cargo.

Although the tent was fairly large (nine by seven by five feet), it had to accommodate our gear as well as its two occupants. We placed our duffel bags at the head so that they would double as pillows, and we put the day packs next to us at either side. My six-foot-one frame was just accommodated by the tent's length. Dressing involved lying down, crouching, kneeling, or twisting until the best position was achieved to slip off or put on clothing. It also involved searching though your duffel bag to find the right garment, which always seemed not to be where you swore you had put it. Even at this altitude of 8,200 feet, and at the end of a comparatively easy afternoon's hike, it was a tiring effort to hunt out clothes and dress in the tent. How much harder and uncomfortable would it be thousands of feet higher and at the end of a full day's strenuous trek?

Dinnertime finally arrived, and we stumbled in the dark to the wooden hut where our long-awaited first evening meal would be eaten. We ate in a bare, dark twelve-by-twelve-foot room with slightly tilted walls and ceiling, which reminded me of those cockeyed amusement park crazy houses. Two long, old, battered-looking wooden tables with benches accommodated the twelve of us along with Jim and Ved. Completely dark and intermittently stuffy and chilly, the room was lighted by a flickering kerosene lamp. To say the least, this crowded, poorly ventilated, and dimly lit room wasn't a comfortable or pleasant setting.

Dinner came in large aluminum pots, which were carried in by the kitchen staff. All of the pots, cups, plates, and utensils were made of aluminum and stainless steel, which had the well-scrubbed, dull, and worn-out appearance that comes with long, rough use and being washed in boiling water. This eagerly anticipated meal began with a small bowl of tasty bean soup ladled out from a large pot. Next came plates piled high with a gluey rice and vegetable mixture in which were strips of tough yak meat—a special and rare treat. A thick, spicy, curry-flavored gravy was poured over this mixture, which was mushy and not at all appetizing. The only flavor came from the curried gravy, and unfortunately, spices are not pleasing to me. The meal was a great disappointment, especially when I thought about the delicious rice pilaf we had for lunch in Lukla. I compensated by gulping down an extra mug of tea, which was always satisfying. Although I was hungry, I was too tired and enervated to eat much. Nevertheless, I looked forward to having dessert, since some sweet always compensates for a meal's shortcomings. When Jim told us that dessert would be a tasty pudding, I anticipated making up for this disappointing dinner. No such luck. The grayish, lumpy, gelatinous pudding turned out to be inedible. One spoonful was enough. Its pasty texture and taste almost made me regurgitate. Somebody joked that it tasted and looked just like wallpaper paste—not a bad comparison. What a letdown, this meal. I couldn't believe that food could be so bad, especially when I thought of all the supplies that had been brought along and the kitchen help bustling about, preparing dinner with fairly adequate kitchen facilities. If this was what the evening meals would be like, I dreaded the next few weeks of dinner.

As we finished eating, Jim talked briefly about tomorrow's itinerary, the long pull to Namche Bazaar, nearly four thousand feet higher than our present camp. He emphasized that it would be one of the most difficult and strenuous hikes of the entire trek, consisting of endless ascents and descents along the cliffs and gorges up the Dudh Kosi river valley. By now, fatigue was overtaking me, and my thoughts were only on getting to sleep. My annoyance about this interminably long day, unappealing campsite, terrible dinner, and Jim's wordiness was tempered by the rationalization that maybe everything had been planned this way to acclimate us to less than adequate conditions and prepare us for worse to come. I was somewhat ashamed of my reflections and annoyance when I thought of those mountaineers who were my models of heroism and adventure, and who suffered death-defying hardships here in the Himalayas. Comparatively, this trek was a piece of cake, just a stroll down Broadway. Yet most of us were not in a mountaineer's class, and I, at least, had expected better conditions than we had experienced today. In any case, it was encouraging that no one voiced any complaints (except for the joking about the wallpaper paste dessert), and a positive and harmonious attitude pervaded the group. As Jim talked about tomorrow, our unanimity was expressed by a general fatigue that had many of us dozing off.

Not only were Olga and I eager to sleep, but we were excited and curious about what it would be like to sleep and live in a tent. We were rank amateurs as campers and had none of the outdoor camping experience of our fellow trekkers. Despite our inexperience, we felt confident and optimistic about coping and surviving the bumbling and trials to come. Back in the pitch-black tent, we used the four-inch macro flashlights for lighting while we got ready to retire. First, we set out everything for the morning: putting out water bottles to be filled, placing boots at the foot of the tent, and arranging the miscellany of toilet, personal, and clothing items in the narrow foot of space to either side of us. Then, after spreading out the goose-down sleeping bags that stretched the length of the tent, we crouched to undress.

It was mild but damp out, about forty degrees Fahrenheit. Since the sleeping bag was rated to be warm to as low as minus ten degrees Fahrenheit, we decided to sleep in our underwear. I can still feel the sensation of slipping into that sleeping bag. It was a soothing and sensual experience. The comfort and warmth of that goose-down bag enveloped me and welcomed my weariness. I knew sleep and relaxation would come easily and quickly. Perhaps, on an unconscious level, it brought to mind memories of childhood, when I slept peacefully under the large, billowing mound of a goose-down comforter, or feather bed, that my mother's relatives in Germany had sent us. Although the bag zippered up its entire length to a hood enclosure, which could serve as a cushion, we used the cargo bags placed across the back of the tent as pillows. We quickly learned to upgrade this pillow arrangement by placing our rolled-up down ski parkas on top of the cargo bags.

It was quite cozy and comfortable in the tent, and we decided to read a while before sleeping. To read by, we used a tent candle encased in a six-inch telescopic aluminum and glass holder. We lit the candle, pushed it back into its casing, and hung it from a line strung above us across the tent. The candlelight was adequate, but it made us uneasy when we thought about the possibility of fire. (We stopped using it the next evening when everyone cautioned us against it.) I don't think we read more than a page before sleep overpowered us. It was close to 9:00 PM, and I slept soundly until the early morning hours, when nature woke me. Too drowsy to stumble among the rocks and path to the toilet, I relieved myself in the scrub brush just several feet from the tent. What an annoyance it was to get up in the middle of the cold, pitch-dark night, wearing little clothing. It would surely become colder as we reached higher altitudes, and something more satisfactory than these nocturnal trips would have to be figured out. Luckily I, who am a light sleeper, was able to fall back into the deep sleep I had left temporarily.

The next awakening was soon after daybreak at 5:30 AM as one of the teenage Sherpa kitchen women unzipped the tent flap, sang out a "Good morning," and poured us a cup of scalding hot tea. This would become a daily morning ritual, being awakened by Lhakpadiki between 5:30 and 6:00 AM and greeted by her strongly inflected singsong "Good morning!" Her cheerful spirits, constant giggles, and kettle of tea made getting up less onerous.

I threw on my woolen pants and polypro long john top to go out to wash and shave. It was a sparkling clear mountain morning, with the chill of the dew everywhere. Washing consisted of taking one or two cupped handfuls of hot water dispensed from a homemade faucet attached to a five-gallon can. It was enough water to brush our teeth and wash our hands and faces. Since warm water was not in plentiful supply, everyone was careful not to take more than necessary. I decided to follow as normal a morning schedule as possible and planned on a daily shave. I can't tolerate any beard growth and feel uncomfortable and dirty if I do not shave. Jim had emphasized that we should follow our usual personal routines in order to feel less disrupted by the strangeness of everything. Using the washing water made my skin feel raw to the touch of a razor blade. Shaving and washing under those conditions served the important function of waking me with a start. There was much to do in the next two hours until we were on the trail again, and there was no time for loafing around.

Before breakfast, we had about an hour to take care of our personal needs and begin packing up and getting ready for the day ahead. These chores involved rolling up our sleeping bags, choosing clothing for the day, and having the cargo bags fully packed by 8:00 AM when we broke camp. We would learn to live out of these cargo bags, which became like a large dresser drawer through which we would rummage repeatedly in search of some item. Clothing, gear, and snacks were never in the same place twice, and they shifted constantly within the duffel bags. Although we used various-sized nylon stuff sacks, each of which held a specific type of gear, clothing, or snack, I tended to forget which sack held what item. The only one I could pick out easily was the neat and bulging sack that held the sleeping bag. I was always amazed at seeing how this mummy-type seven-foot-long sleeping bag, because of its goose-down composition, could be pummeled and squeezed into a bag of eight by eighteen inches. It became a challenge each morning to see how quickly I could stuff the sleeping bag into its small sack.

My usual hiking outfit consisted of shorts and a cotton knit shirt, with a bunting jacket, scarf, gloves, and a sweater as backup clothing in my daypack. For extra energy, we took along a raisin-nut mixture and some cheese. My Pentax single-lens reflex camera (with extra rolls of film, lenses, and filters) and two plastic water bottles, freshly filled, completed our daily load. With all these items, the daypack weighed about twenty pounds, a comfortable and far from burdensome load.

By the time we finished our morning ablutions and packing, breakfast was ready. It was now past 7:00 AM, and breakfast would be taken in the large kitchen tent. After last night's meal I wasn't looking forward to a repeat performance. Surprisingly, breakfast wasn't bad, and it satiated the hunger I was feeling after not eating much since yesterday noon in Lukla. For starters, we had a small bowl of porridge that was like a gluey but tasty oatmeal. In addition to tea, there was instant coffee and hot chocolate mix available, and many different herbal tea bags. Served next was a plate filled with fried potatoes and a shriveled fried egg. A stack resembling pancakes, which turned out to be a local bread called chapatis, accompanied breakfast. If eaten while lukewarm, the bread was passable, more so when it was spread with jam or peanut butter, which was always on the large tray with the beverages. When I write of jam and peanut butter, I must note that they weren't the same tasty foods these names bring to mind. Each came out of a jar, looking and tasting quite dry, and made me wonder whether it was leftover food from a former expedition. Still, it was an edible breakfast, and it gave us the energy for the morning ahead.

With breakfast over, we made a last-minute check of baggage and gear as the Sherpas were breaking camp. Tents were taken down, and baggage was being loaded on the yaks. We followed the Sherpas and headed due north up the river valley. The sun was bright and warm in an intensely blue and luminous sky. The morning chill made some of our group put on red or blue long johns, which gave them the appearance of ballet dancers in eccentric-looking warm-up dress as their underwear protruded below shorts or billowing skirts. With the addition of daypacks, dark sunglasses, and baseball caps, the group could pass as itinerant entertainers from the Middle Ages going from village to village.

We saw no villages or houses during the early hours of hiking. The trail was littered with rocks and stones of all sizes. We descended into the river canyon bounded by precipitous cliffs. Parts of the trail were overhung with outcroppings of enormous boulders. And always on one side of the trail was the Dudh Kosi river. Although the riverbed was rarely full, there were sporadic raging and foamy rapids that made one sense the awesome power of this river. All river systems in Nepal are created by the melting Himalayan snows, and these rivers rage through the southern Nepalese valleys, pouring their waters onto the plains of the Indian subcontinent. Over innumerable ages, these torrential waters carved out the deep gorges and ravines that constituted the trek's route.

The steeply rising mountainsides were heavily wooded with giant fir trees, pine, and spruce, and budding rhododendrons were scattered everywhere. In a month or so, and especially in the monsoon summer months, these forests would look magnificent and lush. Now the terrain appeared rugged and forbidding. The first few hours saw us make several steep descents and ascents on rocky trails that became as narrow as a footpath. It was quite tricky navigating these bumpy trails that could suddenly cause you to trip and send you sprawling. The walking was difficult, especially when we came to rock steps descending at a steep fifty-degree angle for fifty to a hundred feet. Although we had to move cautiously and watch every step, we had to avoid becoming fearful and thereby awkward in our movements. When walking, skiing, or skating, we move with a certain assurance and rarely look down at our feet—if we do, our motion becomes inhibited and clumsy. Remembering this, I walked as naturally and confidently as possible while navigating the treacherous rocky steps.

As we hiked this rugged terrain, I wondered how we would get through these precipitous and rocky narrow paths without a twisted ankle or a leg injury. What a thought to be plagued with at the beginning of our first full day of trekking! I quickly put this anxiety out of my mind and focused on the majestic canyons that enveloped us. A succession of descents brought us down to a wide path that ran parallel to the river for a long, winding stretch. Here the trail was bordered on one side by sharp, vertically rising cliffs and overhanging boulders that put us in dark shadows, while the sunlight glistened thousands of feet above us and the blue sky seemed eons away. It was as if suddenly we had been dropped into a dark tunnel coming to the valley floor. Not only were we thrown into eerie shadows, but we were also unexpectedly struck by a blast of wind that made us shiver from the cold. We hurriedly got out sweaters or jackets and bundled up. For a few minutes, the wind gusts were so strong that they seemed to lift us off our feet as we scurried along. Looking at these endless narrow and twisting mountainous valleys, I could understand how they could trap the air currents and create a turbulent wind tunnel. It must be unbearable and perilous during a winter storm, I thought. Now it was just unpleasant and a bit scary with the unexpected wind, cold, shadows, and crags of rock hanging over the trail with the brilliant sun and sky above. The contrasts were unsettling but strangely exciting.

While walking through these river gorges, we would find the trail winding torturously back and forth across the river. We crossed several bridges that morning, each crossing generating mild anxiety and excitement. The first few bridges were about thirty feet long and only several feet above the roaring river. From a distance, they looked like matchbox toys, flimsy and incongruous amidst the ferocious-looking landscape. Some bridges were guarded by ragged foot-wide white prayer flags placed at each end. We certainly felt the need to be protected against evil spirits while crossing these rickety bridges. Constructed of wooden planks about four feet wide, these bridges were roomy enough to cross a trekker and a yak. The larger bridges had a top rail on either side, but the smaller bridges had a rail on only one side or no railing at all. Although some were shaky and prone to sway slightly, they were fairly sturdy. Our anxieties were primarily triggered by the idea of crossing them and by their awesome surroundings: a raging or foaming river below, huge boulders everywhere, and the crowding cliffs and mountainside looking as if they would topple on us.

Leaving the canyon floor, we began a series of ascents on crumbling loose rock and sand defiles that brought us into the warm sunlight. The cold air and ominous, shadowy surroundings were gone, and we quickly shed our heavy clothes. A succession of short climbs brought us to flat roads that looked out onto meadows, terraced farmlands, and mountainsides of coniferous forests. In the distance behind the canyon walls, we saw occasional snow-covered mountain peaks, a dramatic backdrop for the cliffs of rock, dirt, and greening forests in the foreground. Rambling stone walls announced that we were approaching a village consisting of several stone houses and shacks. The shacks were combinations of wood, straw, and mud, and only the size of a room. In contrast stood occasional two-story grey stone houses with their window frames painted red, green, blue, or gold. These glowing colors in the middle of drab dirt and stone surroundings created a weird and incongruous effect. We learned that these garishly painted windows proudly reflected the owner's status and affluence.

In every village, no matter how small, there was at least a lodge where tea, beer, and snacks were sold. These refreshments were customarily advertised on a quaint wooden shingle and by the pleading glances of the local entrepreneur. Their grimy appearance was enough to dissuade us from trying the refreshments, and we settled for the sustenance that came out of our daypacks. I always kept in mind the importance of drinking as much water as possible to prevent becoming dehydrated. This first morning, I tried to maintain a schedule of a five-to-ten-minute break every hour to rest and to quench my thirst. Unfortunately, the water in our plastic canteens not only turned warm after a few hours of hiking but also had a disagreeable kerosene flavor left over from the boiling process. Nevertheless, I forced myself to drink frequently, since I lose body fluids quickly because of my metabolism that causes me to perspire profusely. Jim had repeatedly stressed that in order to ward off fatigue and maintain our energy, we must keep drinking to replenish the body fluids lost by perspiration.

I soon realized that Olga and I did not have the physical stamina of our younger and more experienced colleagues; therefore, I made sure that we followed the basic rules of good hiking techniques. The question of whether we could keep up with the others was always on our minds and our greatest anxiety. We knew that our most powerful asset was our positive spirits. Intensely motivated to succeed and confident of our ability to cope, we maintained an optimistic outlook. I have always believed that our mental or psychic attitude is the single most important factor in deciding the outcome of life's encounters. Life is more an emotional or psychological challenge than anything else. How you view yourself and the world constitutes the deciding edge—or, more aptly put by the athlete's winning motto, "You gotta believe!" And believe we did. We believed, and we were determined to see Mt. Everest and the Himalayas, no matter what. This belief brought us halfway around the world to one of the most primitive and poorest cultures of the world to fulfill a dream. And the tortuous, twisting canyons and gorges, with their endless ascending and descending climbs, were already putting us to the test and challenging our spirits.

It was becoming warmer as we began several ascents that brought us into the sunlight and out of the valley shadows. I was perspiring freely, as it was nearly seventy degrees in the sun, and I was beginning to feel the effects of the physical effort and altitude. The sky was intensely blue and the air clear and intoxicating, although it was becoming humid. The towering, snowy peaks were not yet visible, but at one turn in the trail, we suddenly saw the faint, distant outline of twenty-two-thousand-foot Thamserku backlit by the early morning sun. Looking directly into the sun's glare made this beautiful, classic triangular snowy summit appear to be a fairy mountain in the unreachable distant sky. Diffusely outlined in the morning haze and bright sun, Thamserku appeared to be a mass of shimmering stone and snow. It was an unexpected and thrilling sight that too quickly disappeared behind the valley walls as the trail took us on its winding course.

By late morning, the terrain became gradually greener as the cliffs were mostly covered by forested areas. Enormous spruce, pine, and fir trees turned the rock mountainsides into green walls that towered on either side of us. As the trail climbed higher, I struggled to maintain a normal walking rate. Soaked by perspiration, I had to stop frequently to rest and to slow my pace. It was becoming a chore to take off my pack and get out the water bottle. Even taking photographs was wearying. (I rationalized that the varying light conditions and sameness of the narrow ravines and gorges didn't warrant taking too many pictures.) At least there were no bugs and insects flying around to add to my discomfort. If I had been subjected to the swarms of black flies, mosquitoes, and gnats (the no-see-ums) of our training climbs in Vermont's Green Mountains, my woes would have been much worse. It was disturbing to feel so fatigued after being only three hours on the march since breaking camp this morning. I tried to stop thinking about the strenuous afternoon hike that was in store for us after lunch. The realization that we were close to the village of Jorsale, our stopover for lunch, helped me forget my worries.

Before Jorsale, we passed an attractive lodge resembling an oversized log cabin that was run by a former Japanese monk. Its surrounding vegetable farm and grape arbors gave it an idyllic and welcoming look. It was too bad we couldn't stop here and refresh ourselves. On our return, however, this would be an overnight camp stop and a chance to sleep indoors in wooden bunks. The approach to Jorsale involved another long, rocky descent and brought us to magnificent forests of giant firs, magnolias, and rhododendrons that would be a blaze of color in another month. Far below us in the distance was Jorsale, a small group of dark wooden houses on the other side of the Dudh Kosi.

The bridge crossing here was the most impressive and picturesque yet. About one hundred and fifty feet long, the bridge spanned one of the widest parts of the river that flowed, half full, placidly below. The path leading directly to the bridge became very narrow, winding, and precipitous, like a three-story-high curving staircase. Stepping down gingerly, we could hold onto protruding rock formations and the trunks of trees or shrubs that bordered this path. Olga, who was far ahead of me while I was taking pictures of this magnificent valley, told me later that she tripped here and slid a few yards on her backside. Luckily, she suffered only a blow to her pride and no physical hurt.

Compared to the flimsy structures we had already crossed, this bridge was a major structure, maybe the Golden Gate of the Nepal's southern mountain country. A suspension-type structure, the bridge hung from a network of thick green rope and metal cables. The bridge floor was four feet wide and made of wooden planks that had become warped, uneven, and splintered by wear and weather. The sides were of thin metal latticework topped by waist-high pipe railings. Despite its apparent sturdiness, the bridge swayed gently when crossed.

Arriving on the other side of the river, we came to a wide, flat, sandy road that gleamed brilliantly in the sunlight. Only ten minutes from Jorsale, I couldn't wait to rest, as I was soaked with perspiration and exhausted. I remembered seeing a young woman in her early twenties, dressed in a white blouse and jeans, striding vigorously toward me with a yak by her side. As we passed one another and exchanged greetings, I was startled when hearing her hard American accent and learned that she was returning from Tengboche. Observing this energetic young woman bouncing along the trail, I wondered why she had only gone as far as Tengboche and had not proceeded to the usual trekking goal of Kala Pattar, another five days of hiking beyond Tengboche. Probably because of my fatigued state, the reaction that came to mind was an apprehensive one: maybe our goal was much too ambitious and difficult. I put this worry aside quickly when I saw, with much relief, a row of houses directly ahead on the edge of the trail overlooking the river.

My picture taking and weariness resulted in my being the last arrival at Jorsale, our rest and luncheon stop. Thoroughly bushed, I was ready to collapse, and I slumped on the bench outside the house where Olga was anxiously waiting. Still in a daze after catching my breath, I climbed the darkened narrow staircase to the second floor of the Sherpa home where lunch was being dished out. I was dizzy from exhaustion, and I remember little of that lunch. Unfortunately, the dirty, stuffy, dark atmosphere of the house wasn't conducive to feeling better. I had no appetite, and eating was an effort.

During the meal, I was quite oblivious to everyone, yet I startled when I heard Jim talk about the long, hard pull to Namche Bazaar to come this afternoon. I was incredulous and wanted to scream in protest as Jim, in his low-key and understated manner, informed us that after lunch, we faced one of the most strenuous hours of hiking of the entire trek. Although the trail to Namche Bazaar from Jorsale would be only a third of the distance covered this morning, it would involve a steep climb of three thousand feet, compared to the negligible five-hundred-foot rise in altitude we had just hiked. The constantly ascending trail would become an endless number of switchbacks, twisting up and around the mountains. Therefore, this afternoon's hike would be considerably shorter but steeper and more physically demanding. How would I make it if I already felt so beat? Olga was as exhausted as I was, but we kept the complaining and worrying to a minimum and hoped that this rest stop would recharge us. We were too tired to even talk, but our gestures and looks communicated how we felt. I noticed that Olga's features were becoming puffy as a result of the altitude. She reassured me that, other than being exhausted, she felt fine and was not developing signs of altitude sickness. After lunch, during which I drank a lot of tea and soup but only managed to nibble at the rice and potatoes, we had twenty minutes to see Jorsale before being on the move again.

Built on the riverbank and consisting of a row of several two-story blackened wood and stone Sherpa houses, Jorsale is the official entrance to the Sagarmatha (Everest) National Park preserve, which encompasses 485 square miles of mountains and villages. An official outpost and tourist building, which looks like a large wooden shack built over a five-foot rock foundation, houses an exhibit of maps and photographs and provides general information dispensed by two uniformed Nepalese. These Nepalese park rangers, in their brown boots, dark tan military khaki shirts and trousers, and cavalry hats, gazed at us in the indifferent, patronizing, and humorless manner of bureaucrats the world over. Everyone entering this park preserve had to pay a sixty-rupee (five-dollar) entrance fee, a detail that Jim had already taken care of. Printed on the back of the entrance ticket was a set of rules that made you realize that the reach of government bureaucracy is, like death and taxes, inescapable. Even in the most primitive lands, bureaucracy invades your life. These are the regulations from the back of the ticket:

> This permit is non-transferable and good for one entry only.

> You enter the park on your own risk. His Majesty's Government shall bear no liability for damage, loss, injury or death.

> Trekking is an acceptable challenge, but please do not:

> - litter, dispose it properly

> - disturb wildlife

> - carry arms and explosives

> - scale any sacred peaks of any elevation

> Please keep all the time to the main trek routes.

> Please be self sufficient in your fuel supply before entering the park. Buying fuel wood from local people or removing any wood materials from the forest is illegal. This will apply to your guides, cooks and porters also.

> Park personnel are entitled to arrest any person in charge of having violated park regulations or search his belongings.

For further information visit Park headquarter or ask any park personnel. National Parks Family Wishes Your Trip Pleasant.

The injunctions concerning firewood and being self-sufficient in fuel are the most strictly enforced because of the scarcity of wood that has been caused by soil erosion and the years of indiscriminately cutting down forest lands.

Olga and I had little interest in looking at the tourist exhibitions. We used this precious rest time to sit and be quiet in the hope of regaining some energy and strength for what was soon ahead. It was even a chore going to the toilet, which was situated a few hundred feet off the road. I was grateful that our fellow trekkers were a reserved and somewhat introverted lot who respected each other's privacy and were not given to endless talk. During lunch, no one spoke much, and I hoped that they were also feeling some fatigue. I was angry with myself and ashamed of being so fatigued, emotions that were triggered by thoughts of my boyhood mountaineering heroes who risked their lives and suffered untold hardships to climb these peaks. To them, this trek would just be a walk in the park. Yet everything is relative, and for Olga and me, this trek was our personal Everest. We quickly realized how outclassed we were by the others and accepted our limitations. We were not out to prove anything or trying to compete with anyone. Our goals were to maintain our own pace, stay healthy, and see Everest. We expected no extra consideration and hoped we would not become a burden to the group.

Although the group was characterized by an eager but businesslike attitude, everyone displayed a quiet acceptance of each other and a readiness to be helpful. Cutting through the general reserve of the group were Donna and Jim, in their early thirties, with a down-to-earth spontaneity and an extroverted and joking manner. I still remember Jim's repeated wisecrack when the going got rough: "We paid for this vacation!" Bespectacled, tall, thin, and dark haired, Donna, always candid and straightforward, kept us from getting down on ourselves.

The unspoken leader of the group, Nas, maintained a positive outlook and a stream of pungent wit. A fascinating person in his late forties, he had left Iran as a teenager to become a world-renowned orthopedic surgeon from Columbia University. Nas was forever expressing his opinions and giving advice (sometimes too much) in an emphatic professional manner. His take-charge attitude and wisecracking were never offensive and acted as a diversion to the group's seriousness. Nas's need to display his physical prowess was reflected in the tacit challenge and competition that existed among him, Abby, and John. All were in superb physical condition and avid climbers, hikers, and skiers. Like overeager racehorses at the starting line, they were always itching to be off. I sensed their energy and need to be in front of the pack, quietly glorying in their physical skills and determination to be the best. After breaking camp each morning, they would soon be on the trail and out of sight, and they would be the first to reach a new campsite.

We left Jorsale at one o'clock, after lunch and a brief rest. I shrugged off my worries and made a conscious effort to avoid a negative attitude. I put myself into a better frame of mind by considering the following rationalizations: Jim knew what he was doing, we were in good hands, the afternoon hike couldn't really be as bad as my anticipated fears, and we had no choice but to go on. Besides, the short rest, tea, and soup had made me feel stronger. The weather too would be an ally, as a cool breeze was blowing through the valley, and a growing cloud cover would shield us from the hot mountain sun. Finally, the knowledge that tomorrow at Namche Bazaar would be the trek's first full rest day—and our first chance for a panoramic view of Everest—helped lift my spirits. My energy also began to flow when I heard that we might get a glimpse of Everest at a certain point on the trail late this afternoon, if the weather remained clear.

As we entered the national park and passed through the wooden tollgate-like barrier, I completely forgot my fatigue as I realized that we were only a day away from seeing the greatest mountain range in the world. The trail continued interminably in a winding northerly direction into one valley after another. The valleys were becoming narrower, and the trail was beginning its steep rise. The soaring cliffs and forest walls crowded in on us, creating a claustrophobic ambiance. Forest areas of magnificent pine, spruce, and fir trees appeared in greater abundance; their size and number increased because of the protection these narrow valleys provided against the elements. On this part of the trail, we noticed natives scurrying about in the forests, collecting precious firewood. On their backs were elongated woven bamboo baskets filled with scraps of wood from fallen and decaying trees and shrubs. Interspersed among the trees and shrubs were rhododendrons of all sizes that would make the valley come alive next month with red, pink, and purple colors.

The countryside was becoming more lush, and it resembled the conifer forests found in alpine regions, with one major difference: the forests and mountainsides bordering these endless gorges looked more rugged and primitive than their well-groomed counterparts in the Alps. However magnificent these majestic evergreen trees were, their beauty was diminished by the immensity of the surrounding mountains and the background of shale, boulders, dirt, and withered foliage.

As the trail rose higher and clouds appeared, it became colder and breezier. I needed my bunting jacket and a sweater when descending to the cold valley floor to make a river crossing. With increasing elevation the canyon floors became damper and wetter and the canyon walls narrower. There was no evidence of flat land or habitable countryside on this part of the trail, which explained the absence of any village between Jorsale and Namche

Bazaar. Despite the lack of villages, this was a much-traveled route, as Namche Bazaar is the administrative center of the Khumbu (Everest) region. Akin to a capital city, Namche Bazaar is the hub of trading, commercial, and governmental transactions with its shops, lodges, bank, post office, and police station. Understandably, all trails led to Namche, and at times, our trail seemed crowded as small groups of natives, Sherpa porters, yaks, and other trekkers passed us from both directions. This activity was a welcome diversion from the monotony of climbing the same winding rock and dirt trail. Exchanging pleasantries with the passing travelers also took my mind off my strenuous exertions and growing fatigue.

I kept looking behind and checking on Olga, who was struggling at a snail's pace with Kanchha close on her heels. Thank God for Kanchha's graciousness and sensitivity when, in his firm but unobtrusive manner, he took Olga's daypack as we started out this afternoon. When the twisting trail and overhanging trees partially hid Olga from view, I could still make out her green and white cap (a souvenir from a Vail ski trip) bobbing conspicuously in the distance. From a distance, a half-mile behind and below me, Olga and Kanchha looked as if they were moving in slow motion.

Not only was Kanchha a great help, but Olga was also supported by a walking stick, which she used since leaving Lukla. We were the only ones who asked for a stick, which a Sherpa quickly fashioned from a broken tree limb. After a few hours of walking from Lukla, I found mine too burdensome to lug along. The stick wasn't wasted, though, as Donna gladly took it off my hands and followed Olga's example. Jim remarked that the use of a walking stick, as any other hiking technique, is a personal preference, but he generally recommended against using such an aid. When leaning for support on a stick, your body tends to be off balance, especially on tricky descents and ascents. With your weight off balance, you're more vulnerable to tripping or falling. But Jim emphasized that we should do what made us feel comfortable and secure, and Olga felt quite safe and contented with her wooden staff. (She tripped and fell only once throughout the entire trek.) Jim's opinion seemed to be confirmed by the fact that we rarely saw other travelers with a walking cane.

The route to Namche was gradually becoming steeper and mostly uphill. Usually about the width of a sidewalk, the trail occasionally shrank to a narrow, uneven footpath. The dark blue sky had also changed to a streaky gray overcast caused by the billowing afternoon clouds that obscured the distant peaks. When we arrived at the vantage point where Everest would be first visible, we found the famous peak hidden by the cloud cover. I wasn't too disappointed, because I learned that the clouds usually dropped down to hide the high summits in the afternoon. Besides, I was struggling to maintain a decent pace as exhaustion was slowing me down. Not only were the endless ridges ahead constantly ascending, but the swirling sand and dirt added to our discomfort. Because there was always another ridge ahead, it seemed that we made little forward progress. The damnable character of the trail, with its constant switchbacks, also added to our feeling of getting nowhere. I just couldn't believe that, after negotiating a steep ridge, which looked like the topmost one, there was another one staring you in the face.

During the last few hours to Namche, the trail was an endless progression of rising cliffs. Looking behind us to the southerly direction we had traversed, we saw an enormous snaking valley of rising and falling hills, resembling an ocean of mountain waves. It had taken eons for the rivers to carve out these deep gorges and ravines. Seeing these twisting canyons and the raging waters below, we could begin to appreciate Nepal's serious erosion problem. When these boiling rivers are at their height and overflow, they carry tons of soil away with them to the plains of India. Despite this dramatic landscape, I took no photographs. I wanted to conserve all my strength and minimize the slightest drain on my energy. Getting the camera out of the daypack and going through the paces of composing a picture were energy drains I could do without. The continuous rising ridges were becoming a torture. The going was incredibly slow and exhausting.

Young John, a thirty-five-year-old social worker, helped Olga and me by showing us the hiker's step, consisting of a definite pause after a stride or two, while negotiating these rises. It felt odd hesitating for a count of about a second before taking another few strides, but the technique helped considerably in cutting down the fatigue and adjusting to the ten-thousand-foot altitude.

Walking near us was Caryl, an experienced backpacker, who epitomized the perfect trekking pace, striding slowly and deliberately, like the tortoise eventually outpacing everyone. Caryl told us that years of backpacking had taught her that a slow, steady pace is the most proficient and least physically stressful hiking technique. Appreciatively, we took this advice and walked quite slowly, as if in slow motion, but with five hours of trekking already behind us, the exhaustion was making us numb. I watched Olga leaning on her walking staff for support, as if she were trying to draw strength from it. Later, in camp, Olga would tell me that it was her "best friend" and that without it, she wouldn't have been able to go on. We spoke little of our fatigue, and we kept our comments restricted to observations about the trail and the travelers who passed us. With envy and awe, we watched natives and Sherpas hurrying by with loads on their back so large that it looked as if they were carrying another person. Several Japanese trekkers rushed by, listening to their Walkmans and smiling inscrutably at us. One carried a brightly colored golf umbrella that looked odd and incongruous opened under the gray overcast skies.

The landscape was turning more rugged, with shale and brown dirt replacing the trees, which were becoming sparser. The riverbed was receding farther below us. Looking over the edge of the trail, the precipitous drop to the Dudh Kosi river was a few thousand feet. We were finally approaching Namche Bazaar, over three thousand feet higher in elevation than the Jorsale lunch stop. The last steep ridge ahead before Namche Bazaar showed the trail dividing into a lower and a higher path on the hillside. Noticing that there were trekkers on each path confused us. The question of which one to follow was answered by Kanchha, who looked concerned as we all noticed the tiny figure of Caryl in the distance taking the lower one. Our route led north to the high end of Namche Bazaar, where our campsite would be located. The lower route took one into the southern and lower end of Namche, a roundabout way to get to our campsite necessitating an extra twenty-minute hike. By now, everyone was so exhausted that any unnecessary detour became a major inconvenience. Although we tried yelling and waving at Caryl, she was too far away to notice us. Kanchha reassured us that someone would direct her properly, since it would be hard to get lost in a town that you can easily see from one end to the other.

As we negotiated that last ridge, we left behind the forested evergreen cliffs and saw the rocky mountainsides streaked with snow. We were moving above the tree line and sensed rather than saw the high mountain altitude, since the dark overcast concealed the surrounding peaks. Finally, the dusty and rock-strewn path brought us to our destination.

5

Window to Everest

Entering Namche Bazaar, we could see in a sweeping glance most of the town spread below us like an amphitheater, with irregular rows of two-story buildings rising in tiers. A hodgepodge of shops, houses, and lodges, the town resembled a huge bowl walled in by steep cliffs, and the darkening day and clouds made everything look dreary and dirty. Still a good fifteen minutes to our campsite on the opposite end of town, we wearily followed a dirt and cobblestone street hemmed in by rows of shops and houses. Flat ground is a rarity in Nepal, as even this path through Namche Bazaar was akin to climbing up and down a few flights of stairs. The town seemed deserted, as the villagers were indoors, preparing their evening meals. We saw only a few children playing and some natives peering from their houses or shops. To them, we were just more of the multitude of trekkers and climbers they had seen traipsing by in the last thirty years. Nevertheless, they greeted us with shy smiles and lilting *namastes*.

Our tents would be pitched in the front yard of Nahtang's house, which overlooked Namche Bazaar and was built on the topmost tier at the edge of town. After climbing a crumbling, rocky street, we arrived at our campsite, a neat-looking row of seven colorful tents pitched side by side. Thoroughly benumbed with exhaustion, we had made it here in four and half hours from Jorsale. All together, we had put in nearly an eight-hour day of hiking since leaving Phakding after breakfast. Olga and I were the last to arrive, with the exception of Caryl, whose detour to the wrong part of town caused her to be the last arrival. From the looks of the others, who had already changed clothes and were lolling around comfortably, they must have been in camp a good hour before Olga and me. We had no strength to talk right then; we just wanted to change into warm clothes and lie down.

Dusk was turning into early evening, and the chill of the mountain air at this twelve-hundred-foot altitude was permeating our dead-tired bodies. A heavy ski sweater and woolen ski hat, plus the welcoming hot cup of tea, helped considerably in warming and strengthening us. My physically and emotionally drained condition, however, kept me in a mild state of shivers. Maybe dinner this second evening would be more satisfying and fortifying than last night's excuse for a meal. I smile when I write the word "dinner," which sounds like such an inappropriate word to describe what passes for our evening meal. Tonight we would eat under Nahtang's roof. As is customary on treks, the evening meal was usually served in some part of a Sherpa's house rented for the occasion.

We had an hour before dinner, allowing time to rest, wash, change clothing, and look around. There was nothing much to see because of the emerging darkness and cloud cover. I wondered whether daylight tomorrow would reveal any mountain peaks behind these hills enveloping Namche Bazaar. I concentrated on our immediate surroundings. The tents were pitched in a dirt yard of fifty by fifteen feet, which was directly in front of Nahtang's house. Separated from the house by a dirt path, this rectangular compound was fenced in by a four-foot-high rock and mud wall. The tent site was also several feet below the path, which was reached by a small rickety ladder of six steps. All buildings and grounds in Namche Bazaar were on different levels because of the rising and terraced characteristic of the land.

Nahtang's house was the middle one in a row of eight identical attached two-story homes. Built of stucco and stone and looking as if they were periodically whitewashed, these forty-foot-wide houses were fairly impressive, and they reflected the more affluent status of natives residing in this trading and administrative center of the Khumbu region. Their uniformly graying white facade and large windows, whose frames were freshly painted in shades of blue or green, projected an attractive and bright appearance among the dirt brown hills. Each family home had its own outhouse, or a communal one shared by several families. Usually a six-by-six-foot stone or wooden shack, the outhouses in Nahtang's block of homes were built out front, and Nahtang's sturdy stone outhouse was conveniently located near the campsite. We were all curious to see the inside of these homes, and we awaited the call to dinner.

Night was falling, and the only light came from kitchen fires, kerosene lamps, and sparsely rationed electric light bulbs. Electricity was slowly coming to Namche Bazaar, and each house had only one or two naked light bulbs. We entered Nahtang's house in darkness, guided by a flashlight, to make our way to the ladder leading to the second floor. Typical of most Sherpa homes, the first floor was reserved for the family's animals, usually a yak or two, dogs, and roosters. Essentially a stable, the ground level consisted of a dirt floor and a low-beamed ceiling. We were immediately struck by the dank, smelly, and cold atmosphere that chilled our bones. Stumbling in the dark against the animals and low ceiling, we groped up the ladder to the second floor, the actual living quarters of Sherpa families. Consisting of a kitchen/dining area and a sleeping area, as well as a prayer room, the living quarters were dimly lit and unheated. Indoors, Sherpa families spend most of their waking time in the kitchen, where a fire is constantly burning. Keeping warm is everyone's priority, especially at night, when the dampness of an unheated house and the cold of the mountain air combine to make one uncomfortable.

We walked through Nahtang's large living-cum-bedroom to where we would eat, a fifteen-by-fifteen-foot room that functioned as the family chapel. This room of worship had as its focal point a small altar with Buddha figures and photographs framed by unlit candles. On either side, the walls were decorated with religious wood carvings and painted decorations. A few large chests with carved inlay decorations were pushed against the wall and would be used as serving tables. We sat on low built-in benches behind long mahogany tables no higher than two feet. It seemed odd and disrespectful to use this room as a meeting and eating place, but the atmosphere of reverence was quickly dispelled as we settled in and watched the kitchen pots with steaming food being brought in. Another incongruous note in this templelike chamber was the two portable cassette radios and a shelf of rock and country music cassettes on the window ledge. Obviously, this room served as an all-purpose family room as well as a family chapel.

During dinner, Jim requested that we rotate volunteers each evening to serve the meal family-style. As the food was being ladled out and passed around, I was on the verge of dozing off and eager to be done with eating and talking. The wind that blew through the room's only window kept us cool and awake. We were all feeling the cold, as everyone remained bundled up and kept on their woolen ski hats. It was early spring, and the stucco walls and wooden panels seemed to offer minimal protection against the cold and wind. I could imagine how uncomfortable these homes must be in the dead of winter with the howling mountain winds and perpetual snowstorms. A constantly burning fire is the only real protection against the savage winters that batter the Everest region. It's no wonder that firewood is such a dire necessity and a treasured resource.

While reflecting on the unheated qualities of these homes, I suddenly recognized an unpleasant odor that was everywhere. It turned out to be the smoke from the kitchen fire, which pervaded the atmosphere, since there are no chimneys in these homes. You can't escape the smoke; it's in your nostrils, in your clothes, in the walls, in the air. Truly, the air you breathe and the food you eat have the smell and taste of smoke. Even the walls and furniture had been blackened and permeated with smoke fumes. The smoke that these natives inhale and live with day in and day out must blacken their lungs worse than any inveterate cigarette smoker. It is ironic that the Nepalese, who live in the highest and purest climatic regions in the world, should suffer from polluted air in their homes, as if nature were punishing them for depleting the forests for firewood.

Despite my tiredness, I was looking forward to dinner to revive me. The first course of soup, made from a dehydrated mix, was satisfying and warming in this unheated chamber. I would have liked more, but there was just enough for one portion. Heaping plates of mushy rice with vegetables composed the main meal. I tried to eat as much as I could, but the best I could do was pick at my dinner. I am one of those individuals who dislike spicy flavors and pulpy food textures. Combine that antipathy with my state of exhaustion, and the result was a loss of what little appetite I had. Nevertheless, I forced myself to eat some of this mush, but the taste was too unappetizing for me to finish my plate. I looked at Olga, who was just nibbling at her meal with a look of gloom and resignation. She whispered, "This food is mostly forget-it," an apt description of the few meals we had already eaten and, regrettably, of those to come. Some acceptable canned fruit finished the meal; at least it was refreshing and easy to swallow, despite an odd metallic flavor. From what I had already seen of the grimy old labels on the jars of peanut butter and jam, I suspected that most of the canned food had been languishing in a warehouse before our expedition rescued it.

At dinner, Jim outlined the plans for our rest day tomorrow. Following a late breakfast at 8:00 AM, he would take us above Namche Bazaar to the park plateau that offered a view of Mt. Everest and the surrounding peaks. After that, we were free to do as we pleased—to rest, look around Namche Bazaar, or take an optional afternoon hike of a few hours to the nearby defunct Japanese-built hotel, which provided a spectacular view of Everest. We could also have some laundry done by our Sherpa crew and have our first opportunity to shower in one of the outdoor shower stalls in the village's trekking lodges. I was so weary that all I thought about for tomorrow was viewing Everest and then crawling somewhere into a corner to rest. As dirty and grimy as I was, I couldn't think of getting up enough energy to shower.

Although Olga and I were quite exhausted, we were pleased to have arrived at this twelve-thousand-foot altitude with no signs of mountain sickness. Some of the group complained of mild headaches and nausea. My only discomfort now was an acute stomach cramp that made me rush downstairs to the outhouse immediately after dinner. I would soon learn that the curry gravy acted like a quick laxative for me, and that I had to avoid taking any spicy sauces if I wanted to prevent the sudden diarrhea that resulted. With regard to the altitude, Jim explained that this rest day was important in helping us get acclimated to the altitude and the higher elevations to come.

Once again, Nas expressed concern about preventing altitude sickness and generously offered Diamox medication to anyone wanting it. Since Olga and I were fearful that our physically exhausted condition might make us vulnerable to developing altitude sickness, we opted to take this preventive medication. Although Nas reassured us that there were no harmful side effects, we might, he said, experience an increased need to urinate. This information brought to mind a very realistic practical and personal concern: how could I avoid having to stumble out of the tent into the dark and near-freezing cold to relieve myself once or twice during the middle of the night? At age fifty-eight, my kidneys no longer allow me an uninterrupted night's sleep. And with the large amount of fluid that I was drinking, these nocturnal needs could become more frequent.

Like so many clinicians presented with a problem, Nas listened with an objective, thoughtful, and omniscient manner that implied a solution would be forthcoming. Although I would often become annoyed with Nas's all-knowing attitude, I realized that his intellect thrived on challenges, and his personality revealed a genuine desire to help others. (In honesty, my annoyance at Nas probably reflected an unconscious recognition of myself in Nas, and a tacit intellectual competition between us; besides, I envied his quick and fertile mind that arrived so easily at solutions, compared to my slower thinking process.) With a gleam in his eye and a lively grin, Nas offered a solution. Like all ingenious solutions, this one was the essence of simplicity: use one of the plastic water bottles as a portable toilet. It was an obvious answer, but I had only two water bottles, which we needed to hold our drinking quotas. Leave it to Nas, who had an extra one that he would gladly give me; he himself would also use one.

There were many things that helped me, as a tenderfoot, to cope better with the many arduous and uncomfortable demands of living in the field for nearly three weeks, but none was more helpful and appreciated than Nas's gift of a bottle to urinate in when nature called me in the middle of the night to leave my cozy sack. This pee bottle, as mountaineers call it, is a technique used by climbers when they are at high altitudes or tent-bound on terrain only large enough to accommodate them. On hearing this discourse, Olga expressed envy and annoyance that her physiology wasn't as easily structured so that she could also avail herself of the pee bottle.

While on the subject of toilet needs, Olga and I agreed that until now, using outhouses wasn't as bad as we thought. Although it would take a little more time and practice to become more proficient at squatting, we quickly got used to the position. Olga was pleasantly surprised that the requisite squatting position and primitive toilet accommodations did not cause her to become constipated. In fact, Olga quipped that her bowels were more regular than usual; normally, when we travel, Olga needs a few days to become accustomed to our new surroundings before her physiology functions efficiently again. Up to now, the outhouses were neat and clean, their floors layered in part with hay, and the rectangular floor openings sufficiently large. It amazed us how little odor emanated from these toilet shacks, probably because of the dry air (made drier by a lack of rain for the last six months), the high altitude, and the cleanliness of the natives. This altitude and our strenuous physical effort, which combined to keep us mildly dehydrated, also explained our minimal need to urinate while trekking.

When our material comforts and frills are taken from us and we're forced to live stripped down to essentials, it's astounding how conscious we become of our bodily functions. It's quite understandable, because if there's a breakdown in our physical machinery, we're in serious trouble. In a primitive country, there are no aids to call on to keep going. We are operating completely under our own power. At best, we could stop and not continue the trek if we were ailing badly; at worst, the Sherpas would have to carry us out, or a helicopter would evacuate us if we became seriously incapacitated. At the back of all of our minds was the nagging anxiety that we might become ill and unable to achieve our trekking goal.

Back in our tent after dinner, we felt richer with Nas's donations of the Diamox pills and the pee bottle. It was only our second night in a tent, but it already felt like home, and it seemed as if we had lived under these conditions for a long time. It's amazing how the human organism can adapt to unusual and stressful situations, especially when our mental attitude accepts and does not fight the new threatening circumstances. As a psychotherapist, I learned after many years of experience that the most effective and healthy way of coping with the stresses and conflicts of life is to realize that we can't control the forces bombarding us, but we can control ourselves. We must accept the reality that we can't change the things beyond our control and look to ourselves, to our inner strengths. Go with the new circumstances, join forces with them, and expend energies in developing strategies to cope, rather than waste energies in battling windmills. Culturally, this is not the conventional way of thinking that has taught us to do battle with threats. Our aggressive, macho, and winning-is-all philosophy has focused on the externals and imposing our own ways on others. As a result, we have weakened ourselves as a culture and a force in the world, as evidenced by the steady erosion of our morals and values and our growing internal problems. By focusing on our own being, we can develop the flexibility and creativity to strengthen ourselves so that the reality beyond our control becomes manageable and does not overwhelm us. Neither a civilization nor an individual who has refused to come to terms with its inner core has remained healthy.

The most immediate application of these thoughts was to be constantly aware that the inconveniences assailing us could keep us in a state of agitation if we allowed them to. Therefore, I focused on positive thoughts, such as the soothing comfort of the sleeping bag, the rest day tomorrow, and the thrill of actually seeing Everest in the morning. I also experimented with different and hopefully more proficient routines of dressing and laying out clothes, shoes, and toilet articles in the tent. Before going to sleep, we looked over our variety of snacks and nibbled on the mix of raisins and nuts. Unfortunately, fatigue had taken away our appetites, and even my favorite Lindt chocolate bars did not appeal to me. As always, Olga put it in a positive light by joking that we needed to lose some weight anyway. We tried to read, but the effort of concentrating was too much, and we gave in to the forces of weariness and went to sleep. These coping strategies, when described by the written word, may sound simplistic and banal, but in these actual trying life circumstances, they were powerful tools for coping and surviving.

While dozing off, we both commented on the unbelievable warmth and comfort of the down sleeping bags. We had taken the Diamox pills and were ready to sleep. Our only concern was the prowling and barking dogs that we hoped would not stray into our tent, since the outside flap couldn't close completely because of a broken zipper. The next thing I knew, I was waking with a start from a deep sleep as I saw a large shadow at my feet by the tent's flap. Frightened that a wild dog was coming to visit, I shouted a warning to go away. But the shadow became larger and entered the tent in the person of Olga, who had gone out to relieve herself. What a scare, and how Olga would tease me about it for days! Yet she confessed to being too scared of the ferocious-sounding dogs to walk the twenty feet to the outhouse and said that she had relieved herself outside the tent. Olga explained that she had awakened with bladder nearly bursting, and rushed to get out of the tent. When the zipper to the tent opening got stuck, she panicked, and her struggle awoke me.

The only redeeming feature of her nocturnal outing was the starlit heavens. Awestruck, Olga reported that she had never seen such a starry sky. The stars were massed in profusion, incredibly aglow and huge. Not even the breathtaking evening stars sparkling above the Alps or the Green Mountains of Vermont could compare with this spectacular display. Despite her being so excited and urging me to look, I was too drugged with sleep to move out of the sack. Although we immediately fell asleep, this incident was a harbinger of the interruptions still to come. Repeatedly during the night, both Olga and I were rudely roused by an acute need to urinate, but as soon as we finished, the urge seemed to return quickly. Being more fortunate than Olga, I had only to use my pee bottle, which was filled to the brim by morning. This was the side effect of the Diamox, and the discomfort and inconvenience it caused made us avoid any more medication unless required by illness.

In the morning, our wake-up call and steaming tea came late at 6:30 AM. It had been a cold night with temperatures below freezing, and the dawn was chilly and crisp. No shorts and light clothes today; I put on khaki pants, a long-sleeved cotton chamois shirt, and a bunting jacket to be warm while shaving and washing in the penetrating air. As I stumbled out of the tent and looked up, I startled with excitement to see an enormous snow-covered mountain range on the opposite end of the town. A vast, wide backdrop of rock, glaciers, and snow, Kwangde, at 20,400 feet, blanketed the width of Namche Bazaar's western perimeter. Although a few miles west of the town, this flat, widespread mountain with peaks at either end looked, in this clear air, close enough to touch. Its immensity and proximity made it appear to be towering directly above us. What a view to be greeted by on awaking, and what a preview of panoramas to come!

This thrilling sight not only made me impatient to see Everest, but it revived my flagging energies. Despite a general tiredness, I felt healthy and had some appetite for breakfast. I enjoyed tea, oatmeal, a fried egg, and roasted potatoes flavored with kerosene fumes, nevertheless tasty and satisfying. Once again, Jim explained that after this morning's short climb to view Everest, we were on our own to rest, sightsee, or take an afternoon hike. Before starting out, everyone gathered clothes that needed washing. Shirts, socks, and underwear were handed over to the Sherpas who graciously volunteered to do laundry. It was a relief and a surprise to know that clothing would be washed here and at our stopover at Tengboche.

Done with breakfast and general cleaning-up chores, we assembled at 9:00 AM to climb the steep, wide road that took us north out of Namche Bazaar. A much-traveled trail, it was the main route leading north to the upper Khumbu region and Everest. At this altitude of over twelve thousand feet, I immediately felt the effort of climbing and began puffing. It was only a forty-five-minute climb, but it was quite steep and dusty. The traffic of natives, children, and animals, combined with an occasional breeze, kicked up the dirt, which got into everything.

The town receded below us, and we came to a path veering off the main trail that brought us to an area that was fenced in with wire. A crudely constructed wooden gate with a wooden shingle was inscribed with the words SAGARMATHA NATIONAL PARK. The immediate surroundings were quite barren and arid, consisting of nothing but dried-out shrubs, stones, and dirt. At this point, the path was edged on either side with rock. There was still nothing to see but brown hills, but this crudely made formal path gave me the sense that it was leading to something of importance.

We were now at over twelve thousand feet, the town below had disappeared from view, and the gently rising walk was bringing us to what we had all been waiting to see. As the sloping path rose higher and came to a plateau, the view slowly began to take shape. With each stride forward, the view gradually opened up. Like a theater curtain opening slowly and vertically, the stage before us revealed one majestic mountain after another coming into view. And then suddenly, we gazed at one of the most spectacular mountain views on Earth.

Stunned and awestruck, I felt tears come to my eyes as I saw these great peaks of my boyhood dreams. Seeing Everest seemed like such an impossible dream that I couldn't grasp that this incredible view was a reality. I sensed that the others were experiencing the same emotions, since an awed silence pervaded the group. From the group's reactions, it was apparent that viewing Everest for the first time had much personal significance to each of us. It took several minutes before any spontaneous display of emotions occurred. As the realization took hold of what we were seeing, the tension lifted, and we broke into cheers. If we felt so intensely awed by this sight, I can only imagine the indescribable and extraordinary experience it must be for mountaineers who are climbing and living in the midst of these great heights and views.

Recalling this thrilling experience, a memory that never leaves me, I still find it hard to believe. And as I write these words to describe that moment and spellbinding view, I am troubled by my inability to find the words to evoke the transcendent experience—it was truly beyond what words can convey. This profoundly emotional experience also had, for me, a strange and personal coincidence: the morning we viewed Everest was March 8, the birthday of my deceased mother, who had worked her entire life so that she could give her only child every possible opportunity for self-fulfillment.

A sensational panoramic view of 180 degrees from right to left had unfolded to the north of the plateau on which we stood. The snow-capped summit of Mt. Everest—at 29,028 feet, the world's highest mountain—was directly in the center of this dazzling panorama. On either side of Everest were the great snow-covered peaks of Ama Dablam (22,500 feet), Lhotse (27,923 feet), and Nuptse (25,850 feet), and adjacent mountains spread east and west as far as the eye could see. Beyond this range of mountains lay Tibet, where the full view and impact of Mt. Everest can be best experienced.

From our vantage point, Everest was not an impressive-looking mountain. Most of Everest was hidden from the Nepal side by Nuptse, a wide ridge of jagged peaks. The summit of Everest emerged from behind Nuptse and was bordered by more striking and beautiful mountains. One dramatic characteristic, however, distinguished Mt. Everest from all others: a plume of cloud that constantly rose above its squared-off summit. Crested most of the time by a billowing cloud, Everest seemed to be forcing us, despite the more imposing beauty of its surrounding peaks, to recognize its uniqueness and majesty.

Although these great summits were snow-covered, their gray and black rock faces showed through the sparse snow cover this time of year and gave the mountain range a dramatic appearance. This enormous panorama was framed by a vivid blue sky and in the foreground by deep, arid valleys flanked by dark rock cliffs and mountainsides above the tree line. In early spring, six months since the last rainfall, this landscape looked stark and ugly. Compared to the lush green mountainsides and meadows of the Alps or Rockies, the Himalayas were a world apart. Here, everything was shades of brown and gray, with stunted bushes and faded evergreen trees. The contrast between the giant, snow-capped mountains and the stark, ugly landscape was quite striking. There was not much beauty here in the traditional view of mountain scenery, as the craggy peaks took on a ferocious, even frightening aspect. The beauty and attraction of the Himalayas in the Khumbu region lie in the stark contrasts, the fierce beauty, and their overpowering presence.

The barren plateau on which we stood belonged to the national park preserve and included a stone building housing a museum of mountaineering lore and exhibits. About the size of a football field, the plateau fell steeply away on all sides to the valleys thousands of feet below. From this site, we also saw the beautiful Thamserku (22,000 feet) immediately to the east and the entire tremendous wide wall of Kwangde behind us. Gazing south, we beheld the hills and valleys below from which we had come, fading to the horizon in an undulating pattern reminiscent of ocean waves. Smack in the center of the plateau was a solitary wooden bench, looking incongruous and out of place in the midst of this overpowering scene. We assembled around the bench, dropped our packs to the ground, and got out our cameras. For the next hour, everyone scrambled to all points of the plateau and its sloping perimeters, taking pictures and absorbing the innumerable vistas that presented themselves in every direction. Spurred on by excitement, I forgot my fatigue and explored every inch of ground, anxious not to miss anything. I couldn't stand still in my eagerness to capture it all on film.

While taking pictures, I came upon Jim, who was pointing out tomorrow's trekking destination to some of the group: the village of Thami, a speck in the horizon and in the foothills of a magnificent range of mountains. From this perspective, Thami appeared to be located in nearly the opposite direction from our ultimate goal of Kala Pattar just below Everest. Why this diversion? Why go so far out of our way? Jim explained that the hike to Thami would help us in our acclimatization and take us through some interesting rock cliffs and canyons. Also, on our return, we would make camp at Khunde, the village on the other side of Namche Bazaar, which is well known for being the site of the first Western-style hospital built by the efforts of Sir Edmund Hillary. I kept my mild annoyance and disappointment to myself, wondering why we needed to waste energy on this side trip. I wanted to hoard my strength for the push to the foothills of Everest, and I was impatient to be headed in that direction. It was akin to having finally seen your cherished goal, only to be told that getting there would entail a detour of two days' hiking.

After everyone had exhausted viewing and picture taking, Jim asked how many would be interested in taking a side trip of three hours up and back beyond Namche Bazaar to see the defunct Japanese-built Everest View Hotel that commanded another magnificent view of these Himalayas. Not only were Olga and I reluctant to further exhaust ourselves, but we also did not want to leave this thrilling and spectacular site. Therefore, we opted to remain here until the clouds arrived and obscured the distant summits before we returned to the town to loaf and rest. Only Kirt, Caryl, and Jack decided to stay with us and to picnic, since we had brought snacks of cheese, crackers, and peanut butter.

Although the sun was intense and the temperature mild at around sixty-five degrees Fahrenheit, the winds that began kicking up in late morning brought a chill to the air. Blowing up the valleys from the south, the winds were gusting at a good twenty to twenty-five miles per hour by noontime. These valleys functioned as one enormously long wind tunnel nurturing the winds that brought clouds and cold air every afternoon to the mountain heights. To the north, where Everest and its neighboring peaks reigned, the turbulent air created the swirling clouds that appeared by noon and gradually increased so that they usually obscured the summits by 1:00 PM. Since the park plateau was becoming quite uncomfortable because of its exposed and windswept site, and the peaks were disappearing behind the clouds, we reluctantly decided to depart. But before descending to town, we visited the park's museum.

Resembling a small ski lodge, it was built of stone with a long sloping roof and a huge picture window on its eastern side. Established for only a few years, the museum was sparsely set up with exhibitions. In fact, the limited number and rudimentary character of the exhibits made the museum not only appear deserted but fairly unimpressive. Nevertheless, what we saw held our interest, as it primarily consisted of photo montages describing the characteristics of Nepal's alpine zone, shrubs, forests, and climbing areas. The exhibit that captured our interest displayed photographs of various expeditions and climbers on Mt. Everest and a display of mountaineering equipment. It wasn't much of an exhibit, but it was a good try at public relations geared to the trekker. While walking through these exhibits, which could be seen in about thirty minutes, we were mostly attracted by the museum guard. About sixteen years old, he constantly hovered nearby, smiling shyly and wanting to be friendly. His dress seemed to be the cast-off garb of Western tourists: scruffy, worn-out sneakers, dirty jeans, and a lightweight green ski jacket with orange sleeve stripes worn over a white dress shirt and a brown V-neck sweater. To complete his outfit, he wore a *topi*, the traditional native headgear; it looked incongruously majestic with its colorful crown of red, yellow, and green vertical striping.

I learned how the Sagarmatha National Park came into existence from reading *Many People Come Looking, Looking* by Galen Rowell, a professional photographer and mountaineer. After the first successful summit attempt of Mt. Everest in 1954 by Hillary, the Khumbu region attracted increasing numbers of tourists. The life of the Sherpa mountain people, as a consequence, began to change significantly. Imagine the results of a steady influx of trekkers on the simple native culture and on this unspoiled land. No longer isolated from materialistic values, the Sherpas became panicked by the indiscriminate pillaging and use of their natural resources. Regrettably, little thought and no plan were given to land preservation.

In earlier times, the precious forests were carefully nurtured and protected. Villagers appointed guards to watch over local forests, which were cut judiciously for firewood. When trekkers and expeditions began steadily arriving, the need for firewood heightened. Wood was cut indiscriminately by Sherpas who, employed by expeditions, were away from their own villages and not bound by communal constraints. Nearly four hundred porter loads of juniper firewood were needed for a single climbing expedition in the fifties.

In 1976, Hillary reported, "The whole area up there is just a desert now, which is all eroding." Hillary is a rare human being; he turned away from riches after his ascent of Everest in 1953, setting aside part of each year to help the Sherpas improve their lives. His efforts have helped them build bridges, schools, and a hospital. It was Hillary to whom Nepal's Royal Highness Prince Gyanendra listened when making plans to preserve the Khumbu region. The result was the establishment of Sagarmatha National Park in 1974, an official preserve of 480 square miles of land. Initially, this parkland created more problems by putting the Sherpa homeland under public control and making the Sherpas feel like public wards. These fiercely independent people enjoyed, until now, complete autonomy of their villages and lives. With the park preserve and tourism, which took the Sherpa away from his home for periods of time, the old traditions became more disrupted. As Galen Rowell so aptly wrote, "The trekking Sherpa is now confronted by a moral choice between the approval of his community, the laws governing the national park, and his livelihood"—psychological stresses that did not exist before the introduction of Western influences.

Today we saw at first hand the terrible effects of constant land erosion: burnt-out black and brown hills starkly set in the foreground of spectacular, craggy, snow-covered mountains. We also learned from the museum exhibits and our guides that finally, eight years after the parklands were established, some progress was being made in preserving and watching over this culture and land with projects of reforestation and the restoration of religious monuments. Whether the Sherpas, however, can preserve their way of life in the face of encroaching tourism and Western values seems doubtful. As it has been for most primitive, impoverished countries, the lure of Westernization, with its materialistic outlook, may be too difficult for these mountain villagers to resist.

Looking forward to an afternoon of rest and relaxation, we headed back down to Namche Bazaar. It was a dusty descent as the wind kicked up the dirt, which on one section of the trail oddly changed into beachlike white sand. Swirling around us, the dust invaded our clothes and every part of us. Obviously, dirt, dust, and dryness are typical conditions during the rainless season. We marveled that, even in our tents, the dust pervaded everything. I used to savor the short-lived pleasure of clean hands after our morning's ablutions. However, as soon as I returned to the tent to pack my gear, my hands would quickly become dirty again. Later on the trek, I hit on a strategy to combat the problem. While packing each morning, I wore my thin polypro glove liners. It may sound silly, but this simple technique temporarily warded off the feeling of grubbiness that would soon permeate our bodies after setting out on the trail. Anything I could do to stay clean was a psychological boost, helping me to feel more alive and energetic—and I needed all the energy I could find.

On our descent back to town, I noticed that the trail and town below were quite deserted. Except for an occasional solitary native, the hustle and bustle of the morning's traffic of people and animals was missing. I realized that, like people everywhere, everyone was by now at their place of work in the fields or on the trail. It's strange how when traveling in different cultures, we tend to forget that people's daily routines are essentially no different than ours. People maintain work, eating, leisure, and sleeping schedules, no matter where on Earth. Traveling is a constant reminder that human beings the world over are bound together by similar needs; despite geographic, economic, and cultural differences, people are more alike than different.

When we returned to the campsite, the kitchen crew offered us lunch, but having already snacked, we settled for only tea. Always eager to please and be helpful, the Sherpas, sensing our weariness, spread out a couple of sleeping pads for us to rest. We were quite a sight stretched out, basking in the sun on the dirt sidewalk in front of Nahtang's house, while the family's roosters and dog ogled us. A few yards away was Nahtang's wife, sitting in the doorway, diapering their newborn infant, whose clean appearance looked incongruous in these dirty surroundings.

Most of the Sherpa children we had seen so far looked grimy and slovenly. Dirty hands, grubby faces, and runny noses were a common sight. Like their elders, the children were also dressed in a variety of colorful clothing. Girls wore long skirts topped by blouses, sweaters, and nearly always a shawl; boys wore either shorts or long pants with jackets or sweaters. Whether it was a baseball cap, Adidas sneakers, a Grateful Dead T-shirt, or one with an alligator insignia, nearly every youngster wore some article of clothing that was either a gift or left over from a trekking or climbing group. These Sherpa children were a healthy-looking bunch, except for the runny nose and cough that everyone seemed to have from inhaling the fumes of their indoor fires. In their faces, we could see epitomized the handsome features of the Sherpa Nepalese: high cheekbones; chiseled, symmetrical features; dark, piercing eyes; and straight black hair. Their physical characteristics were clearly of Asian genetic stock. Most Sherpa ancestors originally came from Tibet, just beyond the Himalayan range. Until Tibet was taken over by the Chinese Communists and shut off from the world in the fifties, the Sherpas and Tibetans actively traded with one another. Recently, with the opening of China, the Communists have allowed the outside world to trade again with Tibet.

Too excited with curiosity about Namche Bazaar, we rested only briefly. We were impatient to take a walking tour of the town in the afternoon. Before leaving, we gathered our laundry that had been laid out to dry on the stone wall in front of Nahtang's house. Viewing these clean clothes and Nahtang's wife washing baby clothes, Olga jokingly bemoaned the wasted effort of washing, as the clothes would quickly be grimy and soiled again. The pervasive dirt was not the reason we decided against taking a shower. Once again, we wanted to minimize the drain on our energy that a shower involved: walking several blocks to a local lodge with a change of clothes, soap, and towel, waiting for the water to boil, and dressing and undressing. It seemed just too much to do. We also knew that in another three days, at Tengboche, we would have our next and final chance to shower before the major push to Kala Pattar.

Although we were covered with a few days' dust, strangely enough, neither Olga nor I felt dirty or uncomfortable. We also had no unpleasant body odors, despite not washing. Probably the dry mountain air and the polypropylene underclothes, which prevent the buildup of body perspiration, combined to help us feel reasonably clean. More likely as an explanation, however, was the power of human adaptability: people have an infinite capacity to adapt to new and different sensations and experiences, given sufficient willpower and desire. We accepted the marginal sanitary conditions and the inevitability of being enveloped by dust and dirt, and did not overreact negatively to them. Rather, all of us in the group viewed this set of circumstances with the resignation and humor typically generated by conditions beyond one's control and customary ways of living. Also, knowing that these deprivations were temporary made them easier to endure. In simple behavioristic terms, the reward was great enough to suffer through the punishment.

From Nahtang's house, it was only a short downhill walk to what suburbanites would describe as the center of town. Most of the shops and lodges were located on two streets: one snaking through the town from north to south, the other going east to west, meeting at a busy intersection. A leisurely ten-minute stroll would take us in either direction to the outer edges of Namche Bazaar. The streets were narrow and at times little more than alleyways, and since the town was built in a valley and on a hillside, they were a series of ups and downs and strewn with rocks. We could trip or fall and turn an ankle here as easily as on the trail.

As we navigated Namche's streets, we became more conscious of the town's unique and dramatic physical setting. Surrounded and crowded by steeply rising dirt hills and rocky cliffs, Namche Bazaar seemed to have been scooped out of the earth and nestled in this mountainous terrain. Overhead, the fleecy, white afternoon clouds paraded against the bluest sky imaginable. Splendidly isolated, Namche Bazaar was a good four days' hike from the nearest city, Kathmandu.

The rows of small shops, with their infinite variety of consumer goods and articles, belied Namche's isolation from civilization. Everything conceivable could be found in these small stores. Crowded next door to one another and no larger than an average-sized living room, these stores sold candy, canned food, toilet articles, film, postcards, and all kinds of clothing and footwear. In addition, several offered handcrafted wood carvings, metalwork, and costume jewelry. There was nothing primitive about these stores except their modest physical structures. Most impressive was the neatness and attractiveness of the display of goods. I marveled at how each category of items was obsessively stacked together in neat rows and colorfully arranged in every shop. Most items were laid out on long tables or under glass counters, while clothing hung from wall racks. The well-organized appearance of each store's display was startling, considering the town's isolated and primitive ambience. The single jarring, or amusing, note was that many of the foodstuffs appeared to be of ancient vintage with their faded food labels and crumpled appearance. The candy bars, cough drops, toothpaste, and canned goods looked as if they had either been lying around for years or battered from too much handling. In truth, many of these goods were leftovers or gifts from passing expeditions and trekkers. This also explained the availability of used climbing gear and equipment. There was little that one couldn't find in these shops. We even passed a tailor shop stocked with a modest selection of fabrics, and we were amazed to learn that the tailor could turn out made-to-order shirts, shorts, or trousers. Usually these custom-made clothes could be finished by late afternoon if the order was placed in the morning. Unfortunately, we discovered this tailor shop too late in the day to take advantage of its same-day service.

Our shopping was limited to a handful of items purchased at a shop whose catchall advertising attracted us. In red block letters of varying sizes on a white background, their sign proclaimed: MOUNTAIN EQUIPMENT, RENTING AND CURIO SHOP, ETC. How could we resist the "etc."? Inside, the large selection of bric-a-brac and handicrafts seemed to be of better quality than those found in the commercial alleys of Kathmandu. We told ourselves that these handicrafts were probably better and more genuine because they were made by local artists far removed from the commercialism of tourist-ridden Kathmandu. What naivete—what rationalization! Anyway, we finally succumbed. I found a prayer wheel that appealed to me, made with a nicely turned walnut wheel encrusted with colored stones and a hammered silver handle, and a Buddhist copper bell whose overtones gave out a pleasing and soothing ring. Olga bought a pendant for her mother and a wedding band that was supposed to be genuine jade. Always an easy mark, Olga discounted my skepticism and believed the smiling, shrewd storekeeper, who knew just how to deal with trekking tourists. When Olga asked Ved, back in camp, whether the ring was jade, he responded with a hearty laugh. Still, it was a pretty ring that pleased Olga and lasted several days until it cracked into pieces like the glass it was.

While shopping and browsing, we noticed how much effort the natives put into making their shops and homes attractive. Most of the buildings were made of stucco and stone that had turned a dirty, faded beige from the weather and wind-blown dust. Some of the flimsy corrugated tin roofs were weighted down by large rocks to prevent their being blown away by the savage winter winds and storms. Despite the arid, begrimed, and primitive ambience, the villagers kept their buildings attractive looking by freshly painting their window and doorframes every spring. Colors of royal blue, red, and green gave the town's buildings a cheery, although incongruous, appearance.

In addition, the colorful signs of the lodges and shops, all in English, helped to brighten up the town. The main lodges (Sherpas Trekkers Lodge, Khumbu Lodge, and the International Foot Rest) offered overnight accommodations, either in a dormitory or a single bedroom, at an average price of one dollar per day. Modest in size, these larger lodges accommodated about ten people in their dormitories; their highly sought-after single rooms were limited to no more than six. Each lodge had a small restaurant offering food and drink for quite reasonable prices; one could eat a satisfying meal for less than two dollars. Tea, local beer, and soda were always available, and at the International Foot Rest, there was a surprisingly well-stocked bar of whiskey, gin, rum, and champagne. The smaller lodges provided sleeping arrangements that usually consisted of nothing but a large room with several beds or spaces for sleeping bags.

Finished with shopping and sightseeing, while walking back to the campsite, we noticed several of our group scrambling down the steep western ridge of the town. When I realized that they were returning from their side trip, I couldn't believe their stamina and energy. Here it was past four in the afternoon, and I was still tired from yesterday's hike and mildly puffing from the hours of walking around the high altitude of Namche Bazaar. How I envied them their energy.

Back at the campsite in front of Nahtang's house, we were soothed by what was to become our late afternoon and predinner daily rituals: washing our hands with freshly boiled water and drinking a cup of tea that spread through our weary bones like a tonic. I am not a tea drinker, but I looked forward to this satisfying strong, full-bodied, and tasty tea. An added treat was the plain English butter cookies, somewhat stale and smelling of cardboard but still appetizing. This time of day usually gave us an hour or so to rest, relax, and talk before dinner. Some of those who had taken the jaunt to the Everest View Hotel spoke with amazement about the building and its spectacular site looking up the valley to Everest. Unfortunately, their viewing was limited by the afternoon cloud cover. Maybe, I thought, we would have the chance on our way back to see this much talked-about setting. Jim told us that the hotel had failed because tourists who were flown into a nearby airfield could not acclimate quickly to the twelve-thousand-foot elevation and would suffer from altitude sickness.

While waiting for dinner, I took in these extraordinary surroundings and the people. I became curious about the many terraced areas on the steep hillsides of Namche that were fenced in by stone walls. These large, barren dirt plots showed no signs of any growth; still, they must have had some importance, or why would they be enclosed by such well-constructed stonework? Ved explained that these steeply inclined areas were experimental plots planted with tree seedlings. Attempts at reforestation in these mountainous regions are confronted by two opposing forces: either the monsoon rains wash the seeds away as the dirt slides down the hillside, or the yaks, who are fiercely independent of mind, trample and eat away the seedlings. The natives desperately hoped that these rock-enclosed plots would combat nature's destructive elements and protect the newly planted tree seedlings. I also became aware that wood was a basic life necessity in the Khumbu. Every house in Namche Bazaar and on the trail had piles of firewood stacked nearby. These neat-looking stacks of wood were as much a part of the landscape as the towering mountains. To these mountain dwellers, the amount of firewood they collected indicated how well they would survive the terrible winters, which could keep them snowbound at home for days and weeks.

Usually around early evening before eating, some of the group would be found writing in their diaries, looking concentrated and distracted as only a writer can appear. Olga and I had each brought along a notebook with plans to keep a journal of the trek. Although we both scribbled a few pages after lunch today, we felt it was too much of an effort to write. To me, writing requires the utmost in concentration and thought, a demand I just could not meet, because of my weariness. At this early stage in the trek, I once again was careful to avoid any undue drain on my energy. Perhaps later, when we became better acclimated to these physical and mental strains, we would feel able to record these incredible sensations and experiences.

Since our arrival at Nahtang's house, everyone had noticed the constant presence of a smiling six-year-old carrying an infant on his back. A close friend of Nahtang's family, this youngster was never without the baby nestled in a sling like a human backpack. It was strange to see this inseparable pair always around the house. Other young children were off to school or out playing, but not this boy.

At dinner, Jim told us the tragic story behind the boy's behavior. A few weeks before, the infant's twenty-year-old mother had suddenly became seriously ill. Repeated internal hemorrhaging and dangerously high fevers caused a coma and sudden death. It was already too late to get the volunteer Western physician, an hour away in Khunde, before the young mother died. A runner was sent for the husband, a Sherpa guide, who ran all the way to Namche Bazaar from Kathmandu, where he was working. Frantic with grief, the father fell into a deep depression. Left with three children, he was overwhelmed with despair. Days passed, and the depression and withdrawal from everybody intensified. He refused to eat, became uncommunicative, and was quite unable to function.

Recognizing that he was in the throes of a nervous breakdown, his friends arranged for professional help—a Buddhist priest who would perform a religious ceremony that would exorcize the young father's immobilizing grief and bring him back to life. Precious juniper bushes were burned while the priest delivered his incantations, which put the grieving father into a trance-like spell. As customary in such rituals, the priest instructed him to perform an act that would purge him of the demons within and return him to health. In this case, the holy man entreated the widowed husband to change the name of his middle child. This sacrifice, like a penance, would cleanse him of the evil spirits causing his disturbed behavior. Like magic, the next day, the man's depression began to lift, and within a few days, he was functioning normally.

Astonished and awed by this tale, our group laughed uncomfortably and spoke patronizingly about the powers of a witch doctor. We so-called civilized people, who have been led to believe in the omnipotence of science and technology, become threatened by forces beyond our understanding. With a superior attitude, we tend to discredit and reject ideas and actions that do not subscribe to the scientific methods we worship. As a psychotherapist, I find this attitude an unfortunate and lamentable one. Science and technology do not have all the answers. I have seen the power of suggestion, the powers of faith and belief, or whatever we choose to call them, effect miraculous changes in people. There isn't a practitioner in the healing arts who does not judiciously use the power of suggestion, whenever feasible, to help patients. At least this psychological technique, unlike physical interventions or medication, has no harmful consequences unless used purposefully to foster a destructive belief.

This tragedy also involved the widower's close friends, who assumed the responsibility of raising his three children. The motherless infant was informally adopted by Nahtang's family circle and became the responsibility of the six-year-old boy, who would not be able to attend school or play freely with his friends. Nahtang's family hoped the arrangement would be only temporary, until another family could be found to raise the baby; Nahtang already had more than enough people to house and feed, and he would be hard-pressed to take on this responsibility indefinitely. Meanwhile, from what we observed, this baby seemed far from a burden to the youngster, who walked around with a sense of importance and pride as the baby hung from his back.

Sudden and unexpected death is no stranger to the Sherpas, who live and eke out a livelihood in this inhospitable country. Every season, Sherpas are killed in mountain climbing accidents and by calamitous weather. These mountain villagers live continuously with the dread of unexpected tragedy that can strike any family. When disaster occurs, the Sherpa community, traditionally close knit and mutually supportive, close ranks and extend support. No Sherpa is alone, but lives in an extended family group that is constantly ready to help when misfortune strikes. Haunted by potential tragedy, these people show an understandable fatalistic outlook. They are plagued not only by frequent death from climbing accidents and natural disasters, but also from hunger, filth, and epidemic diseases.

Although Western physicians had come as volunteer workers and there was now a hospital at Khunde, an hour's quick hike from Namche Bazaar, most Sherpas viewed modern medicine with suspicion and were reluctant to avail themselves of medical help. Prone to ravaging diseases because of pollution and undernourishment, most Sherpas did not live to a ripe old age, but died by their forties. The beauty and handsomeness that radiate from them during adolescence gradually fade during their young adulthood. Before reaching thirty, their faces have become wrinkled, their skin shriveled, and bodies bent. We were amazed and distressed to see these proud and hardy people look shockingly old while still in their twenties.

One of the growing medical problems in Nepal is the alarming incidence of iodine deficiency that causes humans, and even mountain goats, to develop goiters. According to Erik Eckolm, who researched this problem for *The New York Times*, "a lack of iodine in the diet is dooming millions of children to mental and physical disabilities"[1] in Nepal. Throughout the trek, we continually noticed young and middle-aged women with neck goiters, which

---

1.   Erik Eckholm, "Iodine Deficiency in the Himalayas," *New York Times*, April 2, 1985.

were the size of a rubber ball or so large that the neck bulged grotesquely. Without adequate iodine, which causes hypothyroidism, the Nepalese child is deficient in a hormone critical to healthy growth. As a result, children develop mental retardation, become physically crippled, and suffer from many kinds of sensory impairments such as deafness and mutism. In some isolated mountain villages, up to half the children are mentally retarded and will never become productive workers. To combat the problem, teams of health workers are inoculating as many as possible with iodized oil, which is slowly released in the body over a five-year period. More important, health officials are educating everyone to eat salt, since the soil and water of the Himalayas are lacking in natural iodine. Furthermore, the Nepalese government is building hundreds of new iodization plants that will produce the necessary salt. Ironically, this is a disability that can easily be overcome, as the annual cost to provide sufficient iodine per person is less than the price of a cup of tea.

Another health problem is the rise of ulcers, which had been unheard of in the Nepalese, but has been emerging over the past several years. In fact, Nahtang recently developed an ulcer for which he needed to be treated in Kathmandu. The medication is quite expensive, and Jim hoped that the group would consider making a donation after the trek toward Nahtang's medical expenses. We speculated that it would be only fair to help Nahtang, since the ulcers were probably caused, to some degree, by the pressures that Westerners have brought to Nepal and by the stresses involved in supervising a crew of Sherpas on a climbing or trekking expedition. Sherpas, who are employed by foreigners, must have a difficult struggle trying to balance their simple lifestyle and the Westerners' complicated and technologically advanced mode of existence. From our observations, the Sherpa's way of life moves placidly and with an air of resignation that accepts whatever life has in store. The Nepalese do not attempt to challenge and change things or strive continually for achievement. No wonder stomach problems are being found in the Sherpa region. Imagine the tension, frustration, and suppressed anger that these easygoing mountain people must experience in trying to understand and adapt to value systems that conflict so strikingly with their own ways.

There is a universal tendency to view poor and underdeveloped countries with disparagement and condescension. Implicitly, we tend to blame them for their backwardness and lack of progress—as if they were doing something wrong and we "civilized" countries were doing everything right. And when these impoverished countries are threatened and eroded by change, we are annoyed by their inability to adapt to new influences. This Western attitude of superiority is an unfortunate one that reflects our own lack of acceptance. There are not many certainties in life, but the fact of change is as inevitable as our ultimate mortality. Like it or not, change is always at our heels, and countries or individuals cannot ignore its presence without peril. Inherently, change is neither good nor bad, and the value that we ultimately assign it is a function of time and place; for some, it may portend disruption and harm, and for others, growth and benefit. How we accept and adapt to change determines its meaning and consequences. The great challenge is to integrate the immutable fact of change into our lives, so that it creates the least conflict and provides the maximum benefit. It is not always an easy task, and it is an ongoing struggle in this age of technological leaps and culture shock, where the media can bring any place and event on Earth into our living rooms. If we understand this, we can be more accepting of the plight that the Nepalese and the Nahtangs of this world must face, just as in our own lives, we must adapt to the beards, drugs, and sexual freedom of our children's generation.

Beginning the trek

Ama Dablam

Ama Dablam in the clouds

Campsite at Tengboche

Ed Neuhaus

Peddlars on the trail

Valley view from Tengboche toward Everest

Future Sherpas

Kanchha

View of Everest from Namche Bazar

A rest stop

The trail gets tougher

Olga Neuhaus

Olga and Kanchha

Below Kwangde range

The group's initial view of the Everest panorama

Views of Thamserku

Monastery of Tengboche

6

Acclimatization Gets Tougher

That evening, Jim explained that tomorrow's hike to Thami would help our acclimatization and expose us to more mountainous terrain and scenery. En route, we would stop at Thami to have lunch at the home of Nahwang's parents. On our return, this trail would take us to Khunde to see the first hospital in the Khumbu region. I secretly wished we could bypass this diversion and trek directly to Everest. I was experiencing no ill effects from the altitude, except for a mild lassitude, which today's rest had alleviated to a considerable degree. Olga was also feeling less tired, despite her puffy face and scratchy throat, which Jim thought came from the pervasive dust. To my mind, which was preoccupied with getting to our destination, this roundabout route would add to my exertions and tire rather than strengthen me. I quickly squelched this negative thought, remembering to believe implicitly in Jim's leadership.

At Namche Bazaar, I began viewing dinner as a challenge, and I adopted the strategy of eating only what was palatable. After the tasty soup, I picked at my plate for the morsels of vegetables and potatoes, avoiding the mushy rice and spicy, thick gravy. Dessert turned out to be canned peaches, which weren't bad but had a metallic taste. If I was still hungry, I planned to have some of our snacks, which we had in abundance. Surprisingly, Olga and I rarely had much of an appetite, and the little we ate during dinner satisfied us, so we rarely snacked before retiring.

While eating, we noticed a small pile of Sherpa woolen hats on the window shelf behind us. Wondering whether we could buy any, we learned they were handmade by the women of the family and were for sale. They were made of yak wool and in the traditional Sherpa design and color. Like a ski hat, the crown was a dull beige with a dark brown Greek key-type design circling the border. Extremely light in weight, the hat was quite warm and comfortable to wear in these damp and breezy indoor rooms. A singular characteristic of yak wool is that whenever it becomes wet, the wool gives off a strong animal odor. Now, when I wear my Sherpa hat skiing, I can smell the yaks when the wool becomes moistened by the snow.

Back in the tent, we decided to read awhile before going to sleep, a nightly ritual we follow back home. About an hour's reading in bed has us both relaxed and drifting easily to sleep. Usually, our vacation books are adventure stories that require no serious concentration. For the trek, we had settled on a pair of potboilers by Robert Ludlum, whose thrillers are truly incredible and well written. We were still trying to work out a satisfactory lighting arrangement. Despite the advice from backpackers and the latest equipment advertised in backpacking magazines, nothing seemed to provide sufficient illumination to read by. Also, where to place the light source presented another difficulty. The much-touted microflashlight, about six inches long, was convenient but gave off a feeble light. Always skeptical of the latest technologies, I had brought along the basic flashlight one buys at the corner hardware store and found it to be our most effective and reliable piece of equipment, particularly for reading, as we balanced it behind us on the cargo bag that doubled as our pillow. Stretched out in the sleeping bag, we felt comfortable enough to be easily transported by our imaginations to the high seas and snowy Swiss Alps of our novels.

Unfortunately, before we were comfortably settled in our sleeping bag and in this blissful state, we had much to do every night to prepare for sleeping and be ready for tomorrow. Clothes for the morning had to be decided upon and searched out from the overcrowded duffel bag; water bottles had to be placed in front of the tents to be refilled; snacks for the day pack had to be replenished; and the innumerable personal and toilet articles had to be laid out for the morning. It seemed that Olga and I were always in each other's way and that everything was always being misplaced and getting temporarily lost. Our patience was sorely tried while moving about in a crowded tent at the end of a tiring day, where the twelve-thousand-foot altitude makes the night air thin and bone-chilling. Sliding into the warm goose-down sack was always a welcome relief after finishing these nightly chores. Although we wanted to read, we lasted no more than fifteen minutes before falling into a deep, bottomless sleep.

The morning found us rested and eager to be on the move after yesterday's restful meanderings. By now, I felt like an old hand at washing and shaving with a bowl of warm water and using an outhouse. Those chilly morning outdoor shaves have become associated with the soothing smell of coconut that came from my post-shave mountain skin cream. Whenever the odor of coconut wafts by me now, I think of struggling to shave in those brisk Nepalese mornings. Another memory is that of using Nahtang's stone outhouse just before breakfast. Never really comfortable and at ease around animals (except for my midsize dachshund at home), I startled when I saw several dogs and a goat sleeping in the outhouse, oblivious to my presence.

As usual, we left after 8:00 AM on the route to Thami. Heading nearly due west, the trail out of Namche Bazaar involved a steep, rocky ascent. By the time we got out of the town and on the main trail, I was puffing and ready to sit and catch my breath. I found that it always took me about an hour after starting out in the morning to acclimate to the high altitude. Early morning and the last hour before reaching campsite were the toughest times of the day for me. I didn't feel right until I'd been under way awhile and my bodily juices were flowing. Tempted to stop and rest, I resisted, because it was harder to get acclimated if you rested too often. Instead, I just slowed my pace until I was breathing easily and moving with less strain.

The trail to Thami began pleasantly enough through a valley of wide expanses, green forests, and snowy mountains constantly in view. A long stretch of forests bordering the trail belied the rough, dirty terrain we found everywhere. Our spirits were lifted not only by the magnificent views, but by the ease of the trail, which was fairly level much of the morning. So far, it was such an easygoing and stimulating morning of hiking that it lulled me into believing that the trek wouldn't be as physically punishing as I feared.

The wide character of the valleys opened up large, breathtaking panoramas of mountain ranges. In contrast to our first two days of hiking through narrow gorges and twisting trails with rock cliffs hovering over us, we were now surrounded by the wide-ranging Himalayas. Across the valley on our left and paralleling the trail was twenty-thousand-foot Kwangde; behind us was twenty-two-thousand-foot Thamserku; ahead of us were the twenty-two-thousand-foot snow peaks of Tengbouche.

In addition to these expansive views, we passed many chortens along the way. The first one was quite impressive: about twenty-five feet in diameter at its base and tapering into a thirty-foot-high spire, it squatted at a large bend in the dusty trail. On either side were rickety poles with the usual shredded prayer flags, and around the base were *mani* (prayer) stones. On this route to Thami, we would see some of the most picturesque carved *mani* stones in all of Nepal. Although we saw *mani* stones carved as high as ten feet on cliffs, most of them were irregular-shaped grey stones about two feet square, on which were carved Buddhist symbols and decorative geometric forms.

As we approached our halfway mark and luncheon destination of Thamel, the valley floor widened and spread out before us, revealing terraced farmlands stricken with drought. The green foliage we had seen earlier was now transformed into low-spreading hills of stunted juniper bushes and scrub brush. And the wide riverbed just bordering the trail was dried out from the six-month lack of rain. We could not escape the arid, unpleasant brown and gray landscape, which only heightened the dramatic background of snow-covered peaks towering to the vivid cerulean sky. What a contrast!

On the outskirts of Thamel, we passed a large, impressive building surrounded by a stone wall. A commercially made sign with red Nepalese and English letters announced that this was the site of a hydroelectric plant that would bring electricity to the region. But if the sporadic appearance of electric light bulbs in homes in Namche Bazaar is any indication of progress, this goal will be a long time in coming. We could sense the skepticism in the voices and joking smiles of the Sherpas, who described this project as if it were an invasion from outer space. Beyond the building, we saw the village of Thamel rising several hundred feet on the hillside bordering the trail. Approaching the village, which was built in a semicircle, I counted about thirty homes that looked across the trail to a wide, rolling valley of farms enclosed by stone fences. In summer, when the daily rains have turned the countryside lush with greenery and alive with crops, this must be an idyllic pastoral scene. But now, it was a land of parched earth and rock, relieved only by the snow-capped summits around us. The brilliance of the sun and sky could do nothing to make this land appear less lifeless. Nevertheless, the substantial size of the Sherpa houses with their adjacent farmlands made Thamel appear prosperous.

Our lunch stop in Thamel was at Nahwang's house, which faced the trail and was approached by climbing several stone steps. Most of the group had already arrived and were gathered in an open courtyard where we would have lunch. A picnic scene greeted us, with kettles, plates, and condiments on a grey tarpaulin spread over the ground. Grimy and battered with use, the tarpaulin became our daily luncheon tablecloth, around which everyone sat or reclined like picnickers. I can still visualize the colorful daily array of jars of peanut butter, jam, and honey, a sugar bowl, ketchup, Cadbury's hot chocolate, and the inevitable Nescafé. How odd it was that these ordinary, everyday objects, which we usually took for granted, could give us a feeling of security in strange surroundings. And even the simplest things, under difficult conditions, can bring pleasure; for example, I remember that lunch for the tasty and invigorating hot orangeade. Today's lunch was the most appetizing and edible meal so far: a slab of sausage meat, large slices of fried potatoes, and a fried egg, followed by a fresh tangerine.

It was a relaxing hour eating and lounging in that sunny courtyard. The hot sun and cool breezes made the temperature ideal, around sixty-five degrees, and everyone was getting some sun and dozing off. The weather was incredibly perfect, but in the distant horizon, we could see the huge, billowing clouds that would turn the beautiful sky into an overcast one by late afternoon. Already well tanned, I had a healthy appearance that belied my fatigue. Everyone was concerned about the intense sun at these altitudes and used sunscreen and hats to minimize sunburn. Since I rarely suffer sunburn and tan easily, I can tolerate more sun than most people, and I don't go overboard with measures to protect myself from the sun. My high tolerance of cold also enables me to wear lighter clothes than most people in cool temperatures. While many of the group wore pants and jackets, I was still wearing shorts and a light wool-knit shirt. After yesterday's rest day and this morning's relatively easy hike, I felt fairly strong, and there was none of my previous exhaustion. It was too bad we had to move on and couldn't remain in this picnic setting.

In contrast to the comparatively busy and well-traveled route to Namche Bazaar, the trail to Thami had few travelers, especially in the afternoon, when the undulating countryside became one narrow rock gorge after another. Our map showed only one village between Thamel and Thami but revealed a string of villages beyond Thami, north to Tibet. The border between Nepal and Tibet was closed in the 1950s when China seized Tibet, forbidding any further travel and commerce. Nevertheless, the Nepalese in the mountain villages continued to trade with their Tibetan neighbors. With packs of rice on their back, they plodded through arduous mountain passes to Tibet, where their goods were exchanged for the rugs and trinkets sold everywhere in Nepal. After over thirty years of distrust and quiet enmity, Nepal and China had recently agreed to open the Tibetan border to foreign travel. Since tiny Nepal has always been fearful of China and India, its giant neighbors, it has maintained a nervous security within its borders and prohibited foreigners from traveling into its northern borders. The political unrest and instability of the countries surrounding Nepal explain the many police checkpoints along the trail that trekkers must observe and the suspicious militaristic attitude shown by Nepalese police and government officials. Even in Nepal, one of the poorest and most primitive countries in the world, the fear of aggression pervades the bureaucratic atmosphere. The reopening of the border will probably attract more visitors who can now enter the once-forbidden land of Tibet from Nepal. Although increased tourism will bring more material wealth to Nepal, it will also create added threats to an already fragile environment in a country that is struggling to save its natural resources.

The route beyond Thami entered one rocky canyon after another, and the trail began its typical roller-coaster ascents and descents. Towering cliff sides and rock overhangs bordered the trails as the farmlands receded behind us. Everywhere we looked, we saw nothing but rocks and huge boulders. It was rare to see an occasional patch of stunted trees or low-growing bushes. The clouds had blotted out the bright sun and sky, and the leaden, overcast sky added to the ominous landscape. Enveloped by cliffs of stark, unearthly beauty, I felt as if I were on a strange and mysterious planet. The narrow gorges, the dank air, the bleakness, and our being alone on the trail heightened the foreboding atmosphere.

The trail became gradually narrower and began to fall precipitously to a river crossing several hundred feet below. Walking cautiously, we descended a path of loose dirt and stones that made the footing dangerous. A stumble here could send us sprawling, with dire consequences. I slowed down to wait for Olga and Kanchha, so that we could be together crossing the footbridge below. I wanted the comfort and presence of another human being in this treacherous and inhospitable terrain.

It was an incredible and awesome scene we came upon. Enormous boulders, as high as two-story houses, and steeply soaring cliffs surrounded a flimsy footbridge that crossed the foaming, turbulent, shallow rapids below. Made of uneven wooden slats that were held in place by several rocks, and with only one rope handrail, the bridge did not appear very stable. Although the crossing was no more than twenty feet long, it was a scary one, made more so by the swirling rapids that crashed against the rocks along the twisting riverbed beneath us. Looking straight ahead, I quickly but gingerly walked across as Olga and Kanchha waited their turn. As Olga delicately stepped across with Kanchha at her heels, I thought of how helpless we were against the forces of nature and of the courage of the Sherpas who live and travel in this unfriendly, harsh, and primitive ambience. I noticed that Kanchha was now carrying Olga's daypack; because of fatigue and a worsening sore throat, it was a twenty-pound burden she could do without.

Beyond the bridge, the path rose steeply and continued an upward course for most of the next few hours to Thami. It was an utterly bleak atmosphere;

we were hemmed in by rock walls and a dark, overcast sky. We walked up and up in gloomy silence for what seemed like an eternity. It was a depressing afternoon, walking for hours through this narrow, sunless canyon on a trail that repeatedly crossed the winding, shallow riverbed. Whenever we asked Kanchha how long it would take to reach our new campsite, his reactions were determined by the time of day. Inquiring too early in the day would elicit an inscrutable smile and a vague response from him. When we posed the question in the late afternoon, Kanchha would give us an exact answer. By afternoon, he knew our pace and state of fatigue and would give us an estimate that turned out to be uncannily accurate. With his sensitivity and tact, Kanchha tried hard to keep our spirits high and to prevent us from becoming discouraged; his answers to our questions were always guided by these considerations.

Nearly four hours out of Thami, the trail suddenly came to a huge, wide plain that was divided by a stream. On one side was a meadow, wet from the melting snow, and on the other side was a wide, gravelly expanse. About half a mile distant stood Thami, a handful of houses nestled in the foreground of a tremendous mountain range obscured now by the clouds. Alone and unsure of which approach to take, I turned left, toward the grassless plain, because it showed a small footbridge leading to the distant houses. On the lookout for us, Jim spied me in the distance and began waving and calling to come through the meadow to my right. Knowing that I must be spent, Jim hurried to my side and led me through the meadow to our campsite. This wrong turn of mine, with its unnecessary expenditure of energy and time, made me realize that a potential problem existed in hiking alone. After a few hours of trekking, most of the group had usually passed me, and Olga's pace was too slow for me to remain with her. Consequently, I usually walked alone, except for those periodic rests when I waited for Olga to reach me. When I had no one nearby, I could easily make a wrong turn when the trail divided into several paths as it entered a village.

In Thami, the tents were pitched in a semicircle next to the Sherpa's house in which we would have the evening meal. Jim took me inside, where everyone was having tea and cookies. Too tired to feel self-conscious about our slow pace and being the last ones into camp, I felt good about the group's gentle kidding and acceptance of our limitations. Twenty minutes later, Olga arrived, looking ready to collapse. Bothered by a sore throat, Olga was completely exhausted by the long afternoon. Slumped next to me on the wooden bench, she revived slightly after drinking the hot tea. I felt responsible for

Olga being on the trek, and I felt somewhat guilty when I saw her struggling. Knowing, however, that Kanchha was always at Olga's side relieved me of worrying, as I was also struggling and in no better shape than my gutsy wife. As we drank our tea and wolfed down the stale English butter cookies, we commiserated silently with each other.

At over twelve thousand feet, the desolate, dreary village of Thami was a stark contrast to the populated and bustling Namche Bazaar. On the valley floor where we camped, we counted no more than eight randomly placed Sherpa homes, set off from one another by four-foot stone walls. On the cliffs above, a cluster of homes, including a well-known monastery, completed the village. The evening chill and the low-hanging clouds reinforced the sense of desolation we felt here. Adding to the primitive setting were the heaps of cow and yak dung scattered everywhere. We had to step carefully to avoid the partially dried droppings that were all over the campsite. Obviously, the cows and yaks grazed and lumbered about freely on this wide valley floor. Everyone stepped in his share of manure, which clung easily to our jagged Vibram-soled boots. Fortunately, the dung odor wasn't strong enough to be offensive. In this thin high mountain air, the blobs of ordure, about the size of a plate, dried easily. When firm and dried out, the dung is saved to be burned in the winter. Since nothing that can serve as fuel is wasted, all villages collect the shriveled cakes of dung, which are stacked like firewood.

We ate the usual inedible dinner in a large, cold, barren room smelling of recently installed pinewood paneling. It had turned cold and windy, and we were all bundled up in sweaters, parkas, and woolen ski hats. The only warmth in the room came from the hot food and the flickering kerosene lamp. Although it was only about thirty degrees Fahrenheit, this temperature felt chilly and uncomfortable indoors, especially since we were wracked with fatigue. Because of my exhaustion, I don't remember much of that evening, except for a comical incident that could have had unfortunate consequences. Returning to our tents after dinner in pitch darkness, we heard a shrill scream coming from the stone outhouse. In the darkness, Donna had misjudged the placement of the outhouse hole and had stepped or slipped into it up to her knee. By the time someone got to Donna, she had extricated herself and was none the worse for this misstep. Fine except for a bad scare, Donna was lucky not to have sprained an ankle or knee, an injury that might have ended the trek for her at Thami. This incident, which became comical in retrospect, made us all more cautious when walking around camp in the incredibly dark mountain evenings. Many of us began using flashlights to navigate among the rocks, dung, unlit Sherpa homes, and outhouses with their resident yaks, dogs, and chickens.

Drugged with exhaustion, we fell into a deep sleep and awakened to an ice-cold morning that quickly revived us. Looming above us was an enormous, craggy, snow-streaked mountain range. Soaring to the sky in a huge wall of rock and snow, this awesome range seemed close enough to touch despite being almost a mile distant from camp. Thami and our group of tents appeared like toy objects nestled in the foothills of these giant peaks, two of which, Tesi Lapsh and Mangpala, rose to nearly twenty thousand feet. Until now, this was the closest we had come to the Himalayas, and their nearness was an overpowering, even scary presence. What would it be like when we finally arrived at Kala Pattar, with Everest staring down at us from an altitude nine thousand feet higher than these giant mountains? This sparsely populated, isolated village of Thami and the proximity of the towering peaks gave me the greatest sense so far of the stark beauty and colossal size of the Himalayan mountain country. The realization of where we were at this point, and where we were headed, kept me in a state of excited anticipation that helped combat the weariness that was now so much a part of me.

Six hundred feet above us rose the outskirts of Thami, a handful of houses and a famous monastery that Jim recommended we visit before leaving. Overlooking the valley and perched on the cliff, the Thami monastery was reached by a steep climb of thirty minutes. This extra effort was reason enough for Olga and me to decide against the visit. It was becoming increasingly apparent that we needed to conserve every ounce of energy and that we couldn't keep up with our group of experienced and younger trekkers. Once we came to terms with our physical limitations, we felt relieved and less self-conscious about being the last ones into camp each day. In our competitive culture, where winning is everything, we tend to pressure ourselves to try to achieve beyond our capabilities. As a consequence, frustration and tension become inherent in our striving for success and achievement. What we should emphasize, rather than being number one, is the quality of our effort. If we do our best, then whatever follows will be satisfying and fulfilling. This requires, however, the personal security to acknowledge our limitations, a fact that most try to deny because of our need to prove ourselves. These thoughts, which have with time and experience become an integral part of my personal philosophy, were being sorely tested at this point in the trek. But our exhaustion and strong motivation to reach Everest's foothills forced us to accept our slow progress and inability to compete with the group. The relief we felt in admitting this came, I believe, from the biblical counsel that in order to feel strength, we must acknowledge our inherent weakness, or in St. Paul's words, "For when I am weak, then I am strong."

Half of the group opted to make the climb to visit Thami's monastery, while the other half took the trail directly back to Thamel. Once again, the morning was sparkling clear and bright. It was incredible how beautiful and fresh the day began each morning, as if nature had to make up for the depressing heavy, gray overcast sky and dampness that blanketed each late afternoon. These invigorating mornings were like a tonic that helped revive our spirits and energy for the daily trek ahead. Compared to yesterday afternoon's dreary walk, these same narrow gorges and rock cliff sides reflected the bright sunlight, making everything look dramatic and suffused with varying hues of tan, brown, and gray. The intense sun also highlighted the budding plants of early spring, which were beginning to peek out of the nooks and crannies of the rocky terrain. Even the ordinary shallow, bubbling streams glistened with rays of light. Everything came alive during these Himalayan mornings and made us forget the drabness and tiredness of the previous afternoon.

Olga and I felt refreshed, and we walked vigorously downhill all morning. We couldn't believe that it took only half the time, or about two hours, to reach the bridge that had appeared so precarious yesterday. Incredulous, I stared as two heavily laden yaks and two Sherpas crossed the small, shaky bridge that Olga and I had crossed the day before. It was still a scary crossing, with boulders as large as houses and narrow cliffs rising all around us. From here, our energetic pace became a plodding uphill walk all the way to our midday stop at Thamel.

At lunch, Jim talked about the village of Khunde, our next campsite, where Hillary built the first modern hospital in the Khumbu. About two miles north of Namche Bazaar, Khunde also served the neighboring villages with its newly built schoolhouse, which was also planned and funded by Hillary's efforts. Khunde was just about two hours from Thamel, with the last part of the trail rising steeply uphill to become a narrow path that dropped precipitously on one side into the canyon below. Jim stressed that we should be careful about taking the correct trail into Khunde, as the trails branched off just before Namche Bazaar, and a mistaken turn could easily be made.

The last few days' experience had taught Olga and me that we should add at least an extra hour to the predicted trekking time; we also knew that the afternoon trek was, for us, the most strenuous and enervating. When starting out after lunch, I always tried to avoid thinking negatively about the hard pull ahead, and I viewed the afternoon's hike as an exciting challenge that would just take us a little longer than the others. Although Olga was always ready with a quip about the trek's difficulties and inconveniences, we both consciously refrained from complaining. For the first time, I came to appreciate Olga's joking manner, which worked wonderfully well to help us acknowledge the tough reality before us, yet imparted a sense of mastery over what we faced. Humor is one of the most effective weapons that individuals can use to cope with the difficulty and absurdity of life, especially when we're tested to our limits, as we were on this trek. Complaining and railing against the world gets us nowhere and becomes counterproductive. Later in the trek, when faced with potentially serious physical problems, I would unfortunately forget this belief and temporarily lose control of myself.

Surprisingly, we maintained a fairly good pace, keeping up with many of the others, except for Abby, Nas, Kirt, and John, who always seemed to race ahead with boundless energy and speed. I often thought they seemed obsessed with being the first ones in camp. Their superb condition and zest automatically shifted their motors into high gear; they just couldn't walk leisurely for too long.

The last two hours of that afternoon gradually turned into a tough hike, especially for Olga, who was still bothered by a sore throat. Going steadily uphill, the trail became a narrow path that twisted and skimmed around the mountain edges. To our left, the cliff side rose steeply, and to the right, we looked down one precipitous drop after another. The river and valley below seemed like a miniature landscape, but up here on the trail at eleven thousand feet, vastness surrounded us. Immediately across the narrow valley was the magnificent twenty-thousand-foot range of Kwangde, and there were endless valleys and mountains as far as the eye could see.

During a ten-minute rest stop, Jim, who had left Thamel much later than everyone, sat with me to admire the craggy Kwangde peaks. For a change, the usual heavy clouds had not yet arrived. It was still a glorious afternoon, with the sun shining through the huge cumulus clouds that were rolling in from the south. Pointing to a ridge below Kwangde's summit, Jim told of a mountain climbing friend who had slept there overnight on a hammock strung between two rock overhangs during his attempt to reach the top. How our efforts paled against such exploits, which are commonplace for Himalayan climbing expeditions. With that rousing small talk, Jim was off at his usual graceful and deceptive easygoing pace that could outdistance the best of us.

This was my best hiking day, and I didn't become fatigued until the last hour. For some odd reason, I enjoyed the narrow, rocky path that made us feel like mountain goats confidently navigating the twisting turns and loose gravel and rocks underfoot. My feeling stronger than usual that afternoon was probably due to being better acclimatized and exhilarated from the breathtaking panoramas.

As the path snaked higher around the cliff side, the sparsely growing trees and shrubs became more stunted, gnarled, and straggly. It was a miracle that any growth could survive on this steep eleven-thousand-foot ridge, exposed to all of the extremes of drought, wind, rain, snow, and ice. Whatever growth there was had to struggle to maintain its foothold on these precipitous slopes of dirt and stone. It was remarkable that a path could exist on this unprotected ridge. At one point on the ridge, the three-foot-wide trail turned into a series of huge, flat rock steps, each about five feet in diameter, strung out nearly the length of a city block. They were set into the precipitous cliff side at odd angles, tilting slightly, and resembling an obstacle course weaving its way between the rising cliff and the void below. Without this bumpy row of stepping-stones, there wouldn't have been much of a trail, because the precipice, which fell away at a 45-degree angle, did not allow enough of a foothold for a path. Whenever I looked for Olga and Kanchha behind me in the distance, it seemed as if they could topple off this twisting trail that edged precariously around the cliffs' steep precipices. Actually, the walking was more stable and safe than it appeared. But it could seem quite hair-raising, especially when gazing at the spectacular panoramas that enveloped us. Still not yet in the Everest region, we already felt overwhelmed by the immensity of the terrain and mountains.

Feeling somewhat cocky because of my surprising late-afternoon energy, I waited for Olga and Kanchha in order to tell them that I would go on ahead. Kanchha cautioned me about taking the right path to Khunde once I climbed the high ridge above us. Olga wasn't too happy about my forging ahead, but she felt too miserable to argue. Kanchha said little but smiled inscrutably. It was three o'clock, and the clouds were finally darkening the skies when I took off for the steep ridge. Nearly an hour later, I arrived at the top, ready to collapse from exhaustion. The ascent was a scramble through low scrub brush, and the trail divided into many small paths. Unsure of which path to follow, I climbed in a zigzag direction up the slope. I swore at myself for being impatient and not waiting for Kanchha, especially when I reached the top and saw that I had strayed from the main trail.

Back on the trail again, I saw Jim, Donna, and Kirt not too far ahead. I couldn't believe that I had kept up with anyone, but there they were ahead, walking slowly over a wide, open plain. This enormous, flat dirt area turned out to be the defunct airfield of Syangboche. Originally planned as the landing strip for those wealthy Asian tourists visiting the nearby Japanese-built Everest View Hotel, the "airport" had failed because of its high altitude. It was found that flying from sea level to an elevation of eleven thousand feet gave most visitors an acute attack of altitude sickness when they deplaned. The story goes that these affluent but not well-conditioned tourists were given oxygen when they stepped off the plane into the thin air. They had to be carried by yaks for the hour's hike to the Everest View Hotel. In time, the tourists, expecting comfort, not hardship, dwindled to nothing. Now both the airfield and hotel were standing unused. In my mind's eye, I had a gleeful picture of those bewildered visitors staring at a bleak, strange landscape, gasping for breath, while being bounced about by the lumbering yaks. These thoughts were a welcome diversion, but the deserted airstrip, which looked quite incongruous in this desolate landscape, brought me quickly back to reality. Khunde was slightly more than a mile distant in a gradual downhill direction. That last climb was the steepest ascent yet, and Olga later described it as "uphill horror" that she made only because Kanchha kept pushing her up the incline. The gently sloping farmlands and grazing areas we came to were a welcome relief.

For once, I wasn't the last arrival at the new campsite, but I was just as exhausted as usual; the last two hours of climbing the steep hill and getting lost had done me in. Olga arrived shortly after me, having caught up as a result of my wrong turns. Deathly pale with fatigue, she headed straight for the tent to lie down until dinner. By now, we were accustomed to the dark, gloomy skies and fading light that greeted our arrival at a new campsite. Unfortunately, this dull gray weather made every new village appear depressing.

Khunde is Namche Bazaar's smaller neighbor, with about fifty houses and the ubiquitous rock walls dividing widely spread-out fields of stone and gravel. While approaching the town, I noticed several villagers digging up large areas of small dirt plots. Looking closely, I saw their precious cache of potatoes that had been deeply buried and stored over the winter. These villagers, who were probably used to a steady influx of foreign trekkers, did not give us a second look. Despite their passivity and lack of curiosity, they were friendly and quick to point us in the right direction to the campsite. More spontaneous were the beautiful, grinning Sherpa children who darted playfully around us and carefully scrutinized our dress and belongings. Although we had been instructed to refrain from giving the children candy, it was hard to resist giving them this gift of welcome. Sweets and chocolate, which trekkers gladly hand out, have contributed to increasing tooth decay and dental problems in the Sherpa children. Since there are no dentistry services in the Khumbu region, decaying teeth can be treated only by extraction. No wonder the Sherpa smile, in most natives, reveals a missing tooth or two.

Dinner at Khunde was one of the more palatable ones, with flavorful dim sum and roasted potatoes in addition to the customary soup, mushy rice, and beverage. Olga was feeling better, and she joked that the soup appetizer, which was strong and tasty at first, was becoming gradually more watery and tasteless. The kitchen crew was probably running low on the dehydrated soup and, in order to stretch out the servings, put in less soup mix with the same amount of water. I'm sure that in the Sherpas' view, the quantity of food was more important than its quality; it was better to have more food than less food, regardless of the taste.

Jim's postdinner briefing about tomorrow's itinerary suggested a visit to Khunde's hospital and school, both of which were built by Hillary's fund-raising efforts dedicated to improving the Sherpas' quality of life. From there, we would hike to join the trail coming from Namche Bazaar and heading directly north to Everest and our camp at Tengboche. It would be a long, long day of walking. Compared to the relatively isolated paths we had been on, tomorrow's trail would be one of the most heavily traveled ones. Usually considered the main route to the Everest and upper Khumbu region, it would be filled with trekkers, natives, and animals. Jim cautioned us to be sure always to stay on the trail's high side when passing or being passed by yaks. If we were on the low side or at the path's edge, and a yak, an erratic and unpredictable creature, bumped into us, we faced the danger of being sent sprawling down the mountainside. This was not an uncommon experience, since the trail was just wide enough to walk two abreast, and yaks were usually prodded by their owners to keep up a good pace in order to pass the slow traffic (like Olga and me). Perhaps this prodding and yelling to keep moving along contributes to the yak's stubborn and crotchety ways. Although the edge of the trail dropped off thousands of feet to the ravines below, the slope was not a steep vertical drop; it angled about sixty degrees at the steepest. So if you were sent sprawling off the edge, you might fall only several yards or roll down hundreds of feet before stopping. In any case, it was not a thing I wanted to experience while trekking, especially here, where medical help is hard, if not impossible, to obtain. Other than at Khunde, the only other hospital or medical service available in the Khumbu region was far north at Pheriche, where there was a trekker's aid post, established by the Himalayan Rescue Association in 1973.

It was difficult enough to bring Western medicine to Nepal, but the Sherpas' resistance to modern medicine had not yet been overcome, according to Jim. These mountain people still viewed Western physicians with suspicion and had a hard time breaking away from their resigned and do-nothing attitude when someone became sick. Quite fatalistic, they invoked magic rituals and superstition when serious illness struck. Despite the fact that a handful of Sherpas lived to a ripe old age in each village, the majority died by middle age, and half the children did not reach young adulthood. Their toughness and strength, which they had developed to exist in the primitive conditions and cruel weather of these isolated mountain regions, have not protected them from the illnesses that everyone suffers. And without the slightest semblance of medical care, Sherpas tended to die at a young age. As Jim spoke about the Sherpas' reactions to medical aid and Khunde's hospital, I remembered Hillary's autobiography and its description of how the hospital was built.

Building a hospital for the Sherpa people was one of Hillary's "greatest ambitions." A fund-raising drive in New Zealand and America brought in thirty thousand dollars in addition to building materials, food, clothing, and medical supplies. Overseeing the entire planning and construction of the hospital, Hillary had twelve tons of supplies shipped to Kathmandu. From there, they were flown in stages to Lukla and then hauled on the backs of porters and yaks to the village of Khunde at 12,700 feet. Construction began in early November 1966 and was completed in six weeks. One of the marvels of the building was a hot water system heated by a wood-burning stove. Hillary recalls how the Sherpas kept coming to turn on the tap and watch the hot water flow—a completely strange and new experience. Upon its completion, the hospital was administered by a Western physician, Dr. John McKinnon and his wife, Dianne, who volunteered to supervise its operation for two years. Today it continues to be staffed by two volunteer physicians who stay for about two years until being replaced by other volunteers. In the twenty years of its existence, the doctors have not only tended the sick, but also have trained local health aides, who staff health posts located in the eight main Sherpa villages. Despite their superstitions and rigid customs, the Sherpas are gradually beginning to avail themselves of the lifesaving skills that modern medical treatment can bring.

Compared to their suspicious attitude toward medicine, which threatens old beliefs, the Sherpas have been more receptive to education. Several years before building the hospital, Hillary built a schoolhouse in Khumjung, which is less than a mile away from Khunde. The schoolhouse was a preassembled aluminum structure donated by the Indian Aluminum Company and flown in by the International Red Cross. Thanks to Hillary's humanitarian efforts, there were now schools in the Khumbu, each of which served several neighboring villages. The school in Khumjung provided for children from Kunde and Namche Bazaar, who walked for miles up the steep hills every day to attend.

In the morning sunlight, the drabness of the previous afternoon vanished, and Khunde took on a cheerful air. Like most Sherpa villages, Khunde was nestled in a little valley; this valley was bordered by craggy nineteen-thousand-foot slopes to the north and a high-bouldered and tree-lined ridge to the south. The ground, which in warmer months was carpeted by flowers, shrubs, and mosses, was plain dirt. The traditional two-story stone houses looked more substantial than most we had already passed, with their slate roofs, brightly colored window frames, and doorways adorned with small stone overhangs. A few sported bright green corrugated roofs and large glass windows. Many houses were set off from one another by chest-high stone walls, as if their owners, like any proud suburbanite, were staking out the borders of their small domains. Khunde's affluence had resulted from the growing tourist trade and the mountain climbing expeditions that made it a major stopover. Large expeditions seemed to favor it because of its smallness and the lack of commercial bustle of its neighbor, Namche Bazaar, over the high ridge. Khunde is also a stone's throw from all the major trails leading to Everest and the great peaks in the northern and eastern Himalayas.

Even in this isolated village, we could not escape the salesman's pitch. Just beyond our tents, a peddler had displayed his wares, which greeted us when we arose. Spread on faded crimson rugs placed on the dirt ground were bracelets, rings, necklaces, vases, bowls, and jewelry boxes of every conceivable size. After breakfast, everyone inspected these attractive wares, which seemed to be everywhere in Nepal. Most of us bought a few dollars' worth of souvenirs, more in response to the sad and impoverished appearance of the peddler than the need for more bric-a-brac. Dressed in a soiled, wrinkled pastel blue parka with brown trousers tucked into knee-length felt boots, the peddler sat on a basket and stared lethargically at us. Looking ageless and of indeterminate gender, his wrinkled face and soulful expression projected a sense of infinite sadness.

The peddler's dress was typical of the men, who no longer wear traditional Sherpa clothes, instead wearing cast-off expedition parkas, down jackets, breeches, and anoraks in various stages of dilapidation. Strangely enough, the women still wore Sherpa-style clothing: long, plain, dark, sleeveless tunics falling to the ankles and brightened by a colorful apron and blouse. Footwear, however, for both sexes was sandals, sneakers, or hiking boots instead of the old-fashioned Tibetan boots. The women's dress symbolized the old traditions and, perhaps, a silent protest against the encroaching changes brought about by the tourist trade.

After the usual breakfast of oatmeal, eggs, potatoes, bread, fruit juice, and hot chocolate, we were ready for the push to Tengboche. The thought of the very long day ahead, which would finally see us at a campsite looking squarely down a valley to Everest, made Olga and me decide against making the effort to see Khunde's hospital and school. The thrill of knowing that we would finally be on the main trail to Everest made us impatient to be under way.

Although the chilly dawn air always put us in a state of shivers, the morning was milder than usual. I followed the example of the others who put on shorts over their polypro long johns despite the sartorial incongruity. We were quite a weird sight, like partially dressed clowns, with colored long underwear appearing under our khaki shorts. The women didn't look as odd because their long skirts covered the long johns. Despite how silly we looked, this attire was quite functional: warm enough to combat the morning chill without being over-clothed and easily adaptable to the growing heat of the day. All we needed to do was to roll up the long underwear under our shorts as the temperature warmed up.

It was a beautiful early spring morning when we left Khunde. The trail became a pleasant, twisting downhill walk. Tufts of green grass were beginning to show, and rhododendrons and trees sprouted buds that would soon burst into color. The parched streams and brooks, fed by the melting mountain snows, were beginning to flow again. I was feeling invigorated, and I bounced down the trail at a pleasingly vigorous pace. For some reason, no matter how tired I am and how difficult hikers say it is to walk downhill, I love the pace of walking downhill. The steepness is exhilarating and brings me to life. In this countryside, unfortunately, the end of a downhill climb usually means the start of an uphill one.

About ninety minutes out of Khunde, we stopped at a trailside teashop, where several peddlers were selling the usual commonplace trinkets. It was quite a display: several red rugs were spread out over thirty feet, covered with gift items. Our group looked like typical tourists, ogling the knick-knacks and the senile, decrepit-looking peddlers. The scene reminded me of those stopovers made by bus tours the world over, which lure the naive and gawking passengers into buying banal local giftware. We were once again seduced by the apparent bargains, and we engaged in the universal business of haggling to make a better deal. Nas was the most successful bargainer, walking away with a handful of bracelets that he later reported cost him only a dollar, or a third of the original selling price.

While everyone relaxed, drank tea, took pictures, and bought souvenirs, my attention was drawn across the narrow valley to the trail that came from Namche Bazaar; it curved around a ridge to join our trail leading to the upper Khumbu and the Everest region. There, we saw a string of mountaineers striding vigorously ahead of the pack. Jim thought they were probably a major climbing expedition, and since they would be reaching us momentarily, we decided to wait for them. Jim's guess was right, as this train of people and animals represented the advance party of a climbing expedition mounted by India to attempt Mt. Everest's summit before the monsoon season in early May. Numbering about eight climbers, they were a handsome and friendly group, and they stopped to talk to us in fairly good English. One of the leaders, a physician, told us that their expedition planned to duplicate China's recent achievement of being the first to put a woman climber on Everest's summit. They hoped, however, to surpass China's success by placing six young women climbers on top of the world's tallest peak. The Indian women would join the expedition a few weeks later, after the main party had established their base camps at the foot of Everest. What a thrill it was when we coincidentally met these courageous young women on our return in the morning of the last day of the trek!

Seeing this expedition put me in a state of excitement and curiosity. I had read innumerable accounts of summit expeditions hauling tons of equipment and gear through the mountains on the backs of animals and men, and I had always marveled at such a feat. The reality was just as incredible as the descriptions I'd read and mused about. As far as we could see on the trail behind us and across the valley, there was an endless stream of Sherpas, porters, and yaks. The porters were hunched over, carrying heavy loads on their backs. The yaks were loaded with large, overstuffed duffel bags that looked ready to burst, and large, white, heavy cardboard trunks were trussed on either side of them. Dwarfed by the huge and unwieldy loads, the yaks lumbered slowly and precariously along the trail. Around their necks hung cowbells that made a constant tinkling din throughout the valley. Adding to this unbelievable traffic were Sherpas running back and forth among the yaks to move them along and guide them around the twisting turns. Yaks are ornery and stubborn creatures, and the Sherpas were constantly prodding and yelling at them.

Before this endless congestion of animals and Sherpas reached us, Jim roused us to be on our way. It would be easier hiking if we stayed ahead of the expedition; otherwise, the traffic on the trail would slow us down and cause much inconvenience. Jim cautioned the group again to stay on the high side of the trail, particularly now, when advance groups of the expedition's yaks might reach and pass us. I was hypnotized by the interminable convoy that kept coming from across the way. It was akin to the spellbound emotion of watching a slow freight train; I could not see the end of the slow-moving string of men and animals.

I noticed that the animals, although similar to each other with their cow-like appearance and long, shaggy black hair, had differing physical characteristics. Ved told us that not all of these beasts of burden were yaks. As a result of crossbreeding, these cows or bulls were related to yaks. In Tibetan, the word *yak* refers only to the male of the species. The female yak is called a *nak*, and most of the pack animals carrying our trek's gear were *dzopkyo* (show-kee-oo), or the infertile male offspring of a yak and a mountain cow. The results of crossbreeding are infinite, and every new variation has an exotic-sounding name such as *dzhumus, kirkos, dimzos, dimsi, dzums, tulmos*, and *pamus*. The Sherpas' interest in developing so many new strains of yak is explained by their agricultural economy and the status it bestows upon the owner. The number and variety of cattle a farmer possesses is a reflection of his wealth and prestige, as is the number of houses he owns, even though they may just be high-altitude summer huts. Cattle fetch a good price, as they are always in demand for their pack-carrying qualities and milk, which is made into butter.

A basic of Sherpa life, butter is a greatly needed product used for burning in votive lamps in monasteries and private homes. As a dairy item, the butter has a mildly rancid taste and can be repulsive to a Westerner's palate. Primarily used in making the Sherpas' strong Tibetan tea, the butter is mixed into the tea, giving it a full body and an acidic flavor. Although a crock of this butter was available during our mealtimes, few in the group used it, because of its peculiar flavor and taste. It was darker in color, lumpy, and less creamy than the butter we knew.

Before we left this version of a Sherpa trailside tourist trap (basically a teashop with peddlers) and got a head start on the encroaching expedition, everyone took pictures of the climbers and the mass of animals crowding in on us.

7

Few Walks in the World More Wonderful

The next few hours on the trail were the most exciting of the trek so far. There was a steady stream of natives, trekkers, and animals, and spectacular views held us spellbound. The sights were overwhelming, and really too much to absorb. It was unbelievable trekking now, the route winding its way around the edge of one precipice after another. At times, the trail ahead seemed to vanish into space as it rose and wound around a bend on the mountain's edge. The thought of navigating those precipitous bends in the trail was scary, but the breathtaking views kept us too excited to be frightened. Also, the concentration and physical effort needed to keep up the pace, gaze at views, and take photos combated our anxiety.

Over an hour from Khunde and Namche Bazaar, the trail rose to thirteen thousand feet and looked north to the great Imja Khola valley nestled below the greatest of Himalayan peaks. Thousands of feet below were the dark-forested slopes, not yet in bloom, and the deep gorges that would soon be filled with the raging waters of the Dudh Kosi river. Above and just ahead were the colossal snow- and ice-covered mountains rising to incredible heights. What a thrill it was to see, so much closer now, Everest, Lhotse, Ama Dablam, and the endless adjacent wall of craggy summits! Their soaring peaks would appear and disappear as the trail made its switchbacks and dropped behind huge boulders that briefly shut out the enormous views.

After a short climb of rock steps, we came to a ledge jutting over the valley below and were startled by the panorama of the twin peaks of twenty-two-thousand-foot Thamserku, which seemed close enough to touch. From this section of the route, Ama Dablam dominated the view. Shaped like a giant tooth in the sky, Ama Dablam, at twenty-three thousand feet, could be a twin of Switzerland's Matterhorn. Its majestic, towering spire is a duplicate of the

Matterhorn, but about ten thousand feet higher and more gigantic in width than its Swiss counterpart. Although we did not see the lush beauty that the countryside shows later in the season, we felt stirred by the same emotions that Hillary wrote about when describing this part of the trail in his book *High in the Thin Cold Air*:

> There must be few walks in the world more wonderful than the track from Namche Bazaar to Thyangboche. The rivers foam through great gorges far below; the hillsides are clothed in forest, broken only here and there by a sheer rock face, a sharp crag, or a steep mountain meadow; and above everything tower the incredible peaks of the Khumbu region—mighty ice-fluted faces, terrific rock buttresses, and razor-sharp jagged ice ridges soaring up to impossible summits.

In the middle of this vast panorama, on a ridge several miles ahead, I could see the faint outline of a tiny plateau where Tengboche, our next campsite, was located. Towering mountain ranges surrounded Tengboche, which appeared as if it were cradled in their foothills. The anticipation of finally being so close to the mountains of my boyhood dreams kept me in a state of euphoria. I was mildly upset, however, because Tengboche looked to be impossibly far away to reach by the end of today's trek. But Kanchha's confirmation that we'd be there by late afternoon—and my high spirits—wouldn't allow me to dwell on the tough uphill climb we faced after lunch. I ruminated about how much easier and quicker it would be getting there if I could ride one of the hundreds of yaks ambling behind us. Oddly, in all the time on the trail, I never saw a person riding an animal. Not even wheels or wagons existed in this wild and rugged terrain. Foot power is the only form of transportation in these mountainous regions. However, when medical emergencies occur and someone needs to be quickly moved, animals will be used to transport the person. More often, though, the stricken individual will be carried piggyback by a Sherpa, since bouncing around on the rump of a yak leaves much to be desired in the way of comfort and safety.

Small groups of the expedition behind us were beginning to catch up and pass us. The passing porters and pack animals caused much delay and inconvenience, and this created pressure on us to stay ahead of them. Whenever they reached us, we had to be careful to stay out of their way as they scurried by. On a twisting, uneven trail no wider than six feet, walking became tricky when being passed by temperamental yaks with trunk loads swinging out from either side. The sense of tension and commotion at that moment was heightened by the noise of the Sherpas whipping the animals and yelling at them to hurry. Everyone was overly cautious to keep close to the mountainside and clear of these overburdened animals.

On one occasion, I had pressed myself against the slope with my back to the narrow trail as a few yaks clattered by. Suddenly, I was slammed into the mountainside. I felt as if a huge crushing weight had fallen on me. As I picked myself up, breathless and in mild shock, I was afraid that I had been hurt. Gingerly touching and stretching my limbs, I was relieved to find neither broken bones nor an injury, only an aching body and very bruised feelings. I was puzzled by the accident and couldn't understand how it had happened, as I had taken every precaution to keep close to the cliff side and away from the yaks. All at once, I realized that my daypack, which jutted out nearly a foot from my back, had caught on the body or load of a yak that was rushing by me. The lateral collision, with a good thousand pounds of animal flesh plus equipment, had knocked me deeper than I thought possible into the cliff side. As with everything in life, no matter how careful and well prepared we may be, there are always unexpected forces lying in wait to disrupt us. If I hadn't observed Jim's warning and taken precautions, this collision could have caught me on the low side of the trail, and I might still be rolling down the mountainside to the valley thousands of feet below.

Unlike humans, yaks are amazingly sure-footed and have incredible balance while traversing these twisting ascending and descending routes. It was common to see these animals, loaded down and bulging with impossible loads, trot off the trail up and down the steep mountainside without stumbling or falling over. Only once did we see a yak in danger of rolling down a steep, treacherous slope. The yak had stubbornly wandered off the trail and fallen over the embankment. The alertness of a few Sherpas prevented the beast from falling down the ravine. They quickly got to the yak, pushing and prodding him until he righted himself and scrambled back up the trail, no worse for wear.

The trail, which had been steadily rising, was now starting its downward course. We were descending into a ravine, where we would negotiate a river crossing and then stop for lunch. The breathtaking views had vanished as the trail curved its way down through lightly forested areas shored up by rocky cliffs and boulders. Underfoot, the track had changed from hard-packed earth into a strange, gray, finely textured dirt. Its unusually smooth, even silky, surface made walking slippery and dusty. While turning a corner, I slipped, stumbled, and slid several feet on my back. Lucky again, I came up undamaged, and I shrugged it off with a growing confidence that I would remain healthy and strong in the tough days yet to come.

At the bottom of the gorge, we were greeted by the rushing sounds of a foaming river thirty feet below the trail's edge. Just ahead was the narrow wooden bridge, bowed and swaying from the weight and motion of the people and animals crossing it. The scene we came upon was a mountaineer's version of a traffic jam waiting to cross a bridge. At least fifty Sherpas and yaks from the Indian expedition, in addition to our group, were waiting their turn to go. Since the bridge was not the sturdiest, and over a hundred feet long, no more than four or five yaks and natives crossed at one time. Of all the bridges we had already traversed, this looked the most challenging and shaky; it closely resembled the stereotypical flimsy rope-and-wooden bridges pictured in mountain travel books. It was just wide enough for a yak with bags bulging from either side, and long enough to create a rolling motion. This colorful and crowded scene, with its backdrop of huge boulders, steep rock cliffs, and roaring white river below, was like a scene out of the movies.

When our turn came to navigate the bridge, we were accompanied, as everyone was, by three or four yaks, which we tried hard to keep at a distance. It wouldn't be advisable to be knocked about by a yak on this shaky narrow span, fifty feet above the river that roared below. Although it seemed similar to walking a swaying gangplank with rope handrails and jostling traffic, I found the crossing exciting and enjoyable, and it was greatly exaggerated as a frightening experience. To insure everyone's safety, Jim and Ved directed traffic for our group, seeing that each of us crossed with no more than an acceptable number of people and animals.

A steep, narrow rock incline confronted us as we came off the bridge. While climbing this arduous path, I suddenly felt the fatigue that had been masked by the excitement and thrills of the last four hours. What a relief it was when we turned the bend and saw our luncheon campsite adjacent to a trailside tea shop, which was part of a small settlement named Phunki Thangka. There were no other buildings nearby, as the village was spread out on the banks of the river. Every passing trekking group used this as a resting place before the climb to Tengboche, and we found it crowded with trekkers. Although there were at least thirty hikers milling around, I noticed a curious absence of noise or conversation. From my observation, trekkers do not seem to be a boisterous or overly talkative breed. Rather, they appear, generally, to be a quiet and determined group, more introverted than outgoing. Perhaps the combination of their intense motivation to achieve a long-desired goal and their unceasing strenuous physical effort explains their composed and taciturn manner. Add the usually shy, soft-spoken, and passive reactions of the Sherpas, and one can see why the emotional climate of a trekking group tends to be subdued. In no way should this be taken to mean that hiking is a humorless and dull affair. The joyous and playful nature of the Sherpas, together with the excited and happy soul of the trekker, results in a spirited and thrilling experience.

Everyone arrived at about the same time in Phunki Thangka because of the repeated slowdowns caused by the traffic of the Indian expedition. Although Olga and I weren't the usual late arrivals, we were feeling exhausted and eager to rest. This afternoon would be quite tough, with the trail going only one way: up and up and up. I made an effort to eat more than usual at lunch, to store up some extra energy for the steep climb ahead. I was becoming increasingly conscious of losing weight, as my trousers were falling down below my waist, despite the belt being buckled on the last notch. My poor appetite and arduous hiking had made me lose at least ten pounds. Despite feeling physically trim, I always felt tired and as if my clothes were growing too big for my shrinking body. So I ate some extra potatoes and eggs, drank more hot tea, and tried to stuff myself. After only five days on the trail, most of us were not only showing some weight loss, but also looking quite grubby.

Our lunch was spread out on a sloping picnic ground next to a teashop where we could see the colorful parade of trekkers constantly passing by. Across the trail, which was about the size of a wide sidewalk, there were a few water-driven prayer wheels, which caught everyone's attention. I'm sure no one thought that these fascinating religious symbols would someday become a tourist attraction. It was ironic that as attractive as this setting was, with its water-powered prayer wheels, running stream, and forest glade ambience, the teashop where we rested was ugly in comparison. Blackened with smoke and dirt, it looked like a ramshackle structure that had been thrown together overnight. Nevertheless, it was a much-needed place to rest and refuel before pushing on to Tengboche.

While eating and dozing off, I noticed a curious silence, which had struck me on my arrival to Phunki Thangka. I gradually realized that after making the turn on the cliff-side trail, we no longer heard the din of the rushing rapids and turbulent river, or the shouts of the Sherpas prodding the yaks onward. In that deep gorge, with rocks and cliffs rising narrowly and steeply upward, these sounds continued to echo throughout the canyon walls. It would have been a perfect time and place to rest longer, with the hubbub and noise behind us and the forest ambience lulling us to relax. Unfortunately, the pressures of making the next campsite by late afternoon were always present, as Jim did not want the group trekking in poor light or darkness.

It was now just past one o'clock, and Olga and I began our usual earlier departure so we would not be too far behind the group by the day's end. We were both quite tired, and we weren't looking forward to the afternoon trek, especially since it would be as tough, if not tougher, as the second day's afternoon push to Namche Bazaar. How I wished we could have camped here and waited until tomorrow to hike to the Shangri-La site of Tengboche. I damned this organizational approach, with its well-laid plans and schedules that did not allow for much flexibility or individuality, or for the weary likes of Olga and me. This annoying thought helped to charge me up; I stirred myself and roused Olga to be on the way again.

From Phunki Thangka, the trail rose steeply through a forested area that enveloped us. It was hard to believe we were at an altitude of eleven thousand feet, with the great Himalayas nearby, while we hiked through this woodland of firs, pines, and deciduous trees that were not yet in leaf. The route twisted around and around like a steep spiral staircase. Underfoot, it was slippery, with rock ledges and hard-packed dirt. The unsure footing occasionally necessitated reaching for a tree as a handhold to help boost us along.

Emerging from this forest, the trail leveled off slightly as it continued its course on the edge of the cliff side. On our right, Ama Dablam and Thamserku rose to dominate the view, but the endless chain of deep valleys below was equally spellbinding. Because of the noontime descent to the river crossing, we were still a couple of thousand feet below our elevation of this morning. Above us in the distance, the ridge of Tengboche was discouragingly far away. In these high altitudes, with ever-changing light, atmospheric conditions, and vast panoramas of sky and mountains, it became very difficult to estimate distances visually. The shifting sunlight, shadows, reflections, and clouds could easily deceive one into misjudging how near or far away an object on the landscape was. And right now, as my fatigue grew, Tengboche looked as far away as the heavens to me. The trail ahead was just one long ribbon, winding up and up.

Suddenly, the afternoon clouds began moving in and descending upon us, thicker than ever. It seemed as if a curtain had fallen over everything. The mountains, valleys, and sky were swallowed up by the thickening cloud cover and vanished before our eyes. It was incredible that such immense views and colossal mountains could disappear from view so quickly and completely. As the fog blanketed the landscape and darkened the day, all that could be seen was a few hundred feet immediately around us. The magnificent bright day had turned dark and gloomy, creating an atmosphere that dampened our spirits. What a depressing climb it now became. The interminable uphill route was becoming strenuous enough without the added psychological stress of limited visibility. There was nothing to see or focus on except the trail in front of us. It became a tedious and horribly tough hike.

After a few hours, everyone in the group had passed us, as our pace became slower and slower. I remembered the advice to go as slowly as possible and to avoid stopping too frequently. I walked at a snail's pace, counting two seconds before taking the next step, but it was the best Olga and I could manage. Despite Jim's advice, our fatigue and shortness of breath forced us to stop every fifteen minutes and rest for at least five minutes. It was a grueling, exhausting uphill climb that sporadically worsened as we hiked through sandy trail sections where the wind kicked up small dust storms. I stayed close to Olga, whose face looked swollen, her eyes glazed with fatigue; she had put a kerchief over her mouth for protection against the swirling dust. I sensed that even inscrutable Kanchha seemed anxious for us. He shadowed Olga, stopping whenever she did, and following at her heels. We were a solemn, plodding trio. Olga and I said little, but we commiserated silently.

As exhausted as we were, there was never a word or thought that we should stop before reaching our campsite. Despite moving in slow motion like robots, we were committed to keep hiking. Although I was much too weary to think of anything but putting one foot after the other, I was getting anxious about our physical condition and ability to reach Tengboche. What helped to keep me going was my intense anger at Overseas Adventure Travel, the agency that had organized the trek. I cursed them repeatedly for encouraging us to undertake the trek. Obsessively, I kept thinking of my telephone calls to them, when I had asked whether we could handle this trek, considering our lack of backpacking and hiking experience. Now I damned them for their easy reassurances. I'm sure that this loss of control was caused by my terrible exhaustion, anger at the difficulty of the trek, and anxiety over Olga's condition. I remembered our son's remark that this experience would test us to the limits, and I thought that we were at that point now. Recalling his words helped calm me down and made me realize that I needed the energy for walking, not fighting windmills. Nevertheless, I believe that my agitation and anger helped mobilize my mental and physical energies. A stronger motivating force, however, was my fanatical determination to go as far as I was able.

I was puzzled about why we were so much wearier than ever before. Although this was the toughest and longest day of the trek, I had thought that the acclimation and experience of the last six days would find Olga and me in better shape. In our case, it didn't work that way; probably the cumulative effects of fatigue had led to this state of near collapse. Also, our poor eating, weight loss, and constantly being at these abnormally high altitudes had contributed to our growing debilitation. I began to appreciate the cautionary words of our guides and the innumerable mountain climbing books that emphasized the subtly encroaching debilitating effects of being at high elevations. We were huffing and puffing continually, trying to catch our breath, and feeling mildly dizzy. Our imploring looks finally brought forth some encouragement from Kanchha, who informed us that Tengboche was only about another thirty minutes away. With that news, our spirits rose, but only for the briefest moment.

All of a sudden, the mist grew thicker and closed in so that we could see only five feet ahead, and the light fluctuated from brightness to darkness. The heavens showered us with a blizzard. A chilling wind and fine snow completely engulfed us. It was a bizarre and frightening moment that only added to our woes. I thought that the group, who were certainly in camp by now, must be worrying about us, since it was now 6:00 PM, much later than any of our previous arrivals. Besides, the unexpected snowstorm must have aroused further concern.

Suddenly, the snowstorm abated and turned into a light, gentle snowfall. In the mist ahead, we heard our names called and saw John, Ved, and a Sherpa appear out of the fog. Worried, they had come looking for us, and they had brought a thermos of hot tea and some biscuits to ease our plight. What a relief it was to see them, knowing that we hadn't too far to go. The refreshment soothed our weary limbs, but the caring and kindness touched our hearts. Unfortunately, they couldn't walk for us, and we still had twenty minutes to hike. But John and Ved urged us along the trail by their encouraging chatter. I can still hear John, in a marked British accent, exhorting Olga, "Come on, old girl, you can do it," while he held her left elbow, gently prodding and supporting her. Just five more minutes of climbing a precipitous curving trail, and we'd be at Tengboche. It was hard to believe that a village was so close, because the steep mountain wall blocked the view completely to the north.

As we turned the last bend in the rising trail that brought us to the small plateau on which Tengboche was built, we noticed that the snow had stopped and the golden rays of the setting sun were filtering through the streaking clouds. Everyone was waiting anxiously for us and standing around the huge, impressive chorten that stood at the edge of Tengboche. As we approached, the heavens suddenly opened, and the stormy dark clouds lifted. The spellbinding view of the great valley and peaks, which had been totally obscured until now, was unveiled before us. An awed silence came over everyone as Everest, Nuptse, Lhotse, and Ama Dablam appeared through the sun-filtered, scudding clouds. Greeted by this dramatic scene, Olga said in a tremulous voice, choked with emotion and exhaustion, "It was worth it." Her remark broke the tension and expressed the deep feelings in all of us at being so close to Everest. It also set off scattered applause, shouts, and whistles at our safe appearance. It was a thrilling and memorable moment that still brings tears to my eyes whenever I think about our arrival in Tengboche.

As quickly as they had lifted, the clouds returned to obscure the landscape, which turned dark and gloomy again as the sun dropped behind the mountains. The brief clearing in the weather and the view of Everest seemed like a quick reward for making it this far. There was no longer much to be seen except Tengboche's famous monastery and scattered buildings. Too tired to do anything but get to our tents, we were nevertheless fascinated by a huge medieval-type tent set up a few hundred feet away on the edge of the village. The tent housed the advanced climbers and leader of the Indian expedition that had passed us earlier. Circular in shape and about thirty feet in diameter, it was made of beige panels that were decorated in a geometric diamond design, each in red, green, or blue; the tent tapered to a point twenty feet high. Not much interested in anything now but resting, Olga and I trudged to the campsite. As Jim walked with us, I apologized for our lateness and complained that OAT shouldn't have allowed us to go on this trek. In his typical unruffled and honest manner, Jim acknowledged our difficulties but firmly reassured us that we were doing fine. "We made it, didn't we?" was his repeated answer. Adding words of encouragement, Jim also noted that some trekkers didn't even make it this far.

The campsite was located only a few minutes from where we had entered Tengboche. Situated in an area the size of a baseball diamond, the camp was bordered by a grove of trees, several Sherpa homes, and the edge of the mountain. A large kitchen tent, where our meals would be eaten, was adjacent to the close row of tents. Our tent never seemed more inviting as we lay down, thoroughly done in. It was nearly 6:00 PM, and we had been on the trail for five hours that afternoon, plus three hours in the morning. It was clearly the longest and toughest day so far. I couldn't believe that Olga and I, now feeling so exhausted, would make it to Kala Pattar. But at that moment, we couldn't think much beyond getting into warmer clothes and just lying still to collect ourselves.

At thirteen thousand feet, we were at our highest altitude, and the penetrating evening air felt colder than any of our previous nights. We just wanted to stay in our sleeping bags and never move again. Even the idea of getting up again to eat was tiring. Jim poked his head into our tent to inquire about our condition. Jim thought that, as a precaution, Olga should be examined by John, who, although a member of the group, also served as the trek's official physician. (Trekking agencies make an effort to have a physician accompany each group by offering them a reduced rate.) Her extreme fatigue, swollen features, shortness of breath, and pale look made him uneasy, as it did me. My concern over Olga's condition was heightened by her high blood pressure, which was well controlled by the medication she was continuing to take during the trek. Jim was also responding to my candid doubts and anxieties about going any farther. I didn't look as sickly as Olga, but I certainly didn't feel much better.

After Olga had rested for half an hour, John came to examine her and found her to have mild symptoms of altitude sickness: a racing pulse, lassitude, and some edema. But her general physical condition was satisfactory, and the symptoms seemed to be diminishing. Although John thought that Olga could continue the trek, he would wait to see what her condition would be tomorrow, after a rest day, before making any final recommendation. As tough as Olga is, and with her never-say-die attitude, she was subdued and far from her exuberant self. We talked candidly about our ability to continue the trek, and we wondered about the wisdom of going on in view of our extreme lassitude. We agreed to make no decision tonight, but to see what tomorrow would bring. By squarely facing the possibility of a disappointment, rather than suppressing the thought and brooding over it, we relieved ourselves of much inner pressure and anxiety. To voice the thing we dread makes it easier to deal with life and what may lie ahead. I knew that we both had made a great effort to get this far, and we were proud of our accomplishment. Even if we couldn't go any farther, we were surrounded here at Tengboche by the great Himalayan mountains of our dreams. This adventure could so temptingly become an ego trip or a means of trying to test ourselves, to prove a false sense of superiority. To succumb to that thinking would be a perfect example of the classic Greek concept of hubris, an exaggerated pride that often brings retribution. And in these circumstances, the refusal to accept one's limits could be foolhardy and dangerous. With these sobering thoughts, we dozed off briefly until dinner.

That evening was the first time we ate in the dining tent, which was the size of a large living room, but without the same comforts. A faded red oriental rug and several scattered pillows, spread on the ground, were the furnishings. It was a cozy and comfortable setting, despite the coldness and discomfort of sitting on the ground and eating. Although the temperature was at the freezing mark and everyone was bundled up, we were slightly warmed by the heat from the fires of the kitchen tent next to us. The mood of the group was quiet; it had been a long, tiring day for everyone. But we listened expectantly, while fighting back sleep, to Jim explain that our goal of Kala Pattar and seeing Everest in full view was only three days away. For tomorrow morning, Jim had arranged a visit to the monastery, where we would experience the rare opportunity to attend a Buddhist religious service. By luck, we had arrived the evening before the monastery had scheduled one of their infrequent morning-long special prayer rituals. Unfortunately, the only thoughts of the future that stirred me were the full day of rest tomorrow and getting closer and closer to Mt. Everest. I don't remember much else about the evening, but I do remember that we slept the deepest sleep imaginable that night.

We awakened to loud, reverberating music coming from the monastery, heralding the special morning prayer ritual. Strange and ear-splitting, this music startled our ears, which were attuned to Western melodies and harmonies. Cymbals, gongs, and drums gave off brilliant clashing sounds that boomed throughout the valley. Weird-sounding wind instruments blared out shrill and wailing tones. It sounded as if each musician was playing by himself, whenever the spirit moved him, quite oblivious to the other instrumentalists. The plaintive horns and banging percussion, which were played with no semblance of tonality or a regular rhythm, produced an overall musical effect that was far from pleasing. The jarring and repetitious rhythms and the mysterious and atonal Far Eastern melodies reminded me of the music of Hovhaness and the minimalist school of Phillip Glass. Under more comfortable circumstances, I could have enjoyed this new music, but not now at daybreak, struggling to wake up and shake off my fatigue of the day before. Dear God, it was an unearthly way to be roused from our deep sleep.

During the night, a snowfall of several inches had fallen, and we awoke to a breathtaking wonderland of snow. The immediate countryside, mountains, village buildings, and campsite glistened with snow in the early dawn. I hurried to dress and take pictures, as the rising sun and warming temperatures would melt much of the ground snow in a few hours. Spurred on by excitement and curiosity, I quickly walked the short, tree-lined path leading to the village.

I came upon a view that stunned and overwhelmed me with its beauty and magnificence. The small plateau on which Tengboche rested was bounded on every side by gigantic peaks and huge, snow-covered mountain ranges. Crowning the enormous rock and ice walls, and the vast mountain glacier, were the majestic summits soaring to altitudes of over twenty thousand feet and presided over by Mt. Everest at 29,058 feet. It was the most awe-inspiring view imaginable. I easily understood why Tengboche had been described as the most spectacular and beautiful place on Earth and could be considered one of the great wonders of the world.

Tengboche was especially beautiful that morning, because the overnight snow had covered the arid, dark brown foothills and lower mountain ranges with a blanket of white. The rising sun's spreading rays were being reflected off the snow, and the entire landscape shone with a shimmering, ethereal quality. It was a transcendent and humbling experience. The great mountains, so close and so colossal, appeared serene, inviolable, and mysterious in this glistening early morning light. And the valley view toward Everest, of tree-lined riverbanks and endless waves of rising mountain slopes, looked idyllic with its mantle of new snow.

The village of Tengboche is built in a semicircle and overlooks a small, grassy, oval plain the size of a football field. Twenty years earlier, the only structure besides the monastery was a shed built by Hillary to accommodate trekkers and climbers. Today, Tengboche consists of about twenty-five buildings, including several inns, native homes, and additions to the monastery. Even with this buildup, the village retained its isolated simplicity and had not been ruined by the growing influx of trekkers and climbers, according to Jeremy Bernstein, a writer and amateur climber who recently revisited the area after an absence of twenty years. The monastery, or *gompa*, in Tengboche is the most famous in the Khumbu region, since it serves as the spiritual center for twenty thousand Sherpa people. Built on a rise, the gilded temple building dominates the village with its majestic appearance. There could be no better location for prayer and meditation than this mountain village that seemed so close to the heavens. Practicing religion is as much a part of a Sherpa's life as breeding yaks and growing potatoes.

Curious and fascinated by the Sherpas' intense involvement with religious rituals, I was looking forward to attending their prayer service later that morning. But first I had to return to camp to shave and clean up, chores that were delayed by my excitement in beholding the views before the snowfall melted.

Our campsite was just a stone's throw away from the monastery, the roofs of which we could see over the tops of the Sherpa homes next to the kitchen tent. Beyond the temple to the north, we also saw the summit of Everest rising above the great wide ridge of Nuptse. Since the camp clearing was set in a slight depression, we saw only the upper parts of the Himalayas that encircled Tengboche. The views from the campsite were like a preview of the great panoramic vistas that were just a few minutes walk away. It was hard for me to attend to the practicalities of cleaning up, with these mesmerizing sights everywhere I looked. Nevertheless, the stark reality of Olga's condition still kept me apprehensive—and wondering whether we would be able to go on. Although Olga felt better after a night's sleep and was as thrilled as I was by our surroundings, she still seemed to be tired and listless.

Breakfast perked us up, as we had our favorites: fried eggs, roast potatoes, and chapati, or flat wheat-bread rounds. Except for the monastery visit after breakfast, the day would be ours to do what we liked. We were scheduled to be at the temple in an hour, which gave us time to gather laundry to have washed. I was looking forward to laundering my own body, as one of the inns offered showers. Jim suggested a few possible climbs on the neighboring ridges, but the thought of any physical activity was repugnant to Olga and me. Today, we planned to just rest and rest and rest. Hopefully, this day of relaxation would revive us, so that we could be on the march again tomorrow. Ahead of us were three more days of hiking before the final long day's climb to reach eighteen-thousand-foot Kala Pattar. Because of my profound weariness, I had to confess that if we went no farther than Tengboche, I could accept that decision, however disappointing it would be. Everything seemed to be an effort, even the thought of the imminent visit to the monastery, which I could have put off to another time.

At around 9:00 AM, the group gathered outside the monastery's entrance, where Jim outlined some basic rules of conduct to observe during the prayer service: shoes were to be removed as a sign of respect, silence would need to be observed, and photographs could not be taken. Also, since we might become uncomfortable standing in our stocking feet in the damp dark chapel, we could leave at any time during the ritual.

I noticed that this short uphill walk of a few hundred yards to the monastery had left Olga short of breath and puffing noticeably. John and Nas also noticed and quickly took her pulse, which was racing at 140 beats per minute, much higher than expected by this effort at this high altitude. Although Olga was feeling better this morning and they agreed that she could make this temple visit, John and Nas were still concerned about her physical condition, and they would make a final assessment this evening. In his friendly and caring manner, Nas cautioned me against being overzealous about our continuing the trek, in view of Olga's condition. With no intent to alarm, only to express his medical opinion, Nas reminded me that at our age, at this altitude, and with the cumulative effects of fatigue, we could be vulnerable to heart attack. It was a sobering thought that would nag at me throughout the day.

As we walked through the monastery's outer gate and up the hill to the main entrance, I marveled again at the incredible beauty and serenity of this setting. My heart leaped every time I looked up at the vast sky, crowded with endless covered mountain ranges. My eyes kept returning to Mt. Everest, where the plume of cloud and snow was already gathering and streaming from its summit. What a place to commune with the gods and live in prayer and contemplation!

Perched on a knoll, the monastery was built like a small fortress, with its square design, begrimed white stucco and stone walls, small high windows, and dull red tiered pagoda roofs crowned by three golden finials. The main building rose in two tiers to a height of three stories above the surrounding lower structures, appearing like a grandstand overlooking this fantastic mountain scenery. Gleaming in the morning sunlight, the gilded edges of the roof, window frames, and sparse ornamentation reinforced the temple's regal appearance.

We entered a small courtyard bordered on one side by the chapel entrance and on the other sides by a low building with balconies. There was an odd familiarity about the place, which baffled me until I realized that the courtyard resembled an Elizabethan theater set and the entire monastery complex was like a medieval citadel. I expected, at any moment, to see knights and royal personages emerge from these medieval surroundings. Despite this archaic appearance, the monastery was only about sixty years old. Tengboche Gompa, its correct name, was built by an old hermit from Khumjung, Lama Gulu, with the help and financial support of all the surrounding villages. Hillary cites the recollections of his Sherpa guide, Dawa Tenzing, who remembered carrying stones to help build it as a child. "People came from all over: men and women, and some brought their children along. So eager were we to build the gompa that the work went on in all kinds of weather, and often at night, and in six months it was done, even the painting." A remarkable accomplishment, made even more so by being constructed miles away from the nearest villages, atop an isolated mountain spur; villagers had to come from afar and provide their own food and shelter while building it. Unfortunately, in 1933, ten years later, an earthquake destroyed the monastery, which was quickly rebuilt. During the earthquake, the old lama was killed while praying in the chapel; the ashes of his cremated body were strewn on the monastery's ruins.

Folklore has it that a Lamaist saint, while flying over the mountains, fell and left his footprints on a rock, which became the site of the Tengboche monastery. In the Sherpa language, *tengbo* is "heels" and *che* is "imprint," so Tengboche literally means "the imprint of heels." The greatest legend, however, is the Sherpa's belief in the *rinpoche* or abbot of the monastery as a reincarnated lama, a belief that lies at the heart of Lamaist or Tibetan Buddhism. Tengboche and the Rongbuk monastery, its neighbor some thirty miles away to the north on the Tibetan side of Everest, represent the center of this religion. When the Chinese Communists overran Tibet decades ago, the Rongbuk monastery was destroyed as a temple of worship and became a barracks for soldiers and frontier guards. The Dalai Lama, the reincarnate head of Tibetan Buddhism and political leader of Tibet, was forced to flee and became an exile. As a result of this upheaval, many Rongbuk priests became refugees and fled south to the Tengboche monastery, where they still worship. When the current abbot of Tengboche was a small child in Namche Bazaar, he was thought to be the reincarnation of the old abbot. After passing many tests, which proved that he was the reincarnated abbot, this fifteen-year-old became the head lama. Today, forty years later, he presided over thirty-five priests who spent their time in prayer, meditation, and study. Their main rituals are sorcery, witchcraft, and sacrifice used to appease the demons and gods they believe reside in the caves, valleys, and mountaintops.

On entering the monastery chapel, we first came to a few large outer rooms whose walls and ceilings were a blaze of color. The wall panels were painted with murals depicting, in a highly primitive style, scenes of nature and mythic Sherpa tales. Scroll work of every imaginable oriental design bordered the paneling. Their designs and symbols alternately clashed and harmonized in a dazzling visual display on the walls around us. Gilded metal and ceramic statues of Buddha of different sizes peered at us inscrutably from niches in the wall. The predominant wall color was a deep, rich red with contrasting accents of pale green, dark blue, and gold. Not to be outdone were the ceilings, decorated in wide stripes of orange, blue, and green interrupted by painted squares of intricate mosaiclike designs. The walls and ceilings also sported oddly placed red velvet drapes and multicolored prayer flags. The clashing colors, designs, and decorative touches were a visual hodgepodge that was quite dizzying to look at. Oddly enough, this decorative jumble that assailed us was strangely pleasing and inviting once we got over the initial visual shock. These artistically embellished foyer rooms communicated a joyousness and reverence for life and the divine that captivated our hearts. The uplifting and exciting effect of the chapel's outer entrance intensified our curiosity about what the actual chapel would be like.

Walking into the chapel was akin to stepping into a different world; the dazzling colors and joyful ambience of the foyer gave way to the darkness and gloom of the chapel's interior. Illuminated by only the light streaming from an overhead window and a lantern on an altar, the chapel and the worshipping priests were shaded by darkness. Our group huddled by the window, where a small bench and a rolled-up rug offered a few uncomfortable seats. The chapel room was the size of an average suburban house and consisted of three small altars flanked by drapery hangings, darkly lacquered walls, and chests. In the center of the sanctuary was a rectangular area where several rows of benches were reserved for the worshiping priests.

The service we witnessed was puzzling, as it was hard to fathom what was going on. An elderly monk, who was reading from a book in front of the main altar, appeared to be conducting the services. While he read and chanted, other red-robed monks came in and out of the room for no apparent reason. Monks would also suddenly begin chanting, blowing on conch shells and horned instruments, ringing bells, and banging a gong. The chanting and musical sounds, which were monotonous and dirgelike quality, went on interminably. I wondered about the meaning of a chant that was recognizable by its incessant repetitions, and learned from Jim that it was the universal Buddha prayer and the inscription found on most prayer wheels. "*Om mani padme hum*" has many interpretations, but it means something like, "Hail to the jewel of the lotus." Since the lotus is a symbol of Buddha, the prayer honors and praises the Buddha.

After an hour of observing the monks' prayer service, we were getting restless and uncomfortable. Without shoes, our stocking feet were becoming chilled from the damp, cold stone floor. With much relief, we eagerly tiptoed out of the sanctuary. Perhaps it was our discomfort in being cold and still fatigued, but we felt that the chapel service and surroundings were fairly depressing. It was a relief to leave the monastery and be greeted by the glorious sunlight, blue heavens, and magnificent mountains. Just across the way from the monastery and at the edge of the small meadow to the east, Ama Dablam rose twenty-five thousand feet to the sky. The proximity of Ama Dablam's huge mass created the illusion that the mountain was looming directly over this tiny village and was close enough to touch.

Although this exhilarating wonderland and the brilliant weather tempted us to explore our surroundings, all of us had many personal chores to do on this rest day before exploring the countryside around us. Returning to the campsite, we were met by a scene that appeared absurd and incongruous in the midst of this unearthly beauty. A rest day is also a washday, and all kinds of clothing were hanging out to dry on clotheslines that had been strung from tent to tent: colorful long johns, underwear, socks, shirts, and pants. The intense sun quickly dried most of the clothes. We had been advised not to bring along any clothing of synthetic fiber, but everyone found that such apparel dried more quickly than cotton. Best of all, however, was all-wool clothing for ease of washing and drying. My most valuable piece of clothing turned out to be a long-sleeved lightweight wool shirt, which I had debated taking along because it might be too warm. Pure wool is one of the great discoveries of man, capable of adapting to either tropical heat or arctic cold.

As we collected our clothes, I noticed that the several inches of snow that had blanketed the ground this morning had completely melted; the foothills around us had lost their snowy mantle and resumed their arid appearance. So far, we had been extremely lucky in not having bad weather conditions. The physical challenge of the trek was tough enough without having to cope with rain and snow and the discomfort they would bring. In the back of my mind, I worried about having to slog through stormy weather, which would add to our physical effort and fatigue. This wasn't an unrealistic concern, since blizzards and rainstorms frequently occurred at this time of year around Tengboche. Perhaps the snows of yesterday afternoon and last night would be our only taste of bad weather—I certainly hoped so.

With everyone gathering laundry, sorting out gear, and dawdling about, the camp was a beehive of lazy activity. Olga and I planned to take it easy the rest of the day and walk around Tengboche later in the afternoon. After lunch, I was looking forward to my first shower since leaving Kathmandu.

This was our eighth day on the trail, and I was feeling quite grimy and eager to wash away the layers of dirt that had accumulated on my body. Some of the group had already showered and were exulting in their new state of cleanliness. Most of them were planning a hike or a climb this afternoon on one of the nearby hills. Considering my state of exhaustion, I couldn't believe that everyone wouldn't want to just lie in the sun and recharge their batteries. It made me pause to wonder about our physical condition and the advisability of continuing the trek, particularly since the next few days would be the toughest of all.

Olga was feeling better and had no more palpitations, nausea, or shortness of breath, but her paleness and mild lassitude told me that she wasn't completely fit. I also had to face up to the fact that my own physical and emotional condition was not up to par. I was still weary, moving slowly, and feeling ambivalent about continuing the trek. In addition, the awe-inspiring views and beauty of Tengboche made me think that I could accept the decision against going on to Kala Pattar. Here at Tengboche, I was in the midst of the great Himalayas that I had read and thought about for nearly a lifetime. If we remained here and didn't continue the trek, I could bask in the magnificent vistas and indulge my insatiable need to look and look. On this small, lonely thirteen-thousand-foot plateau that was Tengboche, I felt exactly like Hillary when he wrote, "Nowhere have I felt such exhilaration, such wondrously primitive joy, as at Thyangboche."

On the other hand, we wanted to reach Kala Pattar and get as close to Everest as possible. We also felt guilty over the possibility of leaving the group and creating an additional logistics problem for Jim, who would have to leave us with supplies and possibly a Sherpa. Many mixed thoughts and emotions about whether we should go on raced through our minds, but Olga and I decided that we would wait until the evening before making a final decision. How we felt tonight, after a day of recuperation, would tell the tale.

These sobering thoughts nagged at me, especially after lunch, when Olga chose to lie around and read rather than shower and walk around the village. She was still quite weary, and she confessed that even the thought of any physical activity was too much of an effort. Trying not to dwell on her condition and its implications, I prepared for my much-anticipated shower.

A sprawling lodge-cum-restaurant fifty feet below the monastery walls provided the only shower stall in town: a three-by-three-foot-square shack just big enough to accommodate a person. From its ceiling hung the makeshift metal five-gallon can whose bottom was punched with jagged holes to provide a homemade showerhead. A reservation to take a shower had to be made at the lodge, so that they had time to prepare the shower water. Since most of the group had already showered, I found only one person before me.

As I entered the lodge, I was nearly overcome by the fumes of the smoke-filled room. The walls were blackened and grimy from the smoke, and a feeling of gloom and mystery pervaded the atmosphere. I arranged and paid for the shower (thirty-five cents), and I was told that it would take about twenty minutes to heat the water for the shower. While the water was being heated up in a huge kettle, I sat outside the shower shack, which was adjacent to the lodge. I couldn't help but smile and wonder at the incongruity of this moment. Here I was, with a change of clothing and some toilet articles, sitting outside of a primitive shower stall in the midst of Everest and the most awesome mountain peaks. Looking at the magnificent beauty around me was hypnotic and incredibly soothing. I could sit and gaze here forever. Time meant nothing and seemed to stand still here, marked only by the passage of day, night, and the seasons. No one rushed, no one was pressured by the hours, and human activity moved slowly and tranquilly.

These thoughts were reinforced by the sight of the Sherpa lumbering toward me with the hot water. Slowly and indifferently, he poured it into the showering can. He showed me how to use the string attached to a contraption that controlled the water flow. I had to estimate how long I needed to shower, since the only control was either a stop or start, a full flow of water or none at all. Also, I couldn't stretch out the showering time, as the hot water quickly cooled in this windy air.

On a bench next to the shower stall, I undressed and laid out my clothes. I entered the stall with my peppermint-scented liquid soap (recommended for camping), excited and intrigued by a daily ritual that assumed the dimension of a challenge in this primitive setting. With a tentative and cautious pull of the shower string, I was suddenly splashed by the most wonderful stream of warm water imaginable. It was a tonic to feel the water and soap wash over me. As if in a contest to get the best of every drop of water, I rapidly soaped myself between intervals of stopping and turning on the water. The dirt that flowed from my hair and body turned the water into a black puddle beneath my feet. I had felt pretty grubby, but I couldn't believe that I was that dirty.

After five minutes of on-again, off-again streams of water, the shower was over. How I longed for a large Turkish bath towel instead of the puny, cheap hand towel I had to settle for. Quickly drying my lanky six-foot frame, I got into my clean clothes as fast as possible, to avoid getting chilled from the afternoon winds that were blowing through the wooden slats of the shower shack. Brief as the shower was, it did its job and made me feel clean and refreshed. I returned to our tent to deposit my old clothes and to describe the intricacies of showering in Nepal to Olga. I found her lounging in the sun, propped up by her duffel bag. She was still too tired to take a stroll, and so I went exploring alone with my camera.

On the edge of the small clearing that was our campsite, I came to a precipice that looked south to a thrilling panorama. In the distance, I could see the park plateau of Namche Bazaar, from where we first saw Everest, and the twisting trails we had hiked. From this viewpoint, they appeared to be a miniature toy countryside, dwarfed by the tremendous wide range of Kwangde that stretched for several miles, twenty thousand feet in the sky. To my left, in an easterly direction, I gasped at the sight of the twin peaks of fluted ice and snow of a pair of twenty-two-thousand-footers, Thamserku and Kantega. It was hard to believe that these huge masses of rock, snow, and ice could rise to summits of delicate spires that looked as sharp as needles. Walking among the brush and the ridge, I took pictures from every conceivable angle and vantage point. These great towering peaks of all configurations, and the endless valley views, provided my amateur photographer's eye with a constant visual feast.

Just before, and parallel to this precipice, was a walk that led to a trekker's lodge, and beyond to an isolated ridge that ended abruptly less than a mile away. I peeked in to see what such a lodge offered in the way of accommodations. A low ranch-type building of stone and logs, it turned out to be a simple shell that housed about fifteen beds, dormitory style. Any shelter, however simple, is a blessing for anyone trekking at these high altitudes.

This busy afternoon passed quickly, as the darkening clouds, increasing chill, and wind announced the end of our active day. It was time to change into warmer clothes, lie down for a while, have tea, and get ready for dinner. While walking back to our tent, I wondered whether Olga's condition had improved or deteriorated. A time of decision would soon be at hand: could we, and should we, continue the trek? Preoccupied with worry, my mind was a jumble of conflicting thoughts.

8

Altitude Takes Its Toll

I found Olga inside the tent, reading and dozing off. She felt much better, but she was still weary. In better spirits than this morning, she expressed a readiness to go on tomorrow. I noticed, however, that she sounded subdued and displayed none of her usual spunky self. Uncharacteristically, she would leave the decision to me, and to John and Nas, who would soon be examining her.

In the early evening's darkness, I paced around the tent while our trekking physicians examined Olga. The results were favorable: Olga's pulse, blood pressure, and breathing were satisfactory, and only mild signs of edema were evident. Physically, Olga could continue the trek, but no one could predict her physical condition after another day or two of strenuous hiking. It would have to be our decision. In the final analysis, it was what life constantly presents us with: a judgment call. Many variables would have to be reviewed and reconsidered before arriving at a final determination. Firstly, I had to discount Olga's eternal agreeableness and note her uncharacteristic subdued and weary manner. I also had to be honest with myself and confess to my own state of exhaustion. I was at the end of my physical tether and dreading the idea of facing the trail again. Yet our goal of Kala Pattar, whose site offered the closest and best full view of Everest, still lured me on. I needed to talk to Jim now for his opinion, and to clarify again what the next three days of trekking would entail.

Jim confirmed that the days to come would be at higher altitudes and under more primitive camping conditions than we had experienced. The last day, or the push to Kala Pattar, would be the toughest. In order to arrive there by noon and have about an hour of viewing Everest before the weather closed in, the group would rise in the dark of night and be on the trail by 4:00 AM. From the campsite at Lobuche, it would be a strenuous, steep ascent to reach eighteen-thousand-foot Kala Pattar. Walking the first few hours in pitch-black darkness, we would climb sixteen hundred feet of mostly crumbling rocky terrain. The estimated noontime arrival would allow an hour of viewing before starting back again; everyone should be back in camp at Lobuche by 5:00 PM. This schedule allowed for at least eleven hours of hiking in the most arduous conditions so far.

If Olga and I were already as much as two hours slower than the others in arriving at our previous campsites, we would take at least fourteen hours to reach Kala Pattar and return to camp—if we made it at all. The facts were brutally clear against our being successful in reaching Kala Pattar. Would it be worth going on anyway to the next two campsites at Dingboche and Lobuche and remaining at either while the group took on the black hill? If the scenery was as spectacular as Tengboche's, the effort might be worth it. My questions of Jim revealed that although we would get closer to some of the great peaks, we would not have the vast panoramas that encircled us now.

Mulling over these negative facts, I asked Kanchha what he thought of our dilemma to stay here or go on. It was understandable that he would prefer to avoid the discomfort that lay ahead, but his strong reaction surprised me. The usually calm and inscrutable Kanchha described the difficulties ahead, emphasizing the potential problems of the higher altitudes and the bitter cold that usually fell to below zero during the night at Lobuche. Furthermore, he predicted, based on his experiences, that not everyone would make it to Kala Pattar. Kanchha did not directly advise against continuing the trek, but his implication was clear. With Olga's stabilized but potentially vulnerable condition and with my weariness, these physical stresses could cause us serious problems.

This was dramatically confirmed by Nas, who gently but firmly advised that we go no further. As a physician, he cautioned me about Olga's weakened condition, which could easily deteriorate under more stress, and reminded me that at our age and state of exhaustion, the possibility of suffering a heart attack was not uncommon at these altitudes. An active sportsman and mountain enthusiast, Nas knew how much it meant to us to see Everest up close. Nevertheless, he thought it unwise and dangerous to attempt the march ahead. He repeatedly reminded me to focus on how much we had achieved. His sincerity, concern, and compliments were genuine, not platitudes aimed to make us feel better. I shall always be grateful to Nas for helping me place things in the right perspective.

After much heart-wrenching inner turmoil as we reviewed all the pros and cons, Olga and I decided to remain at Tengboche. Taking into account

Olga's condition, my exhaustion, and what still faced us, continuing the trek would be foolhardy and probably dangerous. For one of the rare times in our lives together, Olga did not insist on persevering. Her calm acceptance, even resignation, of our decision confirmed that it was the wisest course to take. I knew we did the right thing when each of us felt a surge of relief, knowing that the pressure to keep on going was lifted.

With some degree of guilt for the logistics problems involved, I told Jim of our decision. Although I sensed that he wasn't too pleased about having us separate from the group, Jim was unfailingly cooperative and agreeable. He would leave Kanchha, Pemba (a kitchen boy, who would cook our meals), and two yaks with us. We would be on our own for four days until rejoining the group at Namche Bazaar. I hadn't asked the others about their reactions, since I didn't want to trouble anyone with our problem. However, everyone knew the problem I was grappling with, and they were quite sympathetic; implicitly, they gave the impression that I shouldn't chance the difficulties of the next several days.

At dinnertime, everyone knew of our final decision. Their positive and sympathetic reactions were reassuring and helped alleviate the guilt we felt over creating extra logistics problems. Sensing our deep disappointment, many promised to bring back photos of the views from Kala Pattar. I really wanted some more substantial memento, and I asked Kirt whether he would mind bringing back some stones from the foothills of Everest. Always keenly perceptive, Kirt responded in his typical enthusiastic and magnanimous manner. Remembering fourteen-year-old Kirt, I still marvel at his maturity and poise, which made him a joy to be around. There are few young teenagers who can adapt easily to a group of adults, particularly over a three-week period under these demanding conditions. To say that he was never a bother did not mean that he was a submissive youngster, for Kirt was quick to assert himself and stand up for his rights whenever anyone tended to treat him condescendingly or too paternalistically. Unfortunately, adults the world over are easily prone to telling adolescents how they should act, adopting the age-old, unaccepting, listen-to-me-I-know-better attitude. When glimmers of such behavior emerged, Kirt would have none of it. Our group of trekkers, from age fourteen to fifty-nine, were rugged individuals, yet able to live in harmony with each other.

Just before falling asleep, I wondered anxiously about the next morning, when the group would leave us behind. It would be a difficult separation, and it was a reality that I didn't want to face. But as Olga and I huddled in our sleeping bags, talking and mulling things over, I knew that the decision to stay behind was the wisest course. Olga confessed that she was still uncomfortable with a sore throat, a cough, and some edema in her ankles, and said that she felt so weary that everything seemed like an effort. As for me, I was also exhausted and looking forward to days of resting and hiking at our own pace.

One of the marvels of the mind is its infinite capacity to arrive at reasons for accepting the inevitability of whatever befalls us. Regrettably, this ability can be used harmfully to deceive ourselves by minimizing or denying reality. The challenge that life offers is whether we can remain honest by acknowledging what we can and can't do, to face our strengths and weaknesses unflinchingly. It's not an easy task, as evidenced by the hypocrisies, lies, and half-truths that prevail in the world. Our needs for power, self-esteem, and the crowd's plaudits fool us into believing we must hide our human frailties and flaunt deceptions, as the emperor did with his "new clothes." How sad it is that we can't grasp the realization that strength lies in facing our weaknesses. Self-deception only forces us to weave more webs of duplicity in accelerating spirals. By accepting our limitations, Olga and I felt a renewed vigor and rising spirits about meeting the challenges of being on our own until we rejoined our group.

The next morning, everyone joked about our being able to take it easy and have the equivalent of room service from Kanchha and Pemba while they braved the rigors ahead. After breakfast, it was strange watching the camp being dismantled, packed away on the backs of the Sherpas and yaks, and everyone getting ready to depart. Saying good-bye would be a disappointing and difficult time. Choked with emotion, we walked with the group to the meadow's edge. I can still see them walking across the meadow, looking back and waving to us as they headed up the valley where Everest stood, glorious in the bright morning sun, with its plume of cloud streaming from the summit. I couldn't hold back the tears and the great disappointment in knowing that this was as close as we would come to seeing Everest. Even now, the memory of that moment makes me tearful but strangely at peace with myself.

As we waved good-bye and watched them disappear into the forest, Olga and I felt sad, but we were also quietly content with having come so far. At that moment, I was inspired by a thought that I believe helped me subconsciously accept this moment: the idea that we were comparable to a climbing expedition where not everyone can reach the summit; we were the second team, and making it to Tengboche was as great an achievement for us as the group's arrival on Kala Pattar. I remembered the courageous climbers I'd read about who never made it to their summit, but whose efforts were no less an accomplishment.

The last of the Sherpas and animals, loaded down with gear, soon left, lumbering down the valley after the main group. Suddenly, the silence and solitude struck us. It was an eerie feeling. There we stood, by our tent, which was pitched in the middle of this small deserted campsite, with only Kanchha, Pemba, and two yaks as companions. Alone, we felt overwhelmed by the awesome mountains and countryside that enveloped us. The unearthly stillness and aura of isolation produced a transcendent sensation of tranquility, which seemed to hold us mesmerized. Reluctantly, we returned to the practicalities of our situation.

Kanchha was responsible for our general welfare and in charge of Pemba, who would follow the usual mealtime routine with one important exception: we would sleep at least an hour or so later than our usual 6:00 AM wake-up call. We planned to stay at Tengboche for two more full days and return on the third day to Namche Bazaar. Jim had suggested that we make the long haul back to Namche Bazaar in two days, which appealed to our desire to take things leisurely. He also had recommended that we be there by Saturday, to see the weekly farmers' and merchants' market day. It was Tuesday, eight days since landing at Lukla, and in that short time, we had experienced a lifetime of wonder and thrills. How much more, I wondered, would there still be in store for us?

We couldn't fully grasp the relief and luxury of being by ourselves, without the pressures of a long hike to yet another new campsite. It was a mind-boggling sensation after the strict routine and discipline imposed by the trek. Although we now had no schedule to maintain, Olga and I thought it best to develop a daily plan of activities, so that we would keep in shape and maximize our opportunities for exploring the countryside. This morning, we planned to explore the narrow ridge that stretched out behind us; in the afternoon, dependent on Olga's condition, we thought of climbing a trail that snaked its way up a nearby hill overlooking the village.

We considered sleeping in the nearby trekking lodge, but we had become quite comfortable in the tent, which seemed like home to us. Despite the dusty and chilly air of the tent, we preferred it to the musty, smoky, and dank atmosphere of a primitive lodge. When Kanchha asked whether we might prefer to sleep in the adjacent Sherpa house where they would live, we quickly rejected that offer, knowing that the air would be even more smoke-filled than the lodge, and smelly because of the animals stabled on the ground floor. Besides, camping outdoors preserved the spirit of this trekking adventure, which we wanted to maintain.

After everyone had departed, the ever-present prowling dogs seemed more noticeable. Our group of four people and two yaks was joined by a small, wire-haired, black and white mongrel dog. Many dogs strayed by, looked us over, and went on their way, but this mongrel stayed on and became a temporary member of our new group. This playful dog, which was always good for a laugh, made us think of our own long-haired dachshund, Schatzie, back home. Being reminded of the world we had left behind was a strange emotion, as that life seemed ages away and quite alien to us now.

We spent the morning hours scrambling about and taking pictures on the ridge behind the campsite. At first glance, this narrow shelf of thinly forested land appeared to be a finger of an island, thirty feet wide and extending a half-mile out to nowhere at thirteen thousand feet above sea level. While walking the barely trodden trail, we saw a villager watching over two grazing yaks. Their presence in this isolated and weird extension of land was a reassuring sign that we hadn't ventured too far. The ridge turned out to be a fabulous natural grandstand from which to view Everest and the Himalayas ranging across the sky to the north. On either side of this thin outcropping of land, the precipices dropped steeply to the valleys thousands of feet below. The panoramas were stupendous from this site. Inching carefully down the slope several yards past the openings in the stunted trees and brush on the northern side, we discovered viewpoints that expanded and magnified the view toward Everest and the adjacent mountain ranges. On this island in the sky, we felt as if we were sitting in the heavens, privileged with the most unobstructed close-up panoramic scene of these awesome peaks one could desire.

We had to be cautious, however, not to wander too far down the slope, as a slip or a slide could tumble us dangerously down the mountainside. Several thousands of feet directly below us was the dried-out riverbed of the Imja Khola valley; there was nothing between us and the distant river but the long, long falling slope of scrub brush, dwarfed trees, dirt, and rock. Although this grandstand seat seemed precarious, it was essentially a safe perch, as long as we watched our step while descending the difficult terrain. Enthralled by our discovery, we found that the morning had quickly passed and lunchtime was upon us. We did not want to tear ourselves away from this spot, which we would return to again and again, but we knew that Pemba and Kanchha were waiting with lunch.

Perhaps it was our diminishing tiredness and renewed feeling of energy, but lunch that day was the best ever. I'm sure, however, that it had a lot to do with our private chef, whose appearance belied the possession of any culinary skill. No more than eighteen and just over five feet tall, with shoulder-length, straight black hair, Pemba looked like a happy vagrant. He was always smiling with a crooked, toothless grin, and he displayed a constant glazed stare that made him appear either stoned or drunk. We soon discovered that he had a passion for drinking *chang*, the local beer, or whatever other alcohol was available. Pemba's clothes added to his unkempt appearance. Most of the time, he wore a wrinkled, long-sleeved white dress shirt that was always streaked with dirt; filthy baggy jeans and a wide colorful headband, begrimed with soot, completed his outfit. What a surprise it was to learn that this disheveled, jolly, eager-to-please teenage Sherpa turned out pretty good meals. That first lunch was delicious: thin, round pieces of freshly made bread called chapatis, roasted potatoes, and chunks of fried breaded cauliflower, all washed down with a hot orange drink and then tea. As an added treat, Pemba opened a can of sardines, which we gobbled up. This satisfying meal made us quickly forget our chef's unclean appearance and the dirty surroundings.

We ate in one of the small stucco houses that bordered the campsite. The balcony where lunch was served seemed to be an unfinished room lacking the outside wall. Although it was a pleasant setting with the cooling breeze and streaming sunlight, the atmosphere was contaminated by the dirt that settled on everything, and the animal and cooking odors that permeated the air indoors. We were glad to leave quickly after eating, but we regretted that we couldn't appreciate more the special efforts made by Kanchha and Pemba to make us comfortable. Sometimes the primitiveness, with its filth and odors, became too much to bear in this context of supernatural beauty. I remembered Olga exclaiming, quite out of character from her easygoing and accepting nature, that it was hard to believe that these beautiful surroundings existed "amidst such shit"; also, that beauty engulfed one when looking upward, but dirt, dung, and squalor took over when looking down at the ground. Her comments were not made judgmentally or critically, but out of sheer frustration over the impoverished conditions that existed everywhere in this country.

Feeling refreshed and invigorated after lunch, we decided to climb the ridge that was a few hundred feet across the way from the village and nestled below twenty-two-thousand-foot Kantega. A climb of about five hundred feet or more, the ridge overlooked the village and offered another exciting vantage point to view the panoramas around Tengboche. As we started out, however, the wind began blowing, and the clouds were rolling in from the horizon. All of a sudden, the warm, sunny air turned chilly, and we had to put on jackets. The trail up the hill was no more than a trampled-down, grassy, narrow foot-path that saw little use. It turned out to be steeper than we had anticipated, and I was glad that Kanchha had decided to come along and take his usual place at Olga's side. The ridge would have afforded us another spectacular view if the streaking clouds hadn't thrown a gray curtain over the mountains. The darkening skies and the wind, which suddenly became strong gusts whipping through the trees, made our position cold and uncomfortable. When we were over halfway there, we decided that it wasn't worth the effort to climb higher and explore the area, since there was no longer much to see, and the wind's intensity had increased to the point where it was difficult to stand upright.

As Olga's kerchief flapped in the stiff wind, it reminded me of the snap and crackle of a mainsail coming about. I also thought of the incredible cold and furious winds that can blow at over one hundred miles an hour on Everest, only several miles up the valley from here. Who can ever forget the terrifying sound of the wind when viewing the film of the British expedition that first climbed Everest in 1953? The snarling and howling wind was deafening. Against such savage gales, climbers have struggled fiercely for hours trying to put up their tents; at times, they have clung to their ice axes, plunged into the deep snow, to keep from being blown off the mountain. In our uncomfortable circumstances, we quickly descended the ridge.

Back in the village, we sat leaning against the stone wall of the stupa, watching the scudding clouds cause the peaks to appear and disappear dramatically. We were both feeling slightly winded from the steep climb, but our extreme fatigue was mostly gone. Despite the exhaustion we had felt during the past eight trekking days, there was never a moment when our enjoyment of the awesome views was diminished by any physical discomforts. The glorious vistas kept us constantly thrilled and effectively masked our weariness.

As we sat contemplating the tiny village of Tengboche, I couldn't believe that it was still so primitive and small after forty years of being the major focal point for the innumerable major expeditions, climbing groups, and trekkers going on to Everest. In 1967, the only building besides the monastery was a small wooden shed that Hillary had built for climbers, and it is still standing. Tengboche now has an additional four small, nondescript restaurant-cum-lodge structures, several Sherpa houses, and a two-story stone lodge that the monastery was building for visitors. These newer buildings had done little to spoil the isolated and primitive setting of Tengboche, which could easily be a stand-in for Shangri-La.

There was little sign of noticeable human activity in Tengboche except for an occasional solitary villager going about his chores, or a monk strolling by. Whenever we saw a priest, he was usually walking leisurely, even aimlessly, around, as if he had nothing to do and time hung heavy on his hands. It was ironic to observe the amusement and condescension the monks displayed toward trekkers who were enthralled by the mountain views, when most of the time, they contemplate the same transcendent sights.

While we were so engaged and resting by the stupa, two of the lamas approached us, a huge, hulking six-footer and a small, slight, balding companion, both dressed in grease-streaked parkas hanging over their ankle-length, maroon priest's robes. They were an incongruous sight and looked like an oddly appareled Mutt and Jeff. Wondering what they could want, we were startled when the meek-looking small priest, who acted as the spokesman, bluntly asked whether we would like to see his colleague's craft work collection. Although they spoke hardly any English, and Kanchha had returned to help Pemba with the mealtime preparations, we were able to understand their few words and gesticulations.

Curious, yet suspicious and reluctant to be taken in, we followed them up the monastery steps to the monks' living quarters. We entered an impressively furnished dark room about the size of a small bedroom. The only light came from a single narrow, elongated overhead window. Dark wooden walls that shone with age had shelves displaying a variety of metal artwork and muted colored drapes. Two beds and a bench left little room to walk about. As soon as we sat down, the seemingly passive monk began his sales pitch. Proudly pointing to the large copper plates, bowls, and vases, he instructed his friend to display them before us one by one. It was soon apparent that the priest was the owner of the artwork and the boss behind this operation; our little monk was the shill.

Suddenly, a young teenager appeared who was training to become a lama and apprenticed to the tall priest. The youngster scurried about submissively to help his mentor show off the large pieces of metalwork. When I posed the universal query of "How much?", I was bowled over by the prices. With a wide grin and imperious look, the priest quoted prices of three to five hundred dollars an item, at least nearly double the price of similar items in the shops of Kathmandu. I rationalized that the steep prices had something to do with the monastery's constant need for funds, so I asked if the money went to the monastery. What naivete, I quickly learned, as the priest began thumping his chest to indicate gleefully that all the proceeds belonged to him.

This encounter felt uncomfortable from the very beginning, but our curiosity and desire to please and respect our hosts trapped us into a situation that gradually deteriorated into an unpleasant experience, made more so by the haughty and greedy demeanor of these lamas. Perhaps my perception of this episode shows a lack of tolerance, but I am saddened by the extent to which the commercial philosophy has invaded the values of everyday life. Increasingly, the human spirit is being taken over by the mercenary belief that there is nothing more important in life than making money. Corporations merge, not to effect better services and quality, but to become richer. Sports teams are ready to leave their hometowns if another town beckons with more dollars. Litigation to sue anybody at the drop of a hat is running rampant. As Russell Baker, the resident *New York Times* humorist, wrote, the old values of the modern age—loyalty, excellence, progress—no longer seem important in this everything-is-up-for-sale age. Even in espionage, Baker noted, in the old days, a spy betrayed his country because he believed in his enemies; today, the spy betrays his country because he believes in nothing but the importance of money.

I couldn't wait to tell Kanchha and see what his reaction would be. As always, Kanchha was his reserved and inscrutable self; he simply shrugged and smiled knowingly on hearing our story. Apparently, this is a typical occurrence between the priests and foreign visitors. Although Kanchha maintained a respectful manner toward everyone, his attitude, and those of the Sherpas, toward the native priests was mocking and less than reverential. From my observations, these hard-working mountain villagers appeared ambivalent toward monks. They respected and needed the priests' religious powers but resented their way of life. Working from daybreak to evening, the Sherpas struggled to survive and eke out a living, whereas the monks performed no productive work and lived, comparatively speaking, a parasitic existence. Prayer, contemplation, and serving the ritualistic needs of the community made up their religious activities. Living off donations and the gifts of others, the lamas led a fairly secure life without any need to struggle. Despite the Sherpas' resentment of their priests, they needed to provide for them to believe that they were serving the deities. In this land of great poverty and hardship, these beliefs helped make life bearable.

Formal training in Buddhism begins in childhood, when monks take children between the ages of ten and fourteen as apprentices. These child apprentices and potential priests not only begin to learn every aspect of the Buddhist religion, but also act as servants to their mentor-priests. Chosen subjectively by the monks, who seek out potential candidates throughout the villages, these children have no choice and do not always welcome their apprenticeship. But every child and his parents ultimately submit to these religious demands. This invasion of a child's freedom may be another factor contributing to the Sherpas' mixed emotions toward the Buddhist priesthood, since the Sherpas are a people who dearly value personal liberty.

It was late afternoon, and the wind had abated, but it remained chilly and dark from the low-lying gray clouds. Where I live, usually the end of a sunny day begins as the blue sky pales and whitens, signaling the onset of evening. In these mountains, the skies turned cloudy and dark by midafternoon, and twilight remained until evening fell at around 5:00 PM. The presence of the mountains could be felt as an ineffable stillness that pervaded this time of day. Being by ourselves amid this supernatural beauty seemed like a sacred and privileged honor.

One of the rituals Olga and I began looking forward to as the day grew darker and chillier was teatime. I never could understand the popularity of tea, which I rarely drank before. But its ability to soothe and reinvigorate made me understand its universal appeal. As we sat in front of our tent, savoring a hot brew, a young backpacking couple arrived at the campsite. Looking exhausted, they asked, in a midwestern American twang, whether we would mind if they camped near us. We watched them set up their tent and prepare dinner, and we were grateful that all these chores were done for us by the Sherpas. Sympathizing with their fatigued state, we offered tea and biscuits. Feeling refreshed, they began heating a dinner of beef and vegetables that smelled delicious.

Nowadays, hiking has become more enjoyable because of the availability of all types of meats and vegetables that come prepared in freeze-dried aluminum packets. Just heating the tin on a portable gas camping stove quickly provides a tasty and nutritious meal. The only drawback is the expense of these individual meal packets, which cost three to five dollars each. We envied them their meal and shiny, clean aluminum plates and utensils.

To our surprise, this mild-mannered couple, Pete and Sue, in their late twenties, hailed from Milwaukee, Wisconsin. They planned to go as far north as possible, hopefully to Kala Pattar, but were unsure if their stamina would hold out. Pete had been sick with a sore throat and laid up for a week at the Japanese trekking lodge a half-day's march below Namche Bazaar. A tall and lanky man, he looked pale and sickly now. It seemed ironic that Olga and I, who looked rested and suntanned, were too physically drained to go on trekking while this sickly trekker wanted to keep going. Oh, the unlimited strength and enthusiasm of youth. We learned that both were violinists with the Minnesota Symphony Orchestra. As we wished them well, I joked that I would be in the audience shouting *"Namaste!"* at intermission when the orchestra was scheduled to play Carnegie Hall in ten weeks. However many times we say that it's a small world, the truth of that cliché always startles us when circumstances arise to validate it.

That evening, Pemba served dinner in the open shed behind our tent. With its three-sided stone walls and wooden-shingled roof, the shed was only six feet deep. Except for its sturdier construction, I was reminded of the bus stop shelters at home. We dined off a wooden plank balanced across two large rocks, near a warm fire that Kanchha had built. Although Pemba had improved the menu, our appetites remained poor. Olga felt much stronger, but a hacking cough kept her from feeling fully recovered; the antibiotics, cough medicine, and altitude sickness pills made her feel like a walking medicine chest. Nevertheless, our spirits had revived, and we felt psychologically fit again.

Even the outhouse next to the lodge couldn't depress our mood. Paradoxically, it was larger and better constructed than any of the outhouses used by a Sherpa home, but definitely less appealing. Similar to a row of beach lockers, the outhouse had a concrete foundation raised three feet above the ground. Going up a few steps, we entered a narrow hallway with a row of six individual stalls, each offering the luxury of a waist-high toilet seat. Once inside, however, this luxury was quickly dispelled by a horrible stench. The odor of human waste was so strong that it made us gag. Until now, we had never experienced such odors, as most of the Sherpa outhouses were surprisingly free of pungent smells. The good ventilation and the hay-strewn floors of the Sherpa outhouses combated foul odors, whereas the concrete foundation and wooden stall enclosures of this toilet facility trapped and intensified them. Rather than use this outhouse, we preferred the one we discovered behind the monastery. Just a small shack, it was supported by wooden planks that extended over the edge of a precipice. When looking through the widely spaced floorboards, we saw a drop of several hundred feet to the ravine below—not the kind of ambience that makes for a sense of security while attending to nature's call. We were baffled by the placement of this outhouse, but we realized that its location provided a natural sewage system, as human wastes dropped down the cliff side.

Every day brought new experiences, discoveries, and insights. Time moved slowly, but the days were filled with excitement and wonder. Even in our solitude here, there never seemed to be a dull moment.

9

Contemplating the Himalayas

On awakening Wednesday morning, I realized that this would be our last day at Tengboche. Since Jim had strongly advised us not to miss the farmers' market early Saturday morning at Namche Bazaar, we planned to leave after breakfast on Friday. We both felt strong enough to make Namche Bazaar in one day, rather than a two-day hike as Jim had advised if we still felt exhausted.

While getting ready for breakfast, Olga and I joked about the handful of trekkers who kept passing our tent on their way to the lodge behind the campsite. Although there were no more than several pairs of trekkers, their chatter and presence in this isolated setting made us feel as if we were camped in the middle of a crowd. When alone and in a strange place, it's easy to overreact to everyday occurrences. I couldn't wait until breakfast was over, so that we could return to the ridge we had found yesterday, which overlooked a valley view of Everest and the surrounding giant peaks. I wanted to gaze for hours at these awesome mountains, to imprint them in my mind forever.

That morning, we noticed the foliage and trees losing their blackened, wintry look and showing bursts of green. We saw budding rhododendrons and rosebushes and were amazed that these stunted bushes could survive on this exposed thirteen-thousand-foot ridge, ravaged by ferocious winter snows and winds. Signs of spring were also evident along the endless Imja Khola valley that stretched to Everest. With the snow-capped summits and blue skies crowning this stunning panorama, Olga and I sat all morning just contemplating these spectacular views. My mind raced with thoughts of those climbers I'd read about who had struggled and sacrificed their lives to reach Everest's summit. I still couldn't believe that I was here, enveloped by the greatest mountains in the world—the mountains of my boyhood dreams.

The Himalayas are the most enormous mountain ranges on the face of the Earth. Across the northern border of India, they extend fifteen hundred miles from west to east. Averaging one hundred miles in width, these mountains lie between the hot plains of India to the south and the cold plateau of Tibet to the north. To grasp their immensity, imagine this: if placed on the eastern coast of the United States, these mountains would extend from Maine to Florida. To understand their incredible height, consider this: if the Alps were put on top of the Rockies, the Himalayas would tower over them, and Everest would still soar thousands of feet above them all. And the largest concentration of the Himalayas is in tiny Nepal, which also has eight of the highest peaks in the world, exceeding twenty-six thousand feet, including Everest at 29,028 feet.

Mount Everest is located in the far northeast corner of Nepal, and from our viewpoint, this giant was half hidden by the mountains that rose before it. Just beyond Everest lay Tibet, where it is fully visible and not obscured by a foreground of other peaks. The best view of Everest from Nepal is at the rocky mountain of eighteen-thousand-foot Kala Pattar, where our trek was heading without us. What we saw of Everest from Tengboche was an impressive pyramid of rock and snow, appearing smaller than the mountains that screened it, because they were nearer. Directly in front of Everest was the massive mountain range of Nuptse, which is a vast curtain of rock, ice, and snow. Nuptse is a twenty-five-thousand-foot wall of small, jagged spires and seems more akin to a wide ridge in the sky, rather than the usual triangular-shaped mountain. Next to Nuptse, to the right of Everest, rose the magnificent twenty-eight-thousand-foot Lhotse, in full view, with its lower peaks culminating in a soaring summit. Together, Nuptse and Lhotse blended to form one huge chain of mountains that walled off most of Everest, except for its majestic summit. At this time of year, the upper reaches of these mountains were mostly gray rock and ice streaked with snow. The savage winds around the summits prevent much snow from accumulating during the spring, when snowfalls are relatively sparse and the hot sun quickly melts new snow; whereas in the middle and lower parts of the mountains, the snow remains plentiful and highlighted by sections of icy blue glaciers.

It wasn't until the last century that Mt. Everest was discovered to be the highest mountain in the world, by a geographical survey undertaken by India and Britain in 1949. This 29,028-foot peak was named after Sir George Everest, who initiated the survey of the Himalayas and Asian geography. Protesting the use of his name because it could not be written in the native language and was difficult to pronounce, Sir George recommended that the mountain be called the name used by the people. Throughout the world it remains known as Everest, but the natives, Chinese, and Tibetans refer to it with awe as Chomolungma, or Goddess Mother of the World.

On this magnificently situated ridge, we discovered a small cairn dedicated to two Chinese climbers who were killed climbing Everest. This three-foot, nondescript monument showed a faded photoengraved picture of the young climbers. Their deep-set Asian eyes stared at us pensively and hopefully, unfortunately never to see beneath their feet the summit they struggled to conquer. Surrounded by towering peaks and facing Everest, this simple memorial with the pictures of the dead climbers' boyish, energetic faces was a profoundly moving tribute. It was a forcible reminder that mortal dangers lurked everywhere among these glorious but treacherous mountains. Since 1921, when climbers first set foot on Everest, there had been about fifty known climbing deaths. Climbing fatalities are primarily caused by avalanches and falls, and, to a lesser degree, by altitude illnesses, exhaustion, falling rocks, and ice pinnacles suddenly toppling over.

The English were the first mountain climbers to explore and attempt the world's great mountains. One of the greatest climbers of all time and one of the fathers of mountaineering was Edward Whymper, an Englishman who in 1865 became the first man to climb the Matterhorn. After a few British attempts at climbing minor Himalayan peaks in the late 1800s, the English imagination became captivated by reports of the tremendous size and insurmountable challenge of Everest. In 1921, they mounted the first Everest expedition, which was to be a reconnaissance, mapping and exploring the Everest region. In those early years, Tibet was the normal approach to Everest, a route that entailed a long, grueling march across the flat Tibetan plains. It was not until 1950 that Nepal would permit climbers to attempt Everest from Nepal. Most climbers thought Everest unapproachable from the Khumbu region in Nepal because of the enormous concentration of peaks on the Nepal border. Between 1922 and 1947, the British mounted six expeditions, which all ended in failure. But these attempts revealed the feasible routes to the summit and the obstacles and dangers of scaling Everest. Of paramount importance was the weather, and choosing the best season to climb became a crucial issue. From early June to September, the mountains were bombarded with daily monsoon rains and winds and periodic snow squalls; in winter, the unbearable freezing temperatures and interminable storms frightened away climbers. The general consensus was that late spring, just before the monsoon weather struck, was the most propitious time to try Everest.

Mountaineers eventually discovered that no matter when Everest was climbed, the weather could suddenly become hazardous. The greatest danger at these altitudes was the wind bringing fog and whiteout, a condition when spatial confusion becomes so bad that one becomes disoriented and unable to see more than a few feet. Extreme altitudes also posed a constant peril to the climbers' physical condition and emotional state. Until the Himalayas were attempted, climbers were mostly experienced with the Alps; scaling Everest meant living and climbing for periods of time at altitudes twice as high. Altitude illness became common, and its symptoms of fatigue, respiratory difficulties, and lassitude could easily affect a climber's judgment. It is understandable that the second British team in 1924 experimented with using oxygen as a climbing aid. The use of oxygen would become, among Himalaya climbers, a controversy that rages to this day. Nevertheless, the majority of the expeditions have used oxygen masks at some stage of the ascent to Everest's summit. The biggest argument against using oxygen was that it goes against man's natural resources and is not "sporting."

Another difficulty in climbing the Himalayan peaks was their immensity and isolated location. Even today, there are no types of modern transportation available, and climbers still have to walk distances of many weeks to reach the Himalayas. And this creates a logistics problem of feeding an expedition during the approach march and the summit attempt, which can take many months. An Everest expedition, therefore, resembles an army on the march, with hundreds of Sherpa porters and yaks strung out for miles on the trail. This chain of men and animals carrying food and equipment can easily number four hundred. Sherpas are ideal porters and guides, but the first British expeditions found that they had little skill in mountaineering and had to be taught the basic techniques of climbing. Sadly, the first fatalities on Everest were seven Sherpas, who were killed in an avalanche during the initial British venture in 1922.

These earlier climbers found that the most perilous technical problem was navigating across icefalls, which are stretches of enormous crevasses and ice pinnacles. An icefall is constantly moving downhill at an imperceptible slow pace, which causes the ice to fragment and collapse unexpectedly. Crossing an icefall becomes a chancy and dangerous undertaking. Adding to the nerve-racking crossing are the roaring explosions that occur when huge chunks of ice crumble and fracture like an earthquake; Hillary referred to one area of the Khumbu Icefall as the "Atom Bomb" sector because of its constant ice explosions.

The entrance to the main southern route to Everest's summit is guarded by the Khumbu Icefall, which the famous mountaineer Mallory called "one of the most awful and utterly forbidding scenes ever observed by man." At eighteen thousand feet, it is a tangle of ice formations exposed to sudden avalanches from the rock walls of Everest and streaked with chasms that suddenly open at one's feet. Ice cliffs of fifty feet and crevasses as wide, which drop thousands of feet below, confront the climber at every turn on the icefall. Climbers and porters constantly negotiate this ice wilderness in order to bring supplies and gear to the camps that need to be established higher on the mountain. Getting safely across its deadly crevasses requires caution, skill, and many prayers, as no one can predict when the icy ground will suddenly crack open or when ice pinnacles will topple over. It is a miracle that fatalities have been so few on the Khumbu Icefall; only about a dozen climbers have been killed there.

What also makes Everest so murderous to climb is the combination of gales, extreme temperatures, and dangerous formations that confront the climber at an altitude that has already sapped his strength. Because of the debilitating effects of these altitudes, "on Everest it is an effort ... to talk, an effort to think, almost too much of an effort to live," said Frank Smythe, who reached 28,100 feet during the 1933 expedition.

Until Everest was finally climbed in 1953, there were twelve unsuccessful attempts to reach the summit. All of the expeditions were British, except two Swiss expeditions and two unbelievable solo attempts. The second British expedition in 1924 resulted in the loss of George Leigh Mallory and Andrew Irvine, who were last seen disappearing into the fog at nearly twenty-eight thousand feet; a controversy still continues about whether they reached the summit. One of the most popular climbers of his time, Mallory has gone down in mountaineering lore for his response when he was asked why people climb a mountain: "Because it's there."

The two solo attempts were carried out in 1934 by an Englishman, Maurice Wilson, who froze to death near the North Col, a valley at twenty-five thousand feet; and in 1947 by a Canadian, Earl Denman, who disguised himself as a Tibetan monk and quit Everest just below the North Col. After World War II, Tibet closed its country to foreigners, frustrating any new Everest expeditions. It wasn't until 1950, after Nepal opened its borders, that the first Westerners, a British climbing team, explored the Everest region from the southern or Nepalese side. Ascending Kala Pattar and walking to the edge of the Khumbu Icefall, they were the first climbers to look upon Everest from the area previously forbidden to foreigners.

When a subsequent 1951 British and a 1952 Swiss expedition each succeeded in putting climbers at over twenty-eight thousand feet, or a thousand feet below the summit, before turning back, these efforts proved that the highest peak in the world could be climbed from the southern approach. Since the first attempt on Everest in 1922, twelve expeditions had failed to achieve success. Still unconquered, Everest was one of the very few challenges left in the universe. The world's preoccupation with Everest probably grew from man's repeated failures, which invested Everest with an aura of invincibility.

As climbers learned more about Everest and achieved heights closer and closer to the summit, it was only a question of time and favorable weather before a successful ascent was achieved. It was becoming a far cry from the first expedition in the 1920s, when climbers were attired in tweed knickers and nail boots. New clothing and gear were now better suited for Everest's brutal weather, and the value of using oxygen had been established, despite the diehards who condemned it. Windproof and rainproof clothing, better-insulated boots, and improved food reflected the growing knowledge and expertise of Himalayan climbing. These developments helped climbers cope better with altitude problems, winds that could blow steadily all day at over a hundred miles an hour, and temperatures falling to a bone-chilling minus eighty degrees at night and rising to above one hundred at midday. Most important, previous climbs had developed a group of experienced climbers who were now more familiar with Everest's topography, technical problems, and dangers. All tended to agree with Mallory, who characterized climbing Everest as more like going to war than mountaineering; therefore, the expedition leader had to be daring, experienced, and able to lead a team of independent, opinionated, and courageous men. This was not an easy task, as past Everest expeditions revealed the politics of attempting a famous unclimbed summit: jealousies about who should be chosen for the final summit attempts, and differing opinions about the size of the climbing group, approach routes, and handling the logistics. Like any human endeavor that will bring publicity and fame to those achieving success, some of the strong personalities too easily exhibited their human frailties and inflated egos.

Embarrassed by their repeated inability to scale the top of Everest, the British planned a huge expedition in 1953 under the leadership of Colonel John Hunt, a forty-three-year-old military officer with Alpine and Himalayan climbing experience. The climbing party numbered fifteen climbers who were picked for all the usual reasons of age, health, experience, and, in Hunt's rules for eligibility, "exceptional fire and determination." Described as possessing a genius for organization and military precision, Hunt was the embodiment of responsibility and authority—all greatly needed, as the climbers, Sherpa porters, and animals would number at least three hundred and fifty.

Leaving Kathmandu on March 8, 1953, the expedition was split in half, departing on successive days for the sixteen-day trek to Tengboche. For three weeks, the expedition camped in the Tengboche meadow, which Olga and I walked each day, acclimatizing ourselves to the high, thin, cold air and getting in shape by exploring the valleys and mountain passes. The generally accepted strategy of climbing Everest involved establishing a base camp around the foot of the Khumbu glacier and then setting up additional camps at successive heights up the mountain. Usually about a thousand feet higher than each previous one, these camps consisted solely of a tent stocked with supplies and two or more climbers. Nine camps at altitudes ranging from nineteen to twenty-eight thousand feet were placed on Everest during this attempt. The higher the camp, the less sparsely provisioned it would be, since hauling supplies to the camps was an exhausting and dangerous task. This strategy enabled climbers to break trails, gain experience with their climbing partner, get close to the summit, and be in the best position for a summit attempt when weather conditions were favorable.

Not everyone agreed with such a massive mountaineering attack, especially the great mountain explorers H. W. Tilman and Eric Shipton, who were most responsible for pioneering routes on Everest. Their approach favored using only a handful of climbers and Sherpas, no more than our own trekking group of thirty in all, in a daring attempt on the summit. In the 1953 expedition, climbers were paired off, and Edmund Hillary, a thirty-three-year-old New Zealand beekeeper, and Tenzing Norgay, a thirty-eight-year-old Sherpa guide, were teamed together by Hunt, who considered them the most skilled and strongest of the group. Both had been on Everest climbs before, Tenzing as far back as a nineteen-year-old on the 1935 reconnaissance. In 1952, on the Swiss expedition, Tenzing had reached 28,210 feet higher than anyone had ever climbed.

At their first meeting, Hillary was soon convinced that Tenzing was the ideal climbing partner. Jogging and leaping down the icefall to win a bet that he could get back to base camp in less than an hour, Hillary nearly met an untimely end. Jumping across a chasm, Hillary suddenly found himself falling down the void when his weight caused the ice edge to crumble under him. Tenzing, who was right behind him, keeping up the mad pace, held fast the rope belay, which saved Hillary, who had pressed his shoulders and crampons (iron spikes attached to the boot soles) on either side of the ice wall. Perhaps at that moment, Hillary had an omen that climbing with Tenzing would prove the truth of Tenzing's second name, Norgay, which means "fortunate one."

Beginning in early April, the expedition maintained a daily schedule of breaking trails through deep snow, across crevasses, and up glacial terrain as supplies were laboriously hauled up the mountain to the advancing camps. For seven weeks, the climbers also reconnoitered possible routes and confronted immense climbing challenges as they established the higher camps from which the summit attempts would be made. The camps were staggered along Everest's southern face to the summit. To climb Everest, camps had to be established just beyond the Khumbu Icefall in the Western Cwm (pronounced coom), a glacial valley nearly two miles long and a half-mile wide. Hauling supplies and gear to the camps in the Western Cwm necessitated continuously traversing the dangerous icefall and a daily climb of more than two hours that everyone dreaded.

By early May, successive camps were finally set up in the Western Cwm: Camp III at 20,200 feet, and at the farthest upper edge of the valley, Camp VI at twenty-three thousand. From here, the route headed up to the twenty-six-thousand-foot South Col, a dip in the ridge between Everest and Lhotse's towering walls, and then up through rock and snow to the South Summit, a point that rises narrowly to the final summit.

At these altitudes, climbing becomes a struggle in the thin, cold air. Hunt was the first to mandate the use of oxygen. Inhaled through a mask attached to a cylinder, oxygen combats sleeplessness by maintaining body heat and preventing headaches caused by freezing nights at high elevations. Despite the use of oxygen, some of Hunt's climbers remained incapacitated by altitude sickness. Although the oxygen cylinders were prone to mechanical failure and burdened the climber with forty-one pounds of extra weight, according to Hunt, "it was vital to success. But for oxygen ... we should certainly not have got to the top." Besides these climbing problems, the expedition was periodically plagued by blizzards, gale-force winds, and poor visibility, which typified the treacherous natural forces of an Everest summit climb.

The first assault party of Bourdillon and Evans set out from Camp IV at twenty-one thousand feet for the push to the summit. After two exhausting days, they arrived at the twenty-six-thousand-foot South Col, where they struggled to put up their tents in a fierce wind. Utterly fatigued, they needed to rest the next day instead of mounting the final summit assault as they had planned. Ironically, it would have been a perfect day for the attempt, as the weather turned clear with little wind. After the rest day, on May 26, Bourdillon and Evans started for the summit, climbing at a good rate until the going became precarious: a savage, howling wind was blowing spindrift from the summit, making visibility quite poor, and falling snow was creating potential avalanche conditions. Besides, Evans was having trouble breathing, as his oxygen set was malfunctioning. Nevertheless, the two climbers reached the South Summit, only three hundred feet below the ultimate summit. The corniced dome on which they stood was at 28,750 feet, the highest elevation that man had ever achieved. And they were close enough to see the final ridge leading to the top.

It was 1:00 PM, and they had already been climbing since 8:00 AM. Should they try for the summit? Estimating that it would take about three more hours to reach the summit, and nearly another five hours to descend to the South Col camp, they decided against the risk. Their oxygen would last for three more hours, and weather conditions were worsening. When Bourdillon and Evans finally made it back to the South Col camp, they appeared to Hillary like figures from another world, dressed in bulky clothes, with oxygen cylinders on their back and masks covering their faces. They had been battered terribly by wind and snow during their descent, and they were encased in ice and snow from head to foot.

The second assault team of Hillary and Tenzing started out on the morning of May 28. Pitching their two-man tent on a tiny ledge at twenty-eight thousand feet, they dozed throughout the night on the highest mountain bivouac anyone had ever attained. At 6:30 AM, they began climbing for the summit. Just before the South Summit, they negotiated snow slopes so steep and powdery that an ice axe could not be planted securely. With no chance of a belay, a slip could not be stopped and would be fatal. Tenzing recalled, "It was one of the most dangerous places I have ever been on a mountain."

Deciding to take the risk, they finally made it safely to the firmer snow of the South Summit by 9:00 AM. Now only hundreds of feet below their goal, they scaled a ridge of rock with huge overhanging cornices that formed a rocklike chimney. Knowing that any one of these cornices could suddenly collapse and hurl them off the mountain, they forged ahead successfully. The last obstacle they confronted was a ridge of undulating rises. The weather was clear with little wind as they climbed until there were no longer any rises and there was nothing but the sky ahead.

On May 29 at 11:30 AM, Edmund Hillary and Tenzing Norgay stood on the top of the world. In his typical restrained manner, Hillary shook hands with Tenzing, who threw his arms around Hillary in a bear hug. While Hillary took photographs, Tenzing buried some food as a gift to the gods of Chomolungma. To this offering, Hillary added a crucifix that Hunt had given him. The gods had indeed been good, providing fine weather, sufficient oxygen to reach to top, safe climbing conditions, and, as Hillary had hoped, a summit that was not a precarious cornice, but a safe rounded cone. They found the summit to be a small snowy platform about three feet wide and forty feet long. What a perch from which to view the world below!

Hillary and Tenzing remained just fifteen minutes on the summit before they began the dangerous descent back to the camp at South Col. They stopped midway, where they had camped the previous night, to brew a hot lemon drink and to adjust their oxygen apparatus to a slower rate so that the oxygen would last. As they approached the South Col camp, George Lowe met them with hot soup and extra oxygen. In telling Lowe, a fellow New Zealander, the good news, Hillary resorted to the slang of their rugged country: "Well, George, we knocked the bastard off."

Thousands of feet below, at Camp IV, everyone was anxiously awaiting the news of the climb's outcome. From their vantage point, the waiting group below saw what appeared to be five tiny figures descending the mountain: Hillary, Tenzing, and the three others who had awaited them at the South Col camp. What a relief—no one had been killed! Hours later, the climbers arrived, Hillary wearily waving his ice axe in triumph. This great accomplishment would soon make them the toast of the whole world and the pride of England, for their victory coincidentally came in time as a special gift for Queen Elizabeth's coronation on June 2, the morning on which their achievement would be announced in *The Times* of London.

As if an insurmountable psychological barrier was now broken, this highest peak in the world has been successfully climbed nearly twenty times since 1953. The route taken by Hunt's expedition has become known as the "ordinary route," and by the slightly mocking Sherpa description as the "yak route." As with any challenge finally overcome, human beings are rarely able to rest on their achievements, but constantly need to create new challenges to test and prove themselves. Subsequent summit attempts have sought out different routes or faces of Everest to scale and have climbed in the post-monsoon and winter seasons. Expeditions began to place more climbers on the summit and try approaches that were considered impossible to climb.

In 1963 an American expedition not only put six men on the summit, but achieved the remarkable feat of being the first to traverse the mountain: one group reached the top from the South Col, the other from the unclimbed West Ridge, with both meeting just below Everest's summit. The Chinese expedition in 1975 was the largest, with 410 people. They tried to place forty men and women on the summit, but gales and swirling snow defeated them. Days later, their second attempt placed nine on top, including Phantog, the coleader and the second woman to reach the summit. Only days before, a Japanese ascent had already put the first woman on the roof of the world.

Everest summit attempts have consisted of many incredible and courageous feats, but one of the greatest occurred during the 1975 British expedition when Doug Scott and Dougal Haston faced a mortal challenge after scaling the summit for the first time from the Southwest Face. Having climbed for about fourteen hours, they reached the top at 6:00 PM, with the dark of night soon upon them. They had no chance to descend safely to the last camp thousands of feet below and had to risk the highest overnight bivouac ever tried by anyone. Several hundred feet below the summit, at 28,750 feet, Scott and Haston dug out a snow cave, where they had to survive the night. Oxygen had run out, as had fuel for their stove. Throughout the night, they stayed awake and kept warm by changing position, massaging each other's limbs, and exercising their arms. The lack of sleep and oxygen caused them to hallucinate. Incredibly, they survived for thirty hours without sleep or food, at an altitude and freezing temperatures that no other climber had ever endured. Sadly, on the day of Scott and Haston's return, another climber of the same expedition, Mick Burke, disappeared in mist as he headed for the summit to take photographs. Sadder still, the Himalayas claimed both Scott and Haston's lives many years later.

Another historic occasion occurred in the 1978 Austrian expedition when Reinhold Messner and Peter Haebler reached the summit without using oxygen. Overshadowing even these magnificent feats of skill and daring was Messner's return to Everest in 1980, when he successfully climbed the summit in a solo attempt. Without oxygen, without companions, and without fixed camps, Messner scaled the summit from base camp and back again in four days! It was certainly one of the most spectacular and courageous achievements ever made by any climber.

While recalling these mountaineering feats, I wondered, *Why does man climb, even against the greatest odds and with the probability of a serious or fatal accident?* Since the Matterhorn was climbed in 1965, it has been estimated that 50 percent of the top climbers have been killed in the mountains. It is therefore somewhat of a miracle that Hillary and Tenzing, who continued to climb regularly, are still alive thirty-five years after conquering Everest. (While writing this, I read that Tenzing just died of a lung infection in his home at Darjeeling at the age of seventy-two.) Perhaps Mallory's simple explanation that it is because the mountains are there offers the key to a partial understanding. The world around us confronts us with many challenges, and mountains present a most formidable test to prove ourselves. The title of Hillary's autobiography, *Nothing Venture, Nothing Win*, exemplifies this philosophy of adventure and risk. When scaling peaks, man can not only test his powers, but can also, as many mountaineers have observed, come close to the winds of eternity. Conquering a mountain summit can make a climber feel that he has faced his own mortality and temporarily vanquished death. And part of standing atop a mountain is the transcendent experience of sheer beauty.

In explaining the need to climb, Messner, who was born in 1944 and grew up in the Dolomite region of Northern Italy, stressed two reasons: the need to be active and push himself to the utmost extreme, and the need to know himself. Messner emphasized that the risks of climbing enabled him "to go deeper into the self," to go on an inner journey that has led him to achieve profound tranquility.

Whatever the reasons for man's addictive desire to climb, there are no final answers and no easy explanations. The mystical need to experience eternity and inner peace is just as valid as the more objective ones of overcoming a challenge and testing one's abilities. Common to all these reasons, I believe, is the fact that when man becomes interested in or challenged by anything in the world—mountains, the sea, space—he is trying to define himself, to know who he is and where he stands in the universe. By developing a life interest or meeting a challenge, we create meaning out of a world of absurdity and confusion. To make life meaningful is man's eternal struggle, a task that the explorer and adventurer actively confront. Perhaps we should not always try so hard to explain every human phenomenon. Analyzing and explaining can ultimately be self-defeating, and it can destroy the beauty and pleasure of an experience. We need to acknowledge that human nature is ultimately unknowable and a mystery. The medieval thinkers summed up our limit to knowledge in one of the truest sayings ever spoken: "All things pass into mystery" (*Omnia exeunt in mysterium*).

I felt a kinship with those courageous Himalayan mountaineers as I gazed at the glorious mountains. To climbers, trekkers, and armchair mountain enthusiasts, Everest is the ultimate peak. I felt fortunate that Olga and I had made it to Tengboche and had these many days in their overpowering presence. Only this afternoon and evening remained before we left the next morning for Namche Bazaar.

Before leaving, I planned to visit the monastery again and take pictures of its fascinating temple. Luckily, we met a lama who was eager to show us the temple. A short, muscular, handsome young priest in his early twenties, he proudly pointed out the alluring colored and gilded murals and altars. While I took picture after picture, the lama donned his red priestly robe and posed for me. Unlike our gift-selling and materialistic monk of yesterday, he was the epitome of friendliness and generosity. As we left the temple, we noticed a group of monks and Sherpas playing cards on the monastery steps. Apparently, the arrival of Sherpas with trekking and climbing groups provides the monks with a chance to gamble and break their monotonous routine. Once again, I was struck by their lack of piety, even irreverent behavior, carried out on their own religious premises, behavior that seemed difficult to reconcile with their rigorous monastic life.

Like all other mornings, Thursday, March 15, the day of our departure, sparkled with clear blue sunny skies and snow-covered summits. Olga and I were reluctant to leave Tengboche, which, with its spellbinding beauty and ineffable tranquility, could pass for paradise. After three days of leisurely exploring and resting, we felt strong again and ready for the hike back to Namche Bazaar. Olga was still prone to a sporadic hacking cough, which she couldn't shake off, but she was otherwise fit again.

We left Tengboche at around 9:00 AM without Kanchha and Pemba, who would meet us at Phunki for lunch. Although they would leave more than an hour later, they would easily catch up to us by noon. Jim had suggested that we make Namche Bazaar a two-day trek and stop overnight at Phunki, a major river crossing for the Everest region. Since we felt physically fit again, and since we remembered the dirty condition of the Phunki lodge and campsite, we doubted that we would follow Jim's advice. Upon leaving Tengboche, we descended a narrow, rocky trail that wound precipitously downhill until it flattened out and skimmed the cliff. Although the views remained beautiful, with endless undulating valleys and snow-capped mountains to the south, we could no longer see Everest and the semicircle of peaks to the north. After descending that steep incline at the village's edge, a curtain of cliffs rose to shut out completely the panorama we had feasted on at Tengboche.

10

Energies Restored

What a difference three days of rest and recuperation meant to us! We felt refreshed and eager to be trekking again. The route back from Tengboche was not too steep, but, to keep us on our toes, there was always a section of trail that ascended and descended along a twisting, narrow path. We maintained a good pace, hiked close together, and gloried in our renewed strength.

In about three hours, we arrived in Phunki, wondering when Kanchha, Pemba, and our yaks would arrive, since we never saw them behind us. While waiting, we reconnoitered the Phunki lodge and sparse campsites. Everything was just as dirty, unkempt, and depressing as we remembered. Olga and I decided against making an overnight stop here. We felt spry, and we wanted to reach Namche Bazaar that day. Kanchha and Pemba arrived twenty minutes later, despite having left camp two hours after our departure.

(I still complained about the estimated hiking times listed by the trekking guide we were using. Olga and I always took more time than listed for a destination. From Tengboche to Phunki, the estimated walking time was about two hours, or a third less than the three hours we had just took. I cursed the guidebook as being biased toward trekking speedsters and unfair to middle-aged hikers.)

Our two Sherpas were happy that we wanted to continue on to Namche Bazaar, where they could be with their friends again. Unfortunately, we wouldn't be able to depart Phunki quickly. Just around the bend from the Phunki lodge, the banks of the Dudh Kosi river were spanned by one of the larger bridges in the area. Both riverbanks and the bridge were crowded with people and animals milling about. It was an impossible traffic jam created by the simultaneous arrival of an Indian and a Bulgarian climbing expedition. Nearly an hour passed before our turn came to cross the bridge. It was a shaky crossing, as the bridge swayed under the weight and motion of too many people and animals.

While hurrying up the hill across the river, we were stunned to see an impeccably turned out and coiffed petite woman striding energetically toward us. Her belt, emblazoned with a large initial G, announced that she was part of the universal Gucci groupies who know no boundaries. As we exchanged quips in passing, her New York accent made us feel momentarily as if we were strolling in Central Park. Although my description of her stylish dress might imply that this was a frivolous woman, her vigorous pace, trim physique, and businesslike manner reflected an extremely well-conditioned and capable trekker. In truth, I was somewhat envious that I could not hike at such a fast pace.

The delay at the bridge and the darkening cloud cover would make this hike to Namche Bazaar seem longer than it actually was. Although the stretch of trail ahead was easy and pleasant, the increasing cloudiness and fog made for an uninteresting hike. But when we arrived at the junction where the trails from Khunde and Namche Bazaar joined, we stopped at the dilapidated teashop and enjoyed an entertaining display of salesmanship. Two peddlers in their middle twenties had spread out all kinds of trinkets on maroon oriental rugs laid out at the edge of the trail. One peddler was playing a homemade banjo constructed of light oakwood. As we approached, he began serenading us, while his partner interjected enthusiastic comments about their products. They were two jolly hawkers who tried hard to sell us something. We needed to buy some bracelets as gifts, but their price of one hundred and thirty rupees was considerably more than the usual eighty-rupee cost. While we joked and offered them one hundred rupees, they refused to compromise. It was a stalemate and no sale, but they hoped to meet us and try again at the Saturday morning market at Namche Bazaar. As we left, they began serenading us and laughingly shouted, "One hundred and thirty rupees," and we yelled back, "One hundred!" The shouts, singing, and banjo strumming were strange sounds to hear in this isolated valley. This encounter reminded us that no matter how primitive and "uncivilized" a country, people still share the same feelings of friendship, joy, and competition.

We were now less than an hour from Namche Bazaar, and the swirling mist gave everything an ominous appearance. Unable to see more than a hundred feet in any direction, we were hemmed in by the brown cliffs disappearing into gray fog and sky, and the walking became oppressive in this gloomy ambience. It was in this bleak atmosphere that we saw an eagle soaring below us with its enormous outstretched wings. Kanchha told us that hawks, eagles, and vultures emigrated from Asia and were not uncommon at high altitudes. Farther along, we were excited to see a few iridescent, multicolored pheasants running up a hillside. Kanchha explained that the pheasant was the national bird of Nepal and that Nepal had an amazing diversity of birds. Nearly four hundred species existed in the Kathmandu valley alone.

Grazing animals and an occasional Sherpa indicated that we were on the outskirts of Namche Bazaar, which we could see several hundred feet below us. Unlike the uphill approach on first entering Namche Bazaar, we had a vigorous downhill hike. Slipping and tripping, we had to traverse a steep hill of rocks and sand. Always amazed that these tricky conditions didn't lay us low with a sprain or a bad fall, we arrived weary but intact at Nahtang's house. It was past 6:00 PM, and we had completed a long nine-hour day. Nahtang's family insisted that we sleep in their chapel room instead of pitching a tent in the front yard. The chapel was the room in which our group had eaten dinner on first arriving at Namche Bazaar. Every night, we had dined under the eyes of Buddha statues amid religious trappings.

It was strange to be sleeping beneath the homemade altar, but the chance to be out of the blowing dust dispelled our discomfort. Although the frigid wind blew through the broken windowpanes, sleep came quickly. Awakening indoors was pure luxury. What a comfort it was to have enough room to move about and put on gear without being cramped by a tent. Pemba arrived with two washbowls and a kettle of hot water. For the next few days, I would not have to wash and shave outdoors, shivering in the chilly, dewy mountain air. The luxury continued as Pemba brought a hot breakfast of freshly made chapatis, fried eggs, and potatoes. The kindness that everyone showed us was endless and heartfelt, an experience we will always cherish. Their solicitude often made us feel uncomfortable, but their genuine and easygoing manner made it easy to accept.

That morning, Olga and I continued the ritual we had begun in Tengboche of contemplating Everest. After breakfast, we trudged and puffed up the hill that led to the national park plateau where we first saw Everest nine days previously. It was a rare morning—the skies above Everest and the surrounding peaks were quite cloudless. Even the usual plume of cloud around Everest's summit was absent. Without the billowing clouds, the towering summits of snow stood out brilliantly against the deep blue sky. This sparkling Friday morning of March 17 was the day that our group was climbing Kala Pattar. Olga and I hoped that this perfect weather was an omen of success, and I said a silent prayer that all would go well. By now, past 10:00 AM, they would have been on their arduous climb for over six hours; they should be on Kala Pattar by noon, staring at the Khumbu Icefall and Everest's southwest face. Our thoughts were with them as we accompanied them vicariously while viewing Everest from this lonely plateau. Olga decided to return to Namche Bazaar to rest and shower, while I remained, taking photos of the vast panorama. Olga was still plagued with the hacking cough, but she felt in good shape.

On this tiny plateau above Namche Bazaar, I was once again, as at Tengboche, the lonely spectator. I couldn't understand why there were so few visitors to this marvelous viewing site, particularly since Namche Bazaar was the first major stopover for climbers and trekkers and offered the first view of Everest. It seemed odd to be here alone for hours while scores of hikers walked around Namche Bazaar below. Unlike other countries that attract tourists, Nepal did not announce its splendors with signs along the trails. Even the two major trekking guides that described the hiking routes and villages in detail did not describe this magnificent site. It seemed that trekkers were too often more preoccupied with attaining their goal than with the beauty in their midst. My reactions may be unfair because of my obsession with mountain views, but I still felt that the lack of visitors was a sad commentary on the curiosity of the trekkers who were making Namche Bazaar a stopover.

These thoughts made me wonder when my fascination with mountains began, and I remembered that my first introduction to mountains happened when I was eleven years old. That summer, my mother took me to Germany to visit our relatives and see the country of my birth. While in southern Germany in Berchtesgaden, I saw my first mountains, the Bavarian Alps. They were the most magnificent and awesome sight I had ever seen. I can recall quite vividly the excitement they aroused in me, especially the snow-capped Watzmann, which was my favorite. Looking at them was a constant thrill, and I vowed that someday, this spellbinding mountain beauty would be a part of my life. From that moment on, I became an armchair mountaineer, and I began reading every mountain climbing book I could find, especially those about Everest. It took half a lifetime to make that boyhood vow come true. At the age of forty, I built a home in the Green Mountains of Vermont and learned to ski. Eighteen years later, at the age of fifty-eight, nearly a full lifetime for many, I realized the ultimate dream of seeing Everest. As Goethe observed, the desires of youth become abundantly fulfilled in old age. Throughout my life, the wonder and thrill that the beauty of mountains still arouse in me remain as intense as they were for that eleven-year-old boy.

At noon, I was surprised to see that the sky still remained clear and free of the billowing clouds that customarily blanket the summit ranges. This meant that our trekking group was still enjoying excellent weather conditions. They should be on top of Kala Pattar at that moment, I thought. While preoccupied with thoughts of the group's progress, I was startled by the sight of a young couple that suddenly appeared. In halting English, they asked if they could share the park bench. Dressed in matching jeans and sport shirts, they had the unisex look typical of so many young people. Despite their nondescript appearance and self-effacing manner, they were rugged individualists. Both were physicians from the Netherlands who were planning to see Asia and Europe on a shoestring. Leaving their infant in the care of parents, they wanted this adventure before settling down to parenthood and a career. Nepal and the Himalayas were first on their itinerary, since they had become enchanted with the country while on a trek many years ago. I was amused to hear their complaints of how things had changed since their visit in the midseventies. They couldn't believe how crowded and built up Namche Bazaar had become, and how much more expensive everything was. Imagine, nearly seventy-five cents a night now for a room in the local lodge that once charged ten cents!

We spent the remaining afternoon in the restaurant of the Khumbu lodge, which was owned by a famous Sherpa climber. Located on the third and top floor, the restaurant was a forty-foot-square room with walls of wood; from its windows, we could see the village below and the massive Kwangde mountain range that loomed above Namche Bazaar. With its sparse wooden furnishings of homemade tables and built-in benches, the lodge was Namche Bazaar's version of a tourist hotel.

We ordered hot lemonade and egg rolls, and we spent the next few hours reading paperback potboilers and absorbing the atmosphere. Mountain posters and photographs of famous climbers decorated the wood-paneled walls. A small bar served all kinds of liquor, obviously tailored to the Western tourists' tastes and pocketbooks, as the average price was five dollars a drink. As much as we wanted to have some Jack Daniels bourbon, the harmful effect of alcohol on our rundown condition at this altitude made us resist the temptation. Although there was never more than a handful customers sitting around, people kept coming and going. They were a quiet and introspective bunch of trekkers and climbers of all nationalities who were dressed plainly and looked pale and weary. There was little of the conversation or joking typical of any restaurant gathering. Most read, looked at the view, or wrote in diaries. Keeping a journal was a common pastime among hikers, but we found writing too mentally fatiguing.

Later at dinner, we recalled how tasty the egg rolls had been at the Khumbu lodge, and we wondered why our food was consistently poor. It was bad enough that our meals consisted of the same food day after day, but the utter lack of flavor and taste, except for the inevitable touch of curry powder, was appalling. The trekking guides described the Sherpas as being the poorest cooks in the world, but this advance notice had not prepared us for the unpalatable, mushy, and glutinous meals. Only omelets and soup (which became more watery as the soup mix ran out) were satisfying. Roast potatoes were tasty when not overcooked and burnt. Of course, tea was the most satisfying nourishment by far. What made everything also taste unsavory was the kerosene flavor that permeated both food and liquids. After ten days of eating this fare, we still couldn't get used to that repulsive flavor. The best that could be said for the meals was that they were monotonous and well intentioned, since the Sherpas worked hard to please. By now, Olga and I had lost our desire to eat. The high altitude and our habitual state of fatigue also contributed to the loss of appetite. Even the snacks of cheese, nuts, raisins, and chocolate in our duffel bags remained untouched. It amazed us how little appetite we had for anything. Trying to be positive, we joked that our lack of appetite helped us lose weight. Based on how my clothes fit, I estimated having lost at least ten pounds since the trek began.

While we were finishing dinner around 7:00 PM, Kanchha burst into the room to tell me that it was a clear, moonlit night. When we arrived in Namche Bazaar, I had asked Kanchha to let me know when the moon was visible. During the trek, I was always too drugged with fatigue to stay awake and view the unearthly moonlit, starry sky. Hurriedly, I dressed warmly, as temperatures would soon be freezing; I wasn't looking forward to that steep climb to the park plateau, but my excitement fought the inertia that tends to immobilize me by evening. I ran up the hill, impatient to see the moon over the Himalayas.

Halfway up, a heavy mist began to blanket everything, and the clear night turned cloudy. Still, I continued to the top, hoping that the fog would lift. It was not to be, as the mist turned into a thickening fog that made it difficult to see beyond an arm's length. Besides the poor visibility, the night air had become quite warm and humid. I felt clammy, and I was perspiring profusely. To continue would be foolish, as I was beginning to lose my bearings, I could tell the direction only by whether I was going up or down, and the scattered lights of the village hundreds of feet below were invisible. Disappointed and annoyed with myself, I was getting anxious about my orientation in this gloomy dense fog.

Suddenly I heard voices hailing me. On the ledge, barely visible above me, I could make out the figures of two Sherpas. Their ghostly appearance in this swirling mist and darkness made me think of eerie spirits foretelling misfortune. This was no time to have an imagination; it was too spooky and scary a moment. As the figures approached, I saw that they were unkempt and very drunk. Puzzled by my appearance, they asked, "Where you goin', Boss?" They laughed when I said I wanted to see Everest by moonlight. "No Everest, no Everest tonight." Then they inquired, "Boss alone. You alone?" Frightened now, I recalled Jim's warning of peasant thieves who look to rob solitary trekkers. With bravado, I explained that my friends were behind me. Immediately losing interest in me, they left, singing and joking drunkenly in the foggy night. Perhaps I had misinterpreted their intentions, but the eerie atmosphere and my disappointment made me feel threatened. No wonder I felt relief at having survived a potential mugging.

Now I had to find my way back down a trail that was hard to see in this fog and pitch-black night. At one deep, sandy section, the trail appeared silvery and elusive. It seemed as if I were walking on a weird moonscape. As long as I walked downhill, I thought I would be all right. When I began stumbling among sections of scrub brush, I knew that I had wandered off the trail, but I remembered that brush was more plentiful on the base of the hill near the village. Sure enough, I could make out the lights of Namche Bazaar. Ironically, there was no fog in Namche Bazaar, and I found my way easily to Nahtang's house. As I changed my sopping wet clothes and cooled off, I described my experience to Olga. We laughed about the encounter with the drunken Sherpas, but in my heart, I felt relieved at having evaded a mugging.

Saturday morning at Namche brought the weekly farmers' market. Trades persons of all kinds, farmers, and craftsmen displayed their products on the tiered slopes and the two roads on the village's southern approach. The milling crowd numbered several hundred, much more than Namche Bazaar's population, and we had to push forcibly to get through. Natives arrived from the neighboring villages to buy and sell every conceivable type of consumer goods. There were groceries, meats, fruits, toilet articles, housewares, candies, fabrics, clothing, woven baskets, and all kinds of crafts. Large sacks with USA boldly imprinted on them momentarily caught our attention. They were bags of flour and grain with the printed message that they were donated by the

USA and not for sale. Regrettably, someone is always being victimized, whether in the civilized world or in primitive lands. As chance would have it, we came upon the two banjo-strumming troubadour peddlers we had met two days ago outside of Namche Bazaar. The bargaining for the bracelets continued where it had left off.

Those three days in Namche Bazaar restored our energies and made us eager to hike to the defunct, Japanese-built Everest View Hotel, a couple of hours northwest of Namche Bazaar. Kanchha encouraged Olga to go, jokingly reminding her that the hotel was equipped with Western-style toilets. We left early Monday morning, feeling excited about hiking again after a week's rest. Starting out is always difficult in high altitudes, but the beginning steep climb with a precipitous foot-wide trail was hard going. Much to our chagrin, a stream of youngsters, cavorting playfully, kept passing us on their way to school in Khunde, a good hour's hike. Getting to the hilltop took an hour, as we kept stopping to catch our breath. The hilltop opened onto a weird panorama of brown and black granite. Devoid of snow, the countryside was bleak and looked like a lunar landscape. This enormous, barren plateau fell away to the valley below, while the contrasting snowy, twenty-thousand-foot Kwangde range hovered above.

The route ahead revealed the outline of a low building. Situated on a small rise, the hotel was nestled among evergreen trees and junipers. A wide staircase of about seventy-five stone steps led to the entrance. Although the carved wood doors were open, the hotel was deserted, and it reeked of dankness. Grimy wood paneling, a shabby dark gold carpet, and cavernous halls heightened the air of desolation. But from the outside deck, the depressing atmosphere vanished, and a thrilling vista opened before us.

Perched on an oval plot of land whose sides dropped precipitously to the valley below, the hotel faced Everest. It seemed as if we were on a floating island enveloped by towering, snow-capped mountains. Standing on the deck of the hotel, we could better see its architectural design. Built like an oversized ranch house, the hotel was long and narrow, about three hundred by fifty feet, and constructed of stone with a flat tile roof. The elongated building was set on a foundation of rock and surrounded by prisonlike stone walls. Monotonous but impressive, the stone facade was broken up by large floor-to-ceiling picture windows in each room, which looked out to the spectacular scenery. Squatting inconspicuously in the landscape, the hotel appeared to have been dropped intact onto this location, blending with its surroundings.

Soon after we arrived, the skies became overcast, and a wide ribbon of cloud blanketed the summits of Everest, Lhotse, and Nuptse. From this vantage point, most of Ama Dablam, which resembled the Matterhorn, could be seen. With gray and white clouds swirling around its majestic peak, the effect was breathtaking. This site could not have been more perfect for viewing the greatest range of mountains in the world.

Unfortunately, the Everest View Hotel went out of business because of a serious miscalculation. Everyone associated with this venture simply forgot the human element. Apparently, no one considered how the hotel's twelve-thousand-foot elevation would affect the incoming tourists. Visitors were flown from Japan, landed on a nearby airstrip, and were transported to the hotel by yaks in a trip that took over an hour. On arrival, most were exhausted and ill from altitude sickness that lasted for days. Coming directly from sea level to this high altitude without a period of acclimation can be physically dangerous. It was no wonder that people stopped visiting this unique setting. Gossip has it that the Japanese builders plan to reopen the hotel and cater to trekkers. Although hikers would be acclimated to the hotel's altitude by the time they arrived, I doubt they would acclimate to its deluxe costs. Trekkers are a frugal bunch, and it is doubtful that a luxury hotel could compete with the cost of sleeping in a tent.

Kanchha led us back to Namche Bazaar on a different trail from this morning's, a more westerly swing so that we'd see other mountain views. It was on this route that I became bewitched by Thamserku, a twenty-one-thousand-foot mountain whose summit consisted of twin snow-covered spires that barely joined together. These delicate-looking twin spires had always been in view to the east of us, but from this vantage point, the entire formation of Thamserku could be seen. I took countless photographs as the cloud formations floating around Thamserku created stunning compositions. With its classic triangular shape rising to snowy twin peaks and jagged ridges extending from either side, Thamserku was the most beautiful mountain I had ever seen.

Returning to Namche Bazaar from the west, we had to negotiate a steep descent of curving paths where the footing was tricky, as stones and dirt occasionally gave way under us. It was puzzling why some attempt hadn't been made to overcome this hazardous approach, in view of the improved economy and the growing number of trekkers. On reflection, it was naive and pointless to pose such a question, which reflects the values of our progress-ridden culture. For the Sherpas, these trails worked and sufficed, and the summer monsoon and winter snowstorms would probably destroy any constructed path on this precipitous incline. Yet the values of the Western world were strikingly apparent as we arrived at Nahtang's house and witnessed his baby girl playing with a cassette player blaring forth rock music.

As we relaxed at the Khumbu lodge, drinking *chang*, Olga and I were struck by the realization that the trek would soon be over. Nahtang estimated that our fellow trekkers would arrive by noon on Tuesday, March 21, our last full day at Namche Bazaar. Olga and I decided on a final look at the magnificent mountains, which had become a part of our daily existence. After a final viewing from the park plateau, we took the main trail heading north to the Everest region. A half-hour's walk brought us to a sharp bend in the trail that afforded a closer and more dramatic view. We ambled off the trail to a small ledge, whose sides fell away into space, and sat transfixed, looking at the mountains for the last time.

No matter how many times I gazed at Everest, flanked by Nuptse and Lhotse, with Ama Dablam, Kantega, and Thamserku curving away in a southeasterly direction, the sight always thrilled me. The rush of excitement I sensed at those times always brought to mind Wordsworth's words: "My heart leaps up when I behold a rainbow/In the sky." It was soon time to leave this idyllic spot and these shining summits. As we slowly walked away, I kept looking back for a last lingering view. Despite our sadness that this stunning panorama would disappear once we started descending to the village, I felt a surge of fulfillment and joy over our accomplishment. We had experienced what we had always dreamed of, and nothing could take that away from us.

As we hurried down the hill, we could see many familiar figures and piles of gear in front of Nahtang's house. The group had returned, and we were excited to see them and hear of their experience. Their appearance shocked us. Everyone looked very pale, haggard, and emaciated. It was a curious reunion, as they spoke little beyond a perfunctory greeting. They were fatigued and still feeling the effects of the arduous climb to Kala Pattar. Olga and I felt self-conscious and somewhat guilty about being suntanned, rested, and healthy. I remembered Donna joking that we looked as if we had been on vacation while they went to work.

Donna and Jim joined us for a quick snack at the Khumbu lodge before our imminent departure from Namche Bazaar. Over spring rolls and tea, they confirmed what the sirdars had reported last evening. The hike to Kala Pattar was the toughest day of the trek, especially the hours before dawn, walking in pitch darkness, and at noon, climbing the steep incline of crumbling rocks to the top of the black hill. They had all pushed themselves to the limit, and they were groggy with exhaustion in those last hours. At the summit, they were rewarded by unusually clear, cloudless skies and warm weather. They had breathtaking views of Everest and the lower icefall. In their typically candid manner, Donna and Jim stressed that we never would have made Kala Pattar and the effort probably would have killed us. They reassured us that our decision to stay at Tengboche was a wise one. My doubts about remaining at Tengboche completely vanished when I heard their comments and saw the physical condition of the group. Most importantly, though, no one became seriously ill, and everyone felt proud that they had achieved their goal.

11

Kathmandu Belly

Our seven-day "vacation" was now over, and we would soon be back on the trail again with our fellow trekkers. We left at around 2:00 PM, headed for a lodge that was hours away, run by a former Buddhist monk. It felt good being back with the group and on the march again, but the emotion was mixed with sadness over saying farewell to those incredibly beautiful mountains and valleys.

The trail back from Namche Bazaar continuously twisted and descended to the river valley floor. The greening foliage, the riverbed far below, and the steeply rising, tree-lined cliffs seemed more breathtaking than ever as the sun, darting in and out of the clouds, created dramatic shadings of light over the panorama spreading around and below us. The snow-capped mountains had receded, and forested cliffs and valleys now predominated. About an hour out of Namche Bazaar, we came to a wide bend in the trail, from which one could see, if conditions were clear, the summit of Everest in the far distance. This spot afforded the first view of Everest from the main trail, but on our way up two weeks before, the heavy cloud cover had obscured the view. Happily, the skies were fairly clear now, and we could see the clouds streaking over Everest's summit, which looked like a miniature peak from here. It appeared to soar majestically in the heavens and seemed to be on view so that I could say my final farewell.

Both Olga and I maintained a good pace and kept up with most of the others, but we were still the last ones to reach the lodge where we would have dinner and stay overnight. When I arrived, everyone was sitting around two circular wooden tables, sipping small tin cups of homemade peach wine. Jim thought this next-to-last day on the trail deserved an evening cocktail. Olga arrived while I was waiting for my drink, which I gave her, the consequence of which was to lead to serious personal complications tomorrow. I was told that that was the last of the peach wine, until the lodge owner remembered that he had a new batch still aging. Donna, who initially decided against having a drink, changed her mind, and we both had some newly made peach wine. The delicious wine seemed to relax everyone, and the group was now joking and chatting. Their earlier low spirits and quietness had lifted. Kirt proudly informed me that he had gotten the rock mementos from Kala Pattar that I had requested. Jim announced that as a special dinner treat tonight, we would have a tinned baked ham, which had been saved for the end of our journey.

Before eating, however, we had to decide whether to sleep in our tent or indoors in the lodge. Only Caryl and Jack decided on the tent, and the rest of us raced indoors to pick out the best accommodations. The small rooms were quickly taken, and Olga and I settled for two lower bunk beds, side by side in a dormitory-type room. The lodge resembled an oversized Cape Cod house with an interior that reeked of mustiness. The dormitory consisted of two rows of five bunk beds facing each other. There was only one window, which provided light and ventilation. A small dining hall, a kitchen area, and a back hallway with several single bedrooms completed the building's layout. Surrounding the lodge were small vegetable and fruit fields, which provided the lodge with most of its food.

A Japanese man, formerly a Buddhist monk, had built the lodge as a stopover for trekkers and climbers. He was a shy and self-effacing man but a bundle of energy and determination to succeed. Next to the trail, a large sign made of logs painted yellow with black lettering advertised: LODGE—FOODS—HOT SHOWER—BATH. It was no competition for the garish Holiday Inn signs, but it was not bad for the primitive hill country of Nepal. On the outside front wall, there were also some attractive, white-painted, vertical signs with Buddhist-inspired moralistic teachings and exhortations on how to be virtuous and lead a good life. In their simplistic but pompous-sounding English translation, their "do" and "don't" commandments were strangely affecting. Regardless of where one finds oneself on the face of the Earth, people need a moral philosophy, a standard of behavior by which to live. Even so-called uncivilized or primitive societies reveal this universal striving for an ethical code of conduct. Often, we patronize the people of another culture by labeling them uncivilized because of their technological backwardness, without realizing that their moral standards are little different from ours. These uneducated Sherpas, in this primitive region of Nepal, were the kindest, most generous, most honest people I have ever encountered.

We were a happy and talkative bunch that evening at dinner. The wine and the realization that we had achieved our goals contributed to the high spirits. Unfortunately, the meal didn't rise to the occasion. It was the usual thin soup and mushy rice and vegetables, and the tinned ham tasted metallic and rubbery. The highlight of dinner was when we presented the Sherpa kitchen crew with everyone's uneaten snacks. It was a cornucopia of candy and grocery items: chocolate bars, chewing gum, nuts, granola bars, cheese, crackers, peanut butter, jams, tins of fish, and similar staples. After dinner, as was his custom, Jim outlined the plans for the next day. Our final trekking day would be a relatively easy hike to Lukla, with a luncheon stop midway in the field. We would arrive at around 3:00 PM, sleep overnight in Lukla, and the following morning catch the 7:00 AM flight back to Kathmandu. Another special dinner was planned, but this time prepared by the Lukla Lodge chef who had cooked that memorable fried rice and vegetable luncheon on our arrival. After dinner, the Sherpas would entertain us with their native dances and songs.

Excited by thoughts of tomorrow, we prepared for bed. In the pitch-dark dormitory, we laid out our gear, toilet articles, and clothes by flashlight. It was a fitful sleep, periodically disturbed by the arrival of other guests. During the night, we heard weird moaning and saw a few of the lodgers going through odd motions. Puzzled by this behavior, which made us wary, we finally figured out what was happening as daylight broke. Some of the native lodgers had engaged in their nightly prayer ritual, chanting and gesticulating.

Despite the restless night, the morning found us full of anticipation and energy. I felt strong, and I was grateful that I hadn't gotten sick or suffered more than my usual state of exhaustion. I couldn't believe that in the past eighteen days, I was lucky enough to have avoided the physical discomforts that some of the others had experienced: nausea, stomach upset, headache, a sore throat, coughing, diarrhea, or aching feet. Perhaps this was Fate's way of compensating me for my disappointment about not reaching Kala Pattar, but secretly I viewed being able to remain healthy as an accomplishment. (The only mishap of the trek occurred after leaving Namche Bazaar, when Pemba, in a mildly befuddled state from too much *chang*, lost his concentration on the steep trail, tripped, and fell on a sharp rock that gashed his hand. The cut was fairly deep and was stitched up by John, our English physician.) Over breakfast, I bragged to Jim about having been free of physical problems during the trek. Oh, how our egos seek approval and praise, and how I would soon pay for this flash of pride!

As always, after breakfast, Olga and I started out before everyone so that we wouldn't be too far behind later in the day. That last morning greeted us with the usual sparkling sun and intense blue, clear, luminous sky. Olga felt strong again, and she had recovered from the hacking cough. We set a rapid, energetic pace, as if to prove that we could finish with a final burst of speed. The brilliant weather and the emergence of spring flowers—primroses, crocuses, roses—peeping out on the greening, sloping countryside reinforced our vigor and high spirits. We felt as alive as nature springing to new life around us.

Everything added to our animation in those morning hours, especially the added thrill of meeting the last members of the Indian Everest expedition, whose main group we had met twelve days ago. This small group consisted of six female Indian climbers, fashionably dressed in lavender expedition outfits. With their beautiful features and deep-set, twinkling eyes, they looked like attractive next-door teenagers. In a self-effacing manner, they told us of their hope to be among the first women climbers to scale Everest's summit. It was hard to believe that these petite, shy, and vivacious women, who could pass for Hollywood starlets, would soon be pitting their skills against Everest's brutal ridges. Their courage and determination to risk their lives brought tears to my eyes as we waved good-bye and wished them Godspeed. (I later learned that two of them reached Everest's summit.)

Although it had been a steep descent from Namche Bazaar, with tortuous footing that made our knees ache, the route was now descending gradually. No longer were we faced with the sudden drops to the riverbed and then the climb upward. For most of the morning, everyone had been walking close together and conversing cheerfully. The air of camaraderie added to the pleasant hike, and we felt great to be walking with the others, rather than by ourselves. The countryside was looking less and less awesome as the precipitous cliffs and narrow valleys gave way to small farms, which villagers were now planting. The tough hikes and rugged Khumbu terrain were behind us, and after a leisurely lunch and afternoon trek, we would be at Lukla, the end of a thrilling journey.

For the first time during the trek, lunch was prepared and served in the field. In a small meadow off the trail, the kitchen crew were attending to the fire, frying eggs, and stirring large pots of soup. It was an inviting scene: colorful rugs had been spread out for us to sit on, and the Sherpas were in a gay mood, as they would soon be back with their families after the trek ended today. While eating, I noticed that the dreary and somber countryside of over two weeks ago was coming alive with new grass, budding rhododendrons, and, nearby on a grassy knoll, a cherry tree ablaze with delicate pink blossoms. Unfortunately, as lunch ended, the vitality I had felt all morning left me, and I began to feel mildly queasy. While putting on my pack, I felt a stomach cramp and mild nausea. Hoping to prevent a stomach upset, I chewed a Pepto-Bismol tablet.

That afternoon hike was pure horror, an experience of unrelieved pain and fear that I have never forgotten. After ten minutes of walking, the nausea and stomach cramps worsened. From that moment on, the physical distress became so bad that I couldn't walk more than five or six steps before doubling over with pain and stopping for several minutes before starting again. My frustration mounted when John and Nas passed by, offering sympathy but saying that there was nothing they could do for me. I still remember John, with his British accent and low-key manner, telling me, "Just push on, old boy, push on."

How I cursed the heavens and my helplessness! My stomach felt bloated and ready to explode, but I could neither vomit, pass wind, nor defecate to relieve the debilitating discomfort. I resigned myself to the tortuous cycle, which lasted for about two hours. Walking slowly, I counted off five seconds until the next stomach spasm of pain occurred and stopped me in my tracks. It was as if I were being punched in the stomach every five seconds by some terrible force. At those moments, I couldn't move, and I had to stop for a few minutes until the pain subsided. Nothing would help, and I just had to forge ahead.

There were moments when I panicked. I feared that the intense stomach pain and nausea indicated a serious illness. But I knew that this was a panic reaction, since I had a companion in my suffering. At the very moment when I felt sick, Donna came down with stomach cramps and diarrhea. While I had to stop frequently, doubled over in pain, she was forced to stop as frequently with repeated attacks of diarrhea. At least, I thought, she could get some momentary relief, while I couldn't. In the midst of our mutual agony, Donna's distress was signaled by an amusing occurrence. Strips of pink toilet tissue floating in the wind and settling on the brush announced her bouts of diarrhea. Seeing Donna in similar distress, I realized that our symptoms probably had been caused by that new batch of peach wine that only she and I had drunk the previous night.

Olga's emotional distress over my plight may have been as bad as my discomfort. She was frantic with worry, and she and Kanchha kept waiting for me to catch up to them. Her concern and questions were only additional pressures. I yelled at her to stop bothering me, to go on ahead, as I would be all right if left by myself. I wanted to be left alone in my misery and did not want to deal with anyone's solicitude and worry. I wasn't very easy to be around.

What kept me going was a ritual of counting to myself, accepting the inevitability of another spasm, and believing that the symptoms wouldn't last forever. Still, most of the time, I was in a daze from the pain and had to force myself to keep walking. After two hours of watching me struggle to walk, Olga suggested that I try a Tylenol with codeine. Despite our trekking physicians' advice against taking any medication, I was desperate for relief. I took the medication and soon experienced some relief as the cramps became less frequent and intense. Instead of having to stop after every five or six steps, I was able to count from twenty-one up to ninety before another spasm struck. And as the afternoon wore on, the pain lessened.

Luckily, the trail was flat and without any steep ascents; the slightest rise in the path required a physical effort that would quickly trigger a cramp. Just before our destination, however, the pain returned in full force when we had to climb a hill to reach the valley where Lukla nestled. Olga and Kanchha had already disappeared from view, but they informed Nahwang about my plight. With his wife, Chindi, Nahwang came back to accompany me step by step during that last hour. Although I felt self-conscious, their quiet presence soothed and encouraged me to keep going.

I arrived in Lukla at twilight, as the sun's rays between the mountains suffused the village with a golden rosy glow. What a beautiful sight and a thrilling moment for me! I had made it to Lukla. I had finished the trek! It was 6:00 PM, and that agonizing hike had taken five hours. Olga had arrived an hour before me, and the group had been settled in since 3:00 PM. I had never been more exhausted or happier to see Olga, and I just wanted to lie down and collapse. Excitedly, she told me of her good luck in getting one of the few single rooms in the Lukla Hotel, which even had a small bathroom with a sit-down toilet. Nas came by immediately to examine me, and he announced that whatever I had did not reveal itself to his surgeon's hands as he palpated my stomach, which was not distended. He advised me to attend the dinner, but to eat only a little rice and bread. Much encouraged, I felt that my malady would soon run its course. But a half-hour later, when I got up from bed and put on a clean shirt, another wave of stomach spasms struck. Nevertheless, I was determined to attend our last dinner, and I left for the dining room in a shaky condition as the cramps were subsiding.

Everyone, including our sirdars and Ved, sat around a long, low table, drinking and eating. Olga had a scotch, which I yearned for but didn't dare touch. The meal was an appealing array of vegetables, rice, noodles, and beef dishes. Surprisingly, I had a mild appetite, but I ate only some plain rice and bread, as Nas had suggested, although I had qualms about eating anything. Before dinner, I had drunk some Coca-Cola and Pepto-Bismol, which tended to soothe my stomach.

After the meal, Jim asked that each of us briefly tell the group about our most memorable experience during the trek. I don't recall the exact remarks, but everyone stressed the spectacular mountain views, the kindness and industriousness of the Sherpa people, the camaraderie of our group, and the emotional impact of seeing Everest, which, for many of us, was a dream fulfilled. The words and sentiments clearly revealed that this land of transcendent nature and beautiful people had stirred all of us profoundly. Among these great peaks, we sensed the mystery and grandeur of nature. The powerful feelings aroused by the breathtaking Himalayas called to mind Thoreau's stirring reactions to climbing Mt. Katahdin in Maine:

> I looked with awe at the ground I trod on, to see what the Powers had made there, the form and fashion and material of their work.... It was the fresh and natural surface of the planet Earth, as it was made forever and ever—to be the dwelling of man ...

To express our gratitude to the Sherpa men and women who composed the kitchen crew, porters, and guides, Jim presented them with the customary gratuities usually given at the end of a trek. The group collected about three hundred dollars, which turned out to be fifteen dollars for every Sherpa, or the equivalent of two weeks' salary. Additionally, many donated hiking clothes, gear, and footwear to the Sherpas. No one was more generous than Nas, who, with Kirt, gave all his hiking clothes and footwear, as well as a set of surgical instruments and a supply of medication for distribution to the few infirmaries in the Khumbu region. The clothes we gave were for Kanchha, who had earned a special place in our hearts for his personal devotion to us. Kanchha, more than anyone, was responsible for helping us persevere and accomplish what we had.

Earlier, Jim had asked the group to consider donating money to help pay for medication that Nahtang needed to cure his ulcer. Everyone gladly contributed to Nahtang, who beamed with thanks and pride over the gift. It was obvious that our high regard and appreciation, which the gift symbolized, was more important to this shy sirdar than the money.

The evening was memorable for the good fellowship and sense of accomplishment that pervaded the atmosphere. Despite the congeniality, Jim had to plead with the Sherpas to demonstrate their native dances. As he led in a group of five Sherpa couples, they giggled with embarrassment. Reluctantly, they began to dance, if one could describe their stomping and prancing as dancing. As they relaxed, however, their halting steps turned into vigorous gypsylike rhythms. I am sure that this clumsy demonstration was not representative of their dancing and singing. Each year, the Sherpas hold many religious festivals and celebrations in which dance takes a central role. But these times are for themselves and not for strangers, to whom they relate shyly and uncertainly.

It had been a long, tortuous day for me. After dinner, Olga and I turned in and prepared for the early getaway tomorrow. Jim wanted everyone packed by 6:00 AM and ready for an early takeoff. The plane would be arriving from Kathmandu in time to take off by 7:00 AM. Getting a seat on the plane would be the final hurdle. As Jim had cautioned, the weather might be unfavorable and prevent a flight from arriving or departing. But the biggest worry would be getting on a flight. In addition to our group, there were dozens of other trekkers waiting for a plane that made only two flights a day.

Being able to remain at the dinner for two hours and eat some food without pain or any stomach distress was like a minor miracle. I learned that my acute stomach illness was called "Kathmandu Belly." It lasts no longer than twenty-four hours, and the best treatment for the excruciating and debilitating pain is bed rest. Unfortunately, my brief recovery wasn't to last much longer. When I began packing our duffel bags, I was suddenly struck by the worst stomach spasms of the day. The slightest movement caused such painful cramps that I stood in one spot, immobilized and terrified of making the slightest motion. I cursed Nas and myself for eating the rice and bread, as I was certain that this small amount of food had made the pains return. It seemed an eternity—perhaps fifteen minutes—before I could move and attempt to lie down. Olga finished packing as I battled my stomach demons. They finally left, and, groggy from the bout, and with the help of a Tylenol, I slipped into a fairly sound sleep.

12

A Dream Fulfilled

Fearful of the condition I'd be in on awakening, I was overjoyed to find myself free from pain and discomfort. The anticipation that we would soon be flying back to Kathmandu overshadowed my weakened physical condition. Along with crowds of natives and trekkers at the airstrip, our group anxiously waited and watched for the plane to arrive. An undercurrent of excitement gripped everyone; natives and trekkers lined the dirt airstrip, jostling each other, running back and forth to take pictures, and hurrying about with luggage.

Surrounded by mountains looming overhead, the village of Lukla was still in early morning darkness and glistening with dew. The towering peaks were backlit by the bright morning sun, whose rays soon enveloped Lukla in their warming glow. Like everyone, I walked back and forth, restless, watching anxiously for the aircraft. The skies overhead were cloudless, and landing conditions were perfect, for now. Suddenly, the crowd buzzed excitedly as it spotted the small plane in the distance. What a sight it was to see this tiny plane, flying between the mountains, coming closer and closer! Dwarfed by the peaks and valleys, the plane looked fragile and vulnerable. As it landed, bouncing up the sloping, rocky dirt runway, the plane shook and rattled as if it would shatter, then came to a stop in a cloud of dust. This white and blue aluminum machine was no fragile thing, but a heroic bird that braved these dangerous mountains day in and day out.

Just before the airplane arrived, Jim asked us to assemble at a wooden gate about twenty yards from where the plane would stop. He stressed that we must remain close together and, on his signal, quickly follow him to embark. In my excitement, I worried that the other waiting trekkers, clamoring for a seat, would come first and prevent our departure. But I had absolute faith in Jim, who quickly herded us through the gate and onto the plane.

As we settled into our seats, the tension lifted, and we broke into joyous shouting and whistling. Before we realized what was happening, the plane was taxiing down the runway, steadily building speed, and with a roar, it lifted off the edge of the airstrip, which fell away several thousand feet to the valley floor. Lukla rapidly became a speck beneath us as we flew into the luminous sky toward Kathmandu.

Sixteen days ago, we had stepped off this same aircraft in Lukla to begin the trek. In that short space of time, I had experienced nature in all its mystery, beauty, and magnificence. I offered a silent prayer of thanks for my good fortune in having fulfilled a lifelong dream—and remaining healthy while doing so. The beautiful Sherpa people, the awesome, rugged countryside, the spectacular, snow-capped mountain ranges, and, most of all, the great summit of Everest have all become a part of me. The memories of those sixteen days will live with me forever. To this day, they seem as alive and vivid as if they had just happened. They have enriched my being and given me renewed belief in the beauty of our Earth, and in the incredible capacity of people to adapt and survive.

As the plane soared higher, the vast Himalayan mountain ranges, stretching across the distant, wide horizon, came into view. Looking out of the aircraft's window, I held back the tears as I gazed for the last time at the breathtaking jagged peaks shining in the morning sun—and at Everest soaring above them, with its plume of cloud streaming from its majestic summit.

Afterword

Since this trek was made in 1984, there have been many changes that have brought a mixed blessing to climbers and the Nepalese.

Most striking is the number of climbing expeditions and successful summit ascents, which have increased at a dizzying rate. Since Hillary and Norgay's first ascent in 1953, over twenty-two hundred summits have been achieved.

The annual record was made in the spring of 2007, when 514 climbers reached the top of Everest. But Everest remains a treacherous and dangerous mountain: five to ten climbers die annually on its slopes, and 205 climbing deaths have occurred since the pioneer climbers George Mallory and Andrew Levine disappeared on the Northeast Ridge in 1924. A garish statistic is that an estimated 120 corpses lie frozen under snow and rock terrain. Aside from bad mountaineering decisions and falls, the major cause of death is avalanches.

The explosion of climbers has been facilitated by the numerous guided climbing expeditions that offer potential summiteers the thrill of climbing Everest for fees ranging from $60,000 to $100,000 per person. These commercial expeditions, over the years, set in place fixed guide ropes on the slopes of Everest, so that accidents are minimized as long as one uses these ropes. Incredible as it seems, during the peak spring season, there can be long waiting lines of climbers waiting impatiently, sometimes for hours, to reach the summit.

A disturbing result of the enormous influx of mountaineers is the growing amount of trash left on the mountain. About fifty tons of trash has been left by climbers who discard tents, oxygen bottles, pots, stoves, and all kinds of climbing gear. In June 2007, the *New York Times* called the world's highest mountain "the world's highest garbage dump." Even during our trek in 1984, we saw the forerunner of the problem, as soda cans and discarded gear began littering the trails. Teams from Japan and Nepal have removed nearly twenty thousand pounds of garbage since 2000.

In another news item, the Chinese have announced plans to build a sixty-seven-mile paved highway from the Tibetan side to the seventeen-thousand-foot base camp of Mt Everest. Once again, our civilized world erodes the pristine beauty of nature.

Despite the increase of tourists and climbers in Nepal and booming globalization, the Nepalese sadly remain one of the most poor and impoverished people on the globe. Their per capita annual income of $210.66 per person remains at about the same level as it was twenty years ago, when our trek took place.

Finally, a personal note. This trek that helped me fulfill my dream of Everest was the experience of a lifetime and remains a memorable and vivid presence to me.

As this book was going to press, Sir Edmund Hillary died on January 10, 2008 in Auckland, New Zealand. At the end of his lecture tours, he would remark "I am a lucky man. I have had a dream come true and that is not a thing that happens often to men".

Namaste!

Selected Bibliography

Armington, Stan. *Trekking in the Nepal Himalaya*. Oakland, California: Lonely Planet, 1994.

Bonington, Chris. *Everest the Hard Way*. New York: Random House, 1980.

Hillary, Edmund. *High in the Thin Cold Air*. New York: Doubleday, 1962.

Hillary, Edmund. *Nothing Venture, Nothing Win*. New York: Coward, McCann & Geoghegan, 1975.

Hunt, Sir John. *The Conquest of Everest*. New York: E. P. Dutton, 1954.

Krakauer, Jon. *Into the Thin Air*. New York: Villard, 1997.

Messner, Reinhold. *The Crystal Horizon: Everest—The First Solo Ascent*. Seattle: The Mountaineers, 1989.

Ray, Prakash. *Kathmandu and the Kingdom of Nepal*. Victoria, Australia: Lonely Planet, 1983.

Unsworth, Walt. *Everest: A Mountaineering History*. Boston: Houghton Mifflin, 1982.

978-0-595-43972-0
0-595-43972-1